4

DATE DUE

THE UNITED NATIONS IN INTERNATIONAL POLITICS

*Written under the auspices of the
Center of International Studies, Princeton University*

*A list of other Center publications appears
at the back of the book.*

The United Nations
in International Politics

EDITED BY LEON GORDENKER

PRINCETON UNIVERSITY PRESS 1971

PRINCETON, NEW JERSEY

LC Card: 71-132239

ISBN: 0-691-05615-3

This book was set in Linotype Caledonia

Publication of this book has been aided by a grant from the Whitney Darrow Publication Reserve Fund of Princeton University Press

Printed in the United States of America by Princeton University Press

CONTENTS

THE UNITED NATIONS IN INTERNATIONAL POLITICS

INTRODUCTION

LEON GORDENKER

A quarter of a century after the enthusiastic establishment of the United Nations, it strains the imagination to think of international relations without the presence of that world organization and the large variety of intergovernmental institutions that have grown up around it. In 1970, observers and participants in the business of relations among states take for granted that the United Nations is a factor to be considered. It is accepted as a fact, but the degree of its influence, its value, and its future enjoy anything but unanimous appreciation.

In one sense, differences about the role of the United Nations in international relations and, specifically, in international politics, reach back to its creation twenty-five years ago. That event was taken as heralding important, and perhaps even fundamental, changes in the way the governments of the peoples of the world conducted their mutual affairs. Honest men, whether serving governments or scholarship, differed then about how much effect the new organization would and should have; they still differ.

What was attempted remains clear. New controls were to be applied to the use of force at the international level. To safeguard against violent tactics among the members, the United Nations was formally endowed with a range of means to settle disputes, including for the first time in history an international force fundamentally to maintain peace and security. Economic and social problems received a high priority and the promotion of human rights became a principal aim of international cooperation; an elaborate institutional network, which expanded rapidly and enormously in the postwar setting, was to work toward these ends. Colonies were brought under international surveillance, almost under international supervision. Accumulated

3

practice and human ingenuity were to contribute to the improvement and extension of international law.

From the vantage point of 1970, what was established and what was attempted in 1945 can seem both heroic and timid, conservative and daring, faltering and surefooted. The chance to improve the world, according to some, went by default—although the wreckage of the old order left by the war offered the building blocks of the new. Others would say that the construction of institutions and the encouragement of a new regularity of conduct under some agreed standards represent a real gain in a confused world. Yet others would put aside consideration of the relatively new institutions as irrelevant to the real problems of world politics which should be seen in the old light of national power and policies. And some would join in the judgment of irrelevance from another angle, insisting that in 1945, as in 1970, only a radical reconstruction of international society had merit.

Although the meaning of the United Nations in international politics remains controversial and, as in 1945, still defies full understanding in some of its aspects, the judgments of 1970 are based on twenty-five years of experience. The complex of international organizations has reached an unprecedented and unexpected size. Largely unanticipated operations have brought the United Nations system into close contact with governments on their home ground in every part of the world. The United Nations itself has more than doubled in membership. Its recommendations to governments number in the thousands. The tasks assigned by its members reflect adjustments and even distortions of its originally conceived role. Its deliberations range far and wide over the material of international politics and make the United Nations appear as one center—if not *the* center that some of its founders envisaged—for international cooperation or conflict. Some governments may downgrade the importance of the United Nations system, but none disregards it.

4

Scholars have shown a lively interest: the United Nations and its related international institutions have become a subject of specialized study. This seems a natural progression of research, since scholars of an earlier generation had been deeply involved in the creation and justification of the League of Nations, the first global attempt to institutionalize the maintenance of peace. Others during the period between the two world wars made specific the intellectual shortcomings of the concepts underlying the League, and tried to elucidate its place in world politics. Still others devoted themselves to sometimes deplorably unscholarly propaganda on its behalf. The inability of the League to achieve crucial successes in peacekeeping and the simultaneous but unanticipated burgeoning of economic and social cooperation received the attention of other scholars. Representatives of all these approaches contributed to the wartime planning for the new world organization; since then, new crops of scholars have observed, studied, probed, pontificated, analyzed, and theorized on the United Nations.

This volume employs the 25th anniversary of the United Nations as a moment—perhaps largely of sentimental significance—to review and rethink its work and role, and to peer into the future. It rests on the assumption—or the fact —that international institutions and the deliberate organization of world politics associated with them have achieved a more than ephemeral place in the world. Each chapter attempts in its own way to help answer such questions as these:

What is the present nature of the United Nations?
What relationship does it bear to broader frameworks of world politics?
How can we understand this relationship?
How can we understand the actions of the United Nations?
What standards of judgment can be applied to the United Nations?

5

What results are obtained when these are applied?

How can we approach forecasts of the future nature and activities and roles of the United Nations?

What research will better help us to understand the record of the past and the events of the future?

What forecasts may be essayed?

In a world as replete with contradiction, tension, and rapid change as our own, it would be futile to pretend that final or perfect answers can be given to such questions. Indeed, this effort to deal with them reflects both the imperfection of the subject matter and an awareness of the likelihood of change in the international system. Any attempt, therefore, to impose a single framework of analysis on the authors would surely have encouraged misleadingly doctrinaire results.

Yet the essays are clearly related. One source of this relationship can be found in the association of the contributors with the Center of International Studies at Princeton University. For several years they have exchanged ideas, discussed each other's writing, raised unanticipated questions, and sought answers bearing on international politics generally. This volume records some of the results of that association.

All the authors are concerned with the problem of maintaining international peace and specifically with the United Nations as it operates in world politics, but the angles of their approaches differ. In planning for this volume, more emphasis was given to originality of individual research than on symmetry in the finished product. No single methodological pattern guided the authors. Consequently, some chapters emphasize abstract and theoretical points, others empirical referrants. Each author has tried to raise new issues and project new ideas, approaching his problems with fresh thought. Every chapter, implicitly or explicitly has a critical purpose—to improve scholarship within its scope.

6

Another link among the contributors derives from a common conception of the United Nations as a subsystem within the larger system of the world political environment. This figures more prominently in some chapters than in others, but the systemic approach has influenced each one.

Although this volume does not pretend to treat every possible issue, it does seek answers for specific questions of importance in the United Nations system. They include the relationship of the United Nations with the larger international system; differences and likenesses of the League and the United Nations in handling conflict; how member governments respond to the recommendations of the General Assembly; managing international conflict resulting from intrastate disorders; United Nations economic aid and its effect on member government policies; and evaluative perceptions of the United Nations. Young's chapter uses systems theory to make a number of theoretical distinctions and its comprehensive and theoretical nature makes it a framework for the book.

The relationship which Young explores—between an international organization and the system in which it operates—is also the central concern of Stanley Michalak's "The United Nations and the League." But Michalak's chapter differs from Young's and others in the volume in its strong comparative emphasis. Michalak suggests categories for classifying conflicts involving peace and security in which the United Nations or the League of Nations took part. In effect, he reviews the entire record of both organizations in the peace-making field, and shows how the results in the United Nations differ from those in the League and what systematic factors may explain the differences. As Michalak correctly points out, "comparative analyses of these two organizations are exceedingly rare in the literature on international organization."

Gabriella Rosner Lande's "An Inquiry into the Successes and Failures of the United Nations General Assembly," also takes up the conflict-solving functions of the world organization, but from a different angle. Mrs. Lande investigates the responses of member states to resolutions adopted by the General Assembly, thus concentrating on the consequences of the policy-making process within the international organization subsystem, rather than on the operation of the wider international system. Mrs. Lande's analysis is based on a careful examination of 29 important resolutions intended to help maintain international peace, and her conclusions point to a decided capability on the part of the General Assembly to serve usefully (even without compulsion) in a large variety of international disputes.

The source of some of the most dramatic and troubled actions of the United Nations—the conflict within a state that spills over into the international arena—is the central focus in Linda Miller's "International Organization and Internal Conflicts: Some Emerging Patterns of Response." Using a systemic framework, she suggests that the next few decades will see changes in the kind of internal conflict which engages the attention of the United Nations, and therefore new patterns of response. But there is little likelihood, according to Miss Miller, that international organizations will initiate or administer large-scale field operations, or that they will even see the establishment of United Nations precedents as "community authorized norms" for handling internal disputes.

Leon Gordenker's "The United Nations and Economic and Social Change," turns to the less-developed countries and explores the influential relationship between those states and the growing economic and social programs of the UN. It is the only chapter in the book which uses direct field observation. One of several conclusions that suggest the need for additional research is that the economic and social activities of the United Nations tend to produce changes in the nature of the international system.

The final chapter, Richard A. Falk's "The United Nations: Various Systems of Operation," has a more strongly normative and evaluative flavor than the others. His undertaking, Falk writes, "is one scholar's attempt to respond to U Thant's plea for moral strength." Always cognizant of the background of the international political system, Falk suggests a set of alternative models that may characterize the role of the UN in the future. Appropriately, the final passages point out the vital role of scholarship in understanding the United Nations and its place in the international political system.

CHAPTER 1

The United Nations and the
International System*

ORAN R. YOUNG

A notable gap in existing analyses of the United Nations is the relative absence of any systematic treatment of the links between the Organization itself and the international system in which it operates.[1] These links constitute a complex dual relationship, both sides of which are worthy of serious analysis. The functions and activities of the United Nations are molded by the basic dimensions and dynamic processes of the international system, but the UN is itself an actor in the system and is sometimes able to influence its environment significantly.[2] Throughout its history the impact of the systemic environment on the Organization has far surpassed the impact of the Organization on the system. Nevertheless, the influence of the United Nations on world politics should not be underestimated, especially in its more subtle and intangible forms.

I

It is important to clarify the proposition that the United Nations is an actor in world politics. This proposition has been a source of widespread confusion and can be attacked

---

* An earlier draft of portions of this essay appeared in 1968. See Oran R. Young, "The United Nations and the International System," *International Organization*, 22, 4 (Autumn 1968), 902-922.

[1] A similar remark applies to the League of Nations. See Michalak, Chapter 2 below. For a significant, though partial, exception to this general conclusion see Inis L. Claude, Jr., *The Changing United Nations* (New York: Random House, 1967).

[2] For a discussion of two modes of influence on the political environment of the United Nations, see Lande, Chapter 3 below, and Miller, Chapter 4.

from two angles. On the one hand, political "idealists" have commonly argued that the effort to conceptualize the United Nations as an actor in world politics downgrades the Organization and implicates it too deeply in the traditional arena of power politics. Those who take this view tend to equate the United Nations with the international system as a whole and to think of it as operating somehow *above* the arena of interstate relationships. But this interpretation glosses over important realities. The United Nations has not been able to adopt a posture above the hurly-burly of power politics; it is as deeply involved in this arena as most of the other actors. The problems generated by power politics constitute its fundamental reason for existence, and the states which engage in power politics are its constituent units. Moreover, the UN is only one of a relatively large number of actors in the international system, many of whom are considerably more influential, at least with respect to specific issues or specific segments of the system.

This confusion about the United Nations as an actor poses a serious problem: it tends to set up a tension between the intangible ethos of universalism embedded in the mythology of the United Nations and the realities of its position in the international system. Not only is an antipathy to power politics an important feature of the mythology of the United Nations; many commentators also operate on the tacit assumption that the UN should always play a major role in various classes of problems outlined in the Charter (e.g. threats to international peace and security). While it may sometimes be politically desirable to maintain such pretenses, it is important for the analyst to realize that the ability of the United Nations to act in any given situation is delimited both by the characteristics of the international system at any given moment and by the processes of change in the system itself.

The second line of attack by political "realists" holds that the United Nations is not an actor at all; it is merely a reflector of the activities of its component members. But this interpretation also glosses over many nuances.[3] While it is certainly true that the United Nations often reflects the desires and policies of its members, this does not make it unusual in the ranks of actors in world politics. All these actors, including the states and nation-states, can be conceptualized as reflections of the push and pull of their component parts. And though it is true that the central authority structures have a greater degree of autonomy in some actors than in others, the United Nations does not seem very different in this respect from the looser federations among the states in the international system. It has become a commonplace (albeit a true one) to conclude that the United Nations as an actor in world politics is more than the sum of its parts. What is more important in the present context, however, is the fact that the Organization as an actor reflects more than the desires and policies of one or a few of its components. There is no doubt that the United Nations is an actor characterized by a relatively low degree of formal institutionalization. And this may account for some of the confusion regarding its stature, since many commentators on its activities have been steeped in a "world view" that tends to equate actors in world politics with states possessing easily identifiable, formal, and legally constituted institutions of government. Nevertheless, the conceptual biases built into our world view should no longer be allowed to blind us to the important intangible and informal aspects of the roles of the United Nations as an actor in the international system.

The nature of the links between the United Nations and the international system has been shaped by the fact that the system itself has changed rapidly and in far-reaching ways since the end of the Second World War. The United Nations has already survived, though with extensive changes and adaptations, several marked transitions in the

[3] Even such a shrewd observer as Claude tends to fall into this trap. See, for example, *op.cit.*, Introduction.

international system. In the immediate aftermath of the war when the UN was being set up, the international system was characterized by a peculiar juxtaposition of political forces. The principal elements, which proved predictably unstable in combination, were: a new and essentially untried set of basic power relationships; deep-seated revulsion against old procedures for the management of power in world politics crystallized by the war itself; a number of politically unsound and increasingly illegitimate remnants of older systems of world order, notably colonial relationships; and the beginnings of a revolution in technology with far-reaching implications in both military and nonmilitary areas. Though this unstable combination formed the effective environment for the formative activities of the UN, it quickly gave way to the international relationships that lasted from the late forties well into the sixties and that soon became identified with such concepts as bipolarity, the revolution in nuclear weapons, and the Cold War. The UN responded to the dynamics of an essentially bipolar international system with extensive adaptations, both institutional and functional in nature, which carried its activities far from the concepts incorporated in the Charter.[4]

In the middle and late sixties, however, a number of trends in the international system began to cumulate in patterns that diverged too much from those of the period of bipolarity and the Cold War to be called variations on a theme. And the current period is increasingly characterized by a decline, though not a termination, of bipolarity; the growth of significant common interests between the superpowers; polycentric developments in the blocs and the deterioration of major alliance systems; the rise or reemergence of a small number of additional power centers such as the People's Republic of China, Japan, France, and the Federal Republic of Germany; the development of distinct

[4] For a more extended analysis of a number of these adaptations consult Oran R. Young, *The Intermediaries: Third Parties in International Crises* (Princeton: Princeton University Press, 1967), Chapter 4.

and frequently discontinuous regional subsystems within the global system; the increasing salience of North-South tension, and the development of ambiguities concerning the role of the state as the dominant unit of world politics. A central feature of the international system at present is an ambiguity, arising from clear and extensive fluidity with as yet no well-established pattern or direction of change. It is therefore hardly surprising that the United Nations now also gives the impression of great flux without a set pattern of evolution.

In view of the extent of these changes in the international system the basic adaptability of the UN seems remarkable. Despite a number of proximate ups and downs since 1945 the Organization has continuously displayed enough flexibility and resilience in the face of changes in the international system to be considered at least minimally useful and worthy of retention by the great majority of member states. This adaptability appears to emanate from the constitutional fluidity of the United Nations as well as from the fact that most of the leading figures who have operated within its framework over the years have adopted a pragmatic political stance. It should not, however, be thought that this adaptability has been achieved at no cost. Over the years the United Nations has paid a substantial price for continuing relevance: constant and unsettling role fluctuation,[5] inability to move along a clear-cut path of institution building, and general inchoateness.

II

Since the United Nations is only one among a relatively large number of actors in the international system, it does not at any given moment play an important role in all the major issues of international politics.[6] Changes in the inter-

[5] For an evaluative discussion of these roles, see Falk, Chapter 6 below.

[6] It is possible to distinguish different levels of United Nations involvement in international issues. At the most minimal level of

national system itself, moreover, often have far-reaching effects on the extent of UN involvement in specific issues. Consider in this connection the impact of the following factors as determinants of involvement.[7]

Great-power Issues

There are at least three relevant aspects of the question of great-power issues. First, there was a clear presumption when the United Nations was established that the Organization would play no more than a marginal role in issues involving the great powers *inter se*. This presumption was explicitly institutionalized both in the voting procedures of the Security Council and in the division of labor between the Council and the other policy organs. Second, there was a tacit assumption that the Organization would be cautious about taking an active part in a problem that seemed an imminent focus of overt great-power competition. Third, it was generally assumed that the blessing of the great powers would be a prerequisite for active UN involvement in specific issues, especially in the peace and security field.

These early injunctions concerning involvement have shifted substantially. During the Uniting for Peace era,[8] efforts were made by the Western powers to use the UN as an instrument in the Cold War, to legitimize various aspects of competitive great-power diplomacy. In the fifties and early sixties, on the other hand, interest rose sharply in operations involving preventive diplomacy and the insulation of trouble spots from potential great-power involvement. As a result, even though the UN steered away from

---

verbal concern it can be argued that the Organization does become involved in most international issues. Involvement of this kind is insignificant, however, in many cases. The concept refers to more significant levels of involvement in the present discussion.

[7] The following list is neither exhaustive nor cast in the form of a logical partition. It therefore does not lend itself to efforts to attach precise weights to the various determinants of United Nations involvement.

[8] The activities of this period are discussed in some detail in Young, *The Intermediaries*, Chapter 4.

issues directly involving the great powers, it tried to reduce the range of overt great-power confrontations by preventive actions. In the current period of fluidity, these latter ideas remain politically influential. But, as might be expected given the present ambiguities of the international system, they are now being increasingly supplemented by the emergence of great-power interests in coordinating their actions on particular issues,[9] at least tacitly, through the United Nations, and by the emergence of concepts concerning the possibilities for more active UN roles in certain problems involving the great powers *inter se*.[10]

Spheres of Influence

Despite the revulsion against past forms of international politics in the postwar period, *de facto* spheres of influence have remained a basic feature of the international system, especially with respect to East-West politics. The physical locus of a particular problem within a major sphere of influence has always barred significant UN involvement. It is true that the boundaries of specific spheres have sometimes seemed hazy and that such barriers have not totally prohibited the display of UN interest, but cases such as Hungary, Tibet, and the Dominican Republic emphasize the extent to which this factor can effectively limit the degree of involvement.

At the same time, the impact of particular spheres of influence on UN involvement has shifted. The American sphere of influence in Latin America has traditionally been the most formally recognized one[11] and it is still of some importance. But in recent years it has been shrinking to a

[9] The activities of the great powers in such cases as Cyprus and the India-Pakistan clash of 1965 are interesting from this perspective.

[10] The role of the United Nations, and especially the Secretary-General, in the Cuban crisis of 1962 constitutes a case in point.

[11] Thus, the only regional arrangements mentioned in the Covenant of the League were those for Latin America (Article 21). And concern for the sanctity of these arrangements was perhaps the most powerful force behind the drafting of Chapter VIII of the United Nations Charter.

small core of essential issues in terms of barring UN involvement in specific Latin American problems. On a more *de facto* basis, the Soviet sphere of influence in Eastern Europe remains one of the sharpest international barriers to United Nations action. Yet current trends make it doubtful that even this barrier will survive intact in the foreseeable future. Perhaps the greatest shift since the late forties with respect to spheres of influence, however, stems from the growing atmosphere of caution surrounding any United Nations actions on the periphery of China. Though the issue of China itself continues to be aired in the Organization, both the overt policies of China and its generally negative attitude toward the UN are important factors underlying the current avoidance of many Asian problems.

Underlying Doctrines

An understandable, though politically ambiguous, determinant of United Nations involvement stems from the underlying doctrines concerning UN operations at any given time. Regardless of calculations concerning the efficacy of specific actions, there is a strong tendency to take a favorable view of intervention in situations that conform, at least superficially, to the prevailing images of the issues the Organization ought to be handling. This factor also accounts for some of the shifts over time in patterns of involvement, since prevailing images, especially in the peace and security area, have passed through several distinguishable phases since 1945.[12]

The impact of underlying doctrines is doubly important since specific actions identified with a given set of doctrines have sometimes produced backlash effects rather than positive precedents of future relevance. In the aftermath of the Korean intervention, for example, interest in interventions predicated upon the Uniting for Peace image of peacekeeping declined sharply. And the difficulties of the Congo

[12] For a detailed discussion linking these shifts to changes in the international system see Young, *The Intermediaries*, Chapter 4.

17

operation have unquestionably made UN decision-makers wary of involvements in subsequent internal war situations. At the same time, the influence of underlying doctrines has recently become increasingly ambiguous. The United Nations has witnessed both a horizontal spread of simultaneously operative doctrines and a decline in the relative dominance of any given set.[13] Consequently, the Organization is now extremely cautious about new involvements— though when action does seem desirable, some doctrinal justification can usually be found.

Specific Membership Problems

A more tangible but equally important factor affecting UN involvement in concrete issues arises from specific membership problems. The doctrinal foundation clearly suggests a thrust toward universal membership and, therefore, relevance on a global basis. Though the United Nations itself has played some role in increasing the number of its members, it has always fallen significantly short of universality. This is not necessarily a critical problem in the case of small states that are non-members, since the Organization can on occasion take actions directly affecting their interests regardless of their membership status and their attitudes toward intervention.[14] The problem is not so easy in the case of larger powers and their dependencies who resist interference, unless the UN allows itself to become an instrument of particular factions in the international system.

Since 1945 specific membership problems have affected patterns of UN involvement in a number of contexts. The inability of the United Nations to deal effectively with the problems of Central Europe stems from the absence of all German representatives as well as from great-power

[13] For an exploration of some of these developments see Oran R. Young, "Trends in International Peacekeeping," *Research Monograph No. 22*, Princeton Center of International Studies, 1966.
[14] Legal justification for such actions can be found in Article 2(6) of the Charter. The Korean intervention constitutes a clear case of activities along these lines.

competition in the Cold War context. More recently, the marked failure of the UN to play a major role in many Asian problems can be explained, at least partially, in terms of the negative attitudes of China and other Asian non-members such as the two Vietnams. Moreover, the ventures of the Organization into instrumental relationships with partial groupings in international politics have often tended to result in sharp setbacks for the overall relevance of the United Nations. This was certainly the case, for example, during the "westernized" period in the Uniting for Peace era. And it is interesting to speculate whether the same thing will happen if current African efforts to use the UN as an instrument of political change meet with proximate success.

General Membership Questions

By the same token, the general characteristics and basic patterns of interest of the membership of the Organization play a role in determining whether the United Nations will become involved in specific situations. Though all members nominally subscribe to certain common goals as a condition of membership,[15] the actual concerns of the members have tended to diverge considerably from these abstract formulations, and the predominant patterns of interest have shifted greatly over the years. As a result, the UN has fluctuated with respect to the issues regarded as both desirable and politically feasible for involvement.

The fact that the composition of the United Nations has changed rapidly over the years, both in numbers and in coalition patterns, has emphasized the importance of this determinant of involvement. This is another area in which the prior actions of the UN itself have been an important cause of the changes.[16] But in any case, the issue orientation of the United Nations has shifted drastically in the transi-

[15] These are set forth in Articles 1 and 4 of the Charter.
[16] That is, the United Nations played some role in the processes through which many of its current members achieved independence.

19

tion from an organization largely lacking in African and, to an extent, Asian members to a forum whose membership is predominantly southern and whose largest single bloc is African. These developments have had great impact in diverting attention from East-West issues to North-South ones, and have produced a wide range of more specific consequences for decisions on the extent and nature of involvement.

Problems of Recourse

A more negative, though still influential determinant of United Nations involvement in concrete issues stems from problems of recourse. Given the nature and record of the Organization, states with viable diplomatic alternatives for the prosecution of their interests have often chosen either to avoid the UN altogether or else to utilize it only marginally. The prospects are different, however, for intrinsically weak powers and states whose diplomatic position offers little room for maneuver. In such cases, the potential of the United Nations for political legitimation and interest aggregation sometimes looks desirable.

Perhaps the most interesting changes in this area since 1945 relate to the states most interested in thus involving the United Nations in specific issues. In the early days, this posture was left largely to the Latin Americans and various interest groups representing "non-self-governing" entities. During the fifties, however, shifts in membership made such patterns of recourse to a considerable degree the province of the Afro-Asian bloc. And even more recently African and Asian interests have become increasingly divergent, leaving the African states, the largest single bloc, dominating these recourse activities. For reasons discussed in other sections of this chapter, the United Nations has now become cautious about involvement in many Asian problems. The Africans, on the other hand, have strong incentives to pursue their objectives through the UN, because of the sharpness of their revisionist interests[17] and because of their relative lack of diplomatic alternatives (though their behavior indicates that reliance on the UN does not always please them).

Bailing-out Exercises

In a number of specific situations, the United Nations has become involved in a problem through the abdication of the party previously responsible. Handing the problem over to the UN has sometimes seemed an acceptable way of divesting oneself of a burden that has become too great or a commitment that is no longer viable given the shifting nature of the international system. Though the resultant problems have frequently remained extremely difficult ones, the record of the UN in dealing with them is by no means entirely negative.

The most obvious cases of such UN involvement have emerged from the processes of decolonization. It is interesting that the British have shown the greatest propensity to hand over such problems, including Kashmir, Palestine, Cyprus, and Aden. This is in part, no doubt, because of the sheer bulk of the British empire. But it is also linked to differences between British attitudes toward decolonization and those of other imperial powers,[18] and to the related fact that others have tended to move so slowly that problems have tended to reach the UN as full-blown threats to international peace and security rather than as bailing-out exercises. Another interesting point about this form of United Nations involvement is the tendency for such cases to con-

[17] The clarity and insistence of this revisionism have become particularly evident in the recent debates on such specific questions as Rhodesia, South Africa, and South West Africa.

[18] The attitudes of countries such as France and Portugal stand in sharp contrast to those of Britain on this issue. Thus, France and Portugal have always insisted that their problems of decolonization are essentially matters of domestic jurisdiction within the terms of Article 2(7) of the Charter and that the United Nations is therefore barred from intervening.

21

tinue to arise even now. Despite the fact that the most basic questions on the issue of colonialism have been settled in general terms for some years, the amount of time required to play out the process of decolonization to the bitter end is considerable.

Second-order Diplomatic Utility

The United Nations sometimes becomes involved in situations on a limited basis when one or more of the major participants are thereby likely to achieve specific diplomatic advantages. In such cases, the principal determinant of UN involvement is the diplomatic maneuvering of important states, rather than any autonomous role of the Organization as a force committed to the maintenance of international peace and security. Since involvements of this kind are intrinsically *ad hoc*, the influence of this determinant is difficult to forecast in advance or to compare with others in any general assessment of UN activities, but it has played an important part in determining the level of UN involvement in a number of major diplomatic confrontations since 1945. The referral of the Berlin issue to the United Nations by the United States in September 1948, for example, was predicated on American hopes for resulting diplomatic advantages. And the USSR supported a United Nations role in the Dominican Republic crisis during April and May 1965 for similar reasons. The fundamentally manipulative basis of this determinant of involvement, however, does not justify an entirely negative interpretation; calculated efforts to involve the United Nations in a particular problem sometimes provide openings for UN activities that turn out to be of considerably broader significance.

Multiple Issues and Overcommitment

Finally, the patterns of UN involvement are highly sensitive to two facts: many issues compete for attention at any given time, and the Organization's resources are so limited that it is necessary to be extremely selective. The familiar

22

issue of overcommitment is an ambiguous one, however, since there are several distinct procedures that can be employed in defining levels of commitment. The problem is sometimes a very concrete one when several crises occur simultaneously—for example, Suez and Hungary in 1956 and Cuba and the Sino-Indian conflict in 1962. At other times, the problem takes the form of complaints of too much attention to a given set of issues, especially when there is fear of too deep involvement in cold-war situations. And there is always a potential problem of overcommitment in matching limited political and financial resources to specific programs of action.

The powers inclined to sound the alarm on the issue of overcommitment have shifted over the years—it has generally been a favorite issue of those seeking, at any given time, to restrict the influence of the United Nations. Thus, the Eastern states took this position during the Uniting for Peace Era, but in later years the great powers have often been inclined to assume it in response to efforts by lesser states to utilize the Organization for political purposes. And throughout the history of the United Nations, many of the lesser powers have been ready to take a stand on this issue whenever the great powers have shown signs of tacit coordination on a policy of using the UN to guarantee a conservative brand of international stability.[19]

It is evident that the determinants of UN involvement in various international issues are complex, and have tended to shift considerably in response to changes in the international system since 1945. What is less clear, however, is whether decisions concerning involvement either in broad problem areas or in specific cases of conflict are ordinarily based on realistic assessments of the Organization's

[19] In the early years, the lesser powers were distinctly concerned about the possibilities inherent in great power domination of the Security Council. And although the issue remained more or less dormant for a number of years, current indications of great power interest in restoring the original position of the Security Council are producing new signs of uneasiness on the part of many lesser powers.

23

capacity to operate effectively in the arena in question. The frequent failure to make realistic assessments of this kind suggests that the United Nations has tended to "live dangerously" over the years and that its longevity is more fortuitous than calculated. But many large-scale political organizations operate in a similar way, and it is often possible to operate on an intrinsically unstable basis of this kind for relatively long periods.

III

Like any other actor in the international system the United Nations can be thought of in terms of its roles or functions in world politics. A great deal of confusion, however, emanates from a failure to draw sufficiently clear distinctions between the different roles played by the Organization and to assess the problems and prospects of specific activities in the light of these distinctions—which are admittedly difficult to spell out. In the first place, there are several reasons why the different roles of the Organization tend to be somewhat indistinct even within a given time period. The prevalence of conceptual confusion, various types of political mythology, and apolitical perspectives in the atmosphere surrounding the United Nations frequently makes it difficult to discern the true nature of any given set of operations. Moreover, there are sometimes political problems involved in UN activities that make it embarrassing to clarify such matters at all: in order to launch a specific operation it is often necessary to obscure its "constitutional" basis or to make its political underpinnings ambiguous (this is especially true, for example, in the peace and security field). At the same time, the fundamental role structure of the United Nations has shifted quite drastically over time in response to the changing nature of the international system, but not as a uniform progression in a definable direction. On the contrary, roles have tended to come and go and even to reemerge, making it difficult to define any clear-cut pattern of transformation in role structure.[20]

In addition, a simple transfer of the concepts commonly employed in assessing the roles or functions of states and nation-states is apt to lead to additional confusion in analyzing the activities of the United Nations. Not only is the Organization less characterized by formal institutionalization than most states, it is also essentially a non-territorial actor,[21] and its component units (at least in the first instance) are states rather than individual human beings. Consequently, it is necessary to analyze the roles of the UN in the international system *sui generis.*[22]

The United Nations as Regulator

Perhaps the most influential hopes, at least in abstract terms, underlying the establishment of the United Nations were based on the idea that it would play a significant role in maintaining a minimal level of stability in the international system.[23] In this sense, the United Nations assumed the mantle of the League as a substitute for the more traditional practices of "power politics."[24] This conception of the

[20] For a discussion of these trends see Young, "Trends in International Peacekeeping."

[21] For a wealth of historical material concerning essentially nonterritorial actors in world politics consult Adda B. Bozeman, *Politics and Culture in International History* (Princeton: Princeton University Press, 1960).

[22] The following list is neither exhaustive nor cast in the form of a logical partition. It is designed more to establish the strength of the links between the activities of the United Nations and the character of the overall international system than to support judgments concerning the relative importance of the different roles of the Organization.

[23] On this point, compare the concept of "minimum world public order" developed by McDougal and Lasswell. See, for example, Myres McDougal *et al., Studies in World Public Order* (New Haven: Yale University Press, 1960).

[24] Though the League was a failure in many respects, the fact that many originally conceived it to be an alternative to the old balance-of-power procedures is clear. And one influential strand of thinking

role of the UN, which has remained influential, is frequently tied to the corollary that in operating as a regulator the Organization should refrain insofar as possible from influencing the outcomes of specific interactions in the international arena. Thus, the role of the United Nations is that of a rules-keeper who imposes certain regulations or restrictions on contestants, by force if necessary, and who calls a halt to specific confrontations that threaten to get out of hand.

The regulator conception has displayed remarkable resilience over the years despite the fact that its relevance has always been severely limited by certain fundamental features of the international system. Thus, it is impossible for an organization such as the United Nations effectively to adopt a position above "high politics" in the contemporary world. Various forms of power politics are endemic to a states system, and inevitably invade the activities of international organizations concerned with highly politicized issues such as those that fall under the heading of peace and security.[25] And the growing importance of conflict patterns stemming from internal war situations in recent years has only emphasized the difficulties of avoiding political interventions in conducting regulatory operations.[26] Moreover, the regulator conception of the UN has been periodically overshadowed or cast aside by efforts to use the Organization as a partisan political instrument, such as those of the

---

underlying the establishment of the United Nations was founded on the proposition that World War II had made the search for alternatives to "power politics" more imperative than ever.

[25] Whether or not particular balance arrangements fulfill the classical requirements for a balance of power, for example, it is clear that at least some basic balances are necessary for the continued existence of a states system and, therefore, for the operation of an international organization in a states system. Some particularly useful comments on this subject can be found in John Herz, *International Politics in the Atomic Age* (New York: Columbia University Press, 1959).

[26] Cases such as the Congo, Yemen, and Cyprus offer a variety of contemporary illustrations of this problem.

Uniting for Peace Era and those now unfolding in the North-South context.

Nevertheless, the regulator image has remained a powerful one even in periods of adversity. It received new life during the Hammarskjöld Administration, when a series of influential UN operations were presented as predominantly regulatory. And the detailed doctrines formulated at that time to govern regulatory activities still remain politically potent. Consequently, the idea of the United Nations as a neutral regulator is deeply embedded in the political environment of the Organization. But this has made it more and more difficult in recent years to avoid the question of the feasibility of compartmentalizing activities: how can the UN continue to engage in essentially neutral regulatory operations while, at the same time, underwriting other actions which have a distinctly partisan flavor and are therefore incompatible with a regulatory conception?

The United Nations as Effector of
Great-power Agreements

From the start, it was widely assumed that the ability of the United Nations to operate effectively in world politics would be dependent upon the willingness of the great powers to coordinate programs of action or, at least, to acquiesce in activities favored by the majority. By the same token, it was generally supposed that the Organization would in fact proceed to implement any policies actively favored by the great powers.[27] In contrast to the League, therefore, a distinct recognition of the realities of power politics was built into the United Nations despite its incongruity with other doctrines of the time.[28] In particular, the juxtaposition of the UN as an effector of great-power agreements with the regulatory image produced an unresolved

[27] Although this was, from the beginning, a source of unhappiness among the lesser powers, it was widely accepted as a valid postulate.
[28] On this subject see, *inter alia*, Inis L. Claude, Jr., *Swords into Plowshares* (New York: Random House, 1961), Chapters 4 and 8.

ambiguity which has, in subsequent years, served as a focus for a good deal of role fluctuation.

In the early years, great-power agreement, albeit generally minimal in content and tacit in form, did allow the Organization to play a role in such situations as Kashmir, Palestine, Indonesia, and the disposition of the former Italian territories. There followed, however, a long period during which one of the predominant realities of UN politics was the inability of the great powers to coordinate even tacitly, which sharply restricted the activities of the Organization.[29] Throughout both the Uniting for Peace Era and the bulk of the Hammarskjöld Administration the role of the United Nations as an effector of great-power agreements was overshadowed, first, by efforts to utilize the Organization as an instrument of great-power competition, and later by a widespread desire to direct UN attention away from great-power politics insofar as possible.[30]

In recent years, nevertheless, the idea of an effector of great-power agreements has reemerged in several significant forms.[31] The two superpowers have shown a growing interest, still tacit for the most part, in operating through the United Nations in certain specific situations such as Cyprus and the India-Pakistan dispute of 1965,[32] and also in more general areas such as the effort to regulate the spread of nuclear weapons.[33] This conception of the UN

[29] An important exception is the tacit agreement of the superpowers which allowed the United Nations to play a role in the Suez crisis of 1956.

[30] For a more detailed discussion of this point consult Young, *The Intermediaries*, Chapter 4.

[31] For a discussion of the attendant problems see Young, "Trends in International Peacekeeping," pp. 12-33.

[32] Incipient interests in superpower coordination have also begun to appear on matters of internal United Nations policy such as the division of competences between the Security Council and the General Assembly and financial arrangements for United Nations activities.

[33] The functions that the superpowers have projected for the IAEA in negotiations concerning efforts to regulate the spread of nuclear weapons are of particular interest in this context.

role has, however, reemerged with a fundamental difference. Though the United Nations may still be responsive to the interests of the great powers on some specific issues, its composition has changed so much that these powers can no longer automatically determine its issue orientation and action patterns on a variety of important contemporary issues, especially in the North-South perspective.

The United Nations as a Partisan Political Instrument

Though the climate of opinion prevailing in 1945 did not foster the idea, the possibility of using the United Nations as an instrument of partisan politics has always interested a number of states and groups of states. The fundamental point of interest arises from the potential of the UN as a legitimizer of intrinsically partisan interests and as a device for cumulating or focusing the influence of otherwise unstructured interest groups. The basic contradictions between this role and those discussed above, however, are obvious.

Sharp shifts in the influence of specific ideas for using the United Nations as a partisan instrument make this conception interesting in considering the links between UN role fluctuation and the changing international system. When the Cold War got under way in the late forties, the Western states discovered that they could effectively dominate the policy production of the United Nations, and they had good reason to desire legitimation for many activities. There ensued, therefore, the United for Peace Era, which lasted until the aftermath of the Korean episode.[34] Changes in both the composition of the Organization and the international system itself, however, destroyed this relationship during the fifties. But these very changes generated new efforts to utilize the United Nations for partisan purposes: the next period devoted much attention to the role of the Organization as a cumulator of the influence of intrinsically

[34] The Uniting for Peace Era is discussed at some length in Young, *The Intermediaries*, Chapter 4.

29

weak states, especially those nonaligned or neutralist on East-West issues.[35] This relationship, in turn, has begun to fragment in recent years. African and Asian interests have become more and more divergent as the Organization has become less willing to become involved in many Asian problems and as the Africans have increasingly asserted their growing numerical dominance. Consequently, the Africans alone are beginning to spearhead many of the more significant efforts to use the United Nations as a political instrument. At the same time, however, the reemergence of great-power interests in using the Organization as a forum for at least *de facto* political coordination is now restricting these efforts of the lesser powers—though it cannot produce a genuine reversion to the patterns of the early years. In short, therefore, there is currently a growing ambiguity surrounding the partisan role of the United Nations.

The United Nations as a Force for Political Change

Related to all these conceptions are other ideas concerning possible roles for the United Nations in achieving authoritative adjustments in the effective distribution of world values. Indeed, this has always been a major source of confusion (sometimes deliberate) in assessing the position of the Organization in the international system. One of the fundamental problems of international politics in a highly decentralized states system is the achievement of political change without radically disrupting the system itself. And this problem has become increasingly complex in the contemporary world as the use of large-scale violence has become less and less acceptable as a means of achieving political change, both because changes in military technology have made such procedures extraordinarily dangerous and because of essentially normative considera-

---

[35] It is worth noting that such functions could be easily subsumed under Hammarskjöld's conception of the role of the United Nations, which emphasized the importance of steering clear of involvement in East-West issues.

tions.[36] Nevertheless, it remains extremely difficult for the United Nations to play an effective role in this area because political change frequently involves the redistribution of values, and therefore losses, for at least some of the actors in the international system. And it is hardly to be expected that influential actors will find it congenial to preside over their own decline even if the process is facilitated by the intermediate position of the UN.

Throughout its history, therefore, the United Nations has tended to be hesitant in assuming active roles relating explicitly to the achievement of political change even though activities of this kind constitute, in a very real sense, a logical corollary to the less active role of regulator.[37] This has been especially evident in any case where military force would be necessary to achieve political change. Consequently, the United Nations has sometimes displayed a tendency to freeze dangerous conflicts in the interests of regulation without doing much to resolve the underlying issues.[38]

Despite this basic caution, however, the Organization has over the years affected (or has been utilized to affect) processes of political change in a number of areas. It has played a significant part in dismantling colonial relationships where the basic trend was already set by drastic shifts in the overall international system and where a facilitative role was possible.[39] It has on occasion played an important dis-

[36] The United Nations itself has played a role in the development of normative considerations operating to inhibit the use of large-scale violence. On the development of such normative considerations see Klaus Knorr, *On the Uses of Military Power in the Nuclear Age* (Princeton: Princeton University Press, 1966), pp. 38-72.

[37] Note, however, that it is sometimes difficult to square the promotion of political change in general terms with the corollary of the regulatory conception of the United Nations which emphasizes the idea that the Organization should attempt to avoid influencing the outcomes of specific political interactions.

[38] Cases such as Kashmir and the problems arising from the Palestine issue are often cited in this connection.

[39] In this area, the United Nations has been an important, although undoubtedly second-order, cause of political change.

31

guised role in bringing about political change as, for example, in the Congo after the death of Hammarskjöld.[40] But these activities are often delicate, and their significance seems to lie more in *ad hoc* considerations associated with specific cases than in their impact on the long-term evolution of UN role structure itself.[41] In recent years, on the other hand, the Southern states (and especially the Africans) have launched, for perhaps the first time in UN history, a concerted drive to utilize the Organization as a genuine legislative force in international politics—not only on specific problems such as Rhodesia and South Africa but also on more general issues arising from the asymmetrical distribution of economic and social values between North and South. The combination of these efforts with the traditionally hesitant posture of the Organization toward a role as a legislative force, together with the emergence of great-power interests in using the United Nations for coordination on relatively conservative policies, seem likely to ensure that the activities of the UN in the area of political change will be a focus of contention concerning appropriate roles for the Organization for the foreseeable future.

The United Nations as a Creator of Long-term Viability

Since the Second World War, there has been a strong emphasis in many circles on the need to supplement international regulatory procedures with longer-term efforts aimed at fulfilling the underlying requirements of viability in a states system. In contrast to the Covenant of the League, the Charter of the United Nations places considerable emphasis on these longer-term activities, especially in

[40] Thus, under the leadership of Thant the United Nations played a crucial role in terminating the secessionist movement in Katanga during 1962 and 1963.

[41] The delicacy of such actions arises from the fact that controversy concerning the political consequences of the United Nations intervention can produce backlash effects on the ability of the Organization to perform regulatory functions in other situations.

such areas as economic development and human rights. Roles in this area were only gradually built up on an *ad hoc* basis under the League, but they have always been accorded high priority in the United Nations. And in recent years, especially, this conception of a role in the creation of long-term viability has been effectively linked to the worldwide groundswell of attention to problems of economic and political modernization.[42]

The United Nations has, on the whole, played a role of considerable significance in this area. It is of course true that it has not been able to stimulate a massive increase in aid programs for the underdeveloped world, that it has not presided over a wholesale transfer of existing programs from bilateral to multilateral bases, and that many individual observers are dissatisfied with some specific activities in this area. Nevertheless, these longer-term UN activities are unquestionably impressive in contrast with past multilateral efforts, and it is now increasingly accepted that the complex of UN programs directed toward promotion of national viability generate effects more far-reaching than their financial dimensions would suggest.[43] Moreover, the relevant activities of the United Nations have shown some tendency to expand in both volume and significance as the fundamental problems of development and modernization have become more salient in the international system. The continuing shift in the prevailing patterns of UN debate is linked to such developments. And specific new programs such as UNCTAD, UNDP, and UNIDO are indicative of the strength of this link between changes in the overall international system and the evolving pattern in the distribution of UN resources.

[42] The basic idea behind this link stems from the proposition that a states system will be viable in proportion to the internal viability of its component units. This proposition, which is widely held at the present time, can be traced all the way back to Kant's analysis of international politics in one form or another.

[43] The recent work of Leon Gordenker is particularly suggestive on this point. See below, Chapter 5.

The United Nations as Norm Creator

The United Nations has always played a significant role in creating the atmosphere or climate of opinion in which adaptations of the normative structure of the international system occur. This involves the process of law creation in international society,[44] but it is considerably broader in its consequences. It includes the development of both substantive norms of international politics and operative rules of the game for use in the international arena. And it often encompasses the formulation of specific procedures for legitimation of the political activities of individual actors in the international system.[45] The position of the United Nations is of considerable importance with respect to each of these functions: it offers a variety of formal and informal opportunities for wide multilateral contacts, and the acceleration of change in the international system in recent years has made may older procedures for adapting norms and rules less and less adequate.

This role as a creator of norms has expanded markedly in recent years. In the early years, the gap between the premises of the founders and the realities of international politics was so great that the United Nations was, above all, occupied with internal adaptation aimed at carving out at least potentially meaningful roles. Next, during the late forties and throughout the fifties the virulence of the Cold War and the rigidities of bipolarity were such as to minimize temporarily the significance of adaptive processes with respect to norms and rules of the game, and to cast suspicion on the relevance of the UN in this area. During the

[44] For an interesting discussion of this point see Gabriella Rosner Lande, "The Effect of the Resolutions of the United Nations General Assembly," *World Politics*, 19, 1 (October 1966), 83-105. Interesting work on this subject is also being done by Richard A. Falk and Rosalyn Higgins.

[45] For a discussion that focuses specifically on the question of political legitimation see Inis L. Claude, Jr., "Collective Legitimization as a Political Function of the United Nations," *International Organization*, 20, 3 (Summer 1966), 367-379.

sixties, however, several major shifts in the international system have decreased this rigidity. The decline of bipolarity and the rise of new power centers has introduced greater flexibility into East-West relationships, and new elements of fluidity which require the adaptation of old norms are emerging. In addition, the international system is now entering a period of increasingly rapid and extensive change, as yet without clear-cut patterns. In such a world, the need for procedures to facilitate the adaptation of norms and rules of the game is very great, but many of the established procedures, such as the development of customary international law, tend to decline in relevance. The sixties, therefore, saw a considerable increase of UN activity in the area of norm creation.

Several interesting conclusions emerge from this examination of the shifting patterns of UN roles in the international system. First, several of the roles are linked either positively or negatively and, therefore, exhibit a tendency to fluctuate in related patterns. Second, despite incompatibilities between specific roles, the United Nations has seldom displayed such a high degree of integration as to prohibit interesting developments along several of these channels simultaneously. Third, it is evident that the patterns of UN role fluctuation have been highly responsive to changes in the overall international system. In this connection, it is worth emphasizing again that the current period is one of considerable ambiguity in the role structure of the United Nations, just as it is a period of great flux in the overall international system. It therefore seems useful to turn to a more detailed consideration of current problems raised by the links between the United Nations and the overall international system.

IV

The constant presence of change, pervasive but somewhat indeterminate with respect to overall pattern or direction, constitutes a fundamental aspect of the international milieu in which the United Nations operates at present. The resultant fluidity of the international system shapes the activities of the Organization in a number of significant ways. The problems of regulating relationships of power, for example, are highly complex and require constant innovation with respect to both concepts and proximate activities. The role of the United Nations as a creator of norms and a source of collective legitimization tends to be sharply emphasized in a rapidly changing system in contrast to one that is more stable and slower to change. And the opportunities arising from change invite actors in the system to try to harness the influence of the Organization toward the accomplishment of political change. Even more fundamental, however, is the fact that the constant pressures of change tend to impose an inchoateness on the United Nations. Though this is not necessarily a signal of decline in the overall significance of the UN in world politics, it does tend to preclude orderly, long-term processes of institution building.

At the same time, the current fluidity of the international system has produced more substantive developments affecting UN operations. In the first place, the present period is witnessing important trends in the nature or quality of conflict in the international system. The United Nations was originally predicated, to a considerable degree, on the expectation that the principal threats to peace and security in world politics would stem from relatively clear-cut cases of interstate conflict involving the use of overt force across international boundaries. International realities, however, have shifted increasingly away from this expectation in recent years along several different channels. First, even cases of relatively direct interstate conflict are extraordinarily ambiguous in the current era—outside the subsystem formed by the old European states. A wide range of covert forms of coercion and proxy activities are of critical importance in the contemporary world. And as one moves beyond a simple "first-shot" conception of aggression,[46] these changes quickly make the problems of operating a genuine collective security system unmanageable. At the same time, many contemporary threats to international peace and security originate in what are essentially internal wars, a development that poses great problems for UN activities.[47] To begin with there is the problem of determining the point at which an internal war becomes sufficiently intertwined with external problems to be classified as a threat to international peace and security.[48] Moreover, it is increasingly clear that the United Nations cannot expect to intervene in situations of this kind without becoming deeply involved in substantive political issues, a fact that accounts for a good deal of the current hesitancy about such involvement.[49] As far as some Members are concerned, however, it is precisely this last characteristic of internal wars that makes the possibility of UN intervention interesting: in such contexts the prospects for utilizing the Organization as an instrument for the achievement of political changes become increasingly meaningful.

The problems arising from these changes are heightened even further by the fact that many of the most important cases of international conflict in the current period are actually complex amalgams, with elements of civil strife and

[46] The problem of formulating a working definition of aggression has been worked over many times in the contexts of both the League of Nations and the United Nations. Consensus, however, has never been reached. The "first-shot" conception refers to the idea of defining aggression in terms of the initiation of overt hostilities. Though this conception was never very satisfactory, it has become manifestly inadequate with respect to contemporary world politics.

[47] See Miller, Chapter 4 below.

[48] A consideration of the peculiarities of such cases as the Congo, Cyprus, Yemen, Rhodesia, and South West Africa illustrates the range of problems associated with such efforts at classification in real situations.

[49] Hesitancy along these lines rose sharply during the course of the Congo operation. It is important to add, nevertheless, that the Organization has continued to intervene in civil strife situations in cases such as Cyprus.

elements of external (and frequently competitive) intervention. In conflicts of this kind (Vietnam or Yemen) the weight of multiple cross-pressures tends to make the UN position inflexible.[50] As a result the capacity of the United Nations to intervene successfully in at least some of the most dangerous conflicts of the current era, in terms of *any* of its major roles, is apt to be negligible.

A second problem stems from the fact that the geographical distribution of major conflicts in world politics has been shifting in such a way as to create difficulties for the United Nations in its efforts to carve out meaningful roles in the international system. In effect, the shift with respect to serious threats to international peace and security has been characterized by movement in a southeasterly direction. We are moving into a period in which few threats of fundamental significance for the stability of the overall system emanate from the western hemisphere, and in which European security problems, though still important and potentially dangerous, are becoming frozen in patterns that are not likely to produce major disruptions in the immediate future.

The most dangerous areas in terms of international stability are now Africa and Asia, both areas in which there are often substantial barriers to efficacious United Nations activities. African conflicts, which are probably less serious from the point of view of systemwide stability than Asian ones, tend in the current period to emanate either from complex internal war situations[51] or from intractable issues involving racial problems. The latter have a high potential for polarizing political forces in the United Nations and for precipitating complex patterns of conflict involving both

---

[50] Above all, regulatory intervention alone is apt to be impossible in such cases since international operations of significant proportions are almost bound to produce important political consequences at least on a *de facto* basis. And as soon as one moves beyond sharply restricted regulatory activities in such situations, political cross-pressures begin to multiply.

[51] The cases of the Congo and Nigeria illustrate this pattern.

internal and external forces.[52] The result is a kind of unstable political equilibrium in which it is generally conceded that the Organization should take an interest in African problems, but there are sharp disagreements with regard to the specific roles it should play in such situations.[53]

Asian problems, on the other hand, seem both intrinsically more dangerous, and even more difficult from the point of view of successful United Nations operations, which are peculiarly limited by the combined weight of critical membership gaps, hostile attitudes on the part of important local powers,[54] nonacquiescence of relevant outside powers, and perhaps the most delicately balanced patterns of competitive intervention in local conflicts in the world. And, to make matters worse, changes in the alignments of interest groups inside the UN itself are currently tending to focus the effective attention of the Organization on non-Asian problems.[55] In the Asian context much of course depends on the developing role of Communist China and the future course of relationships between that country and the United Nations. But it is now increasingly clear that formal membership for China (even in the doubtful event that the Chinese would accept it in the near future) would not somehow deflate the problems.[56] There-

[52] Both the Rhodesian and South African situations harbor potentially explosive elements of this kind.

[53] The equilibrium remains intact for the moment because the Africans have not yet taken drastic steps to move beyond the postulate that the Organization should take a clear-cut interest in African problems. It is unstable because African frustrations in this area are currently rising sharply and becoming more and more focused on concrete issues such as Rhodesia and South Africa.

[54] This is of course particularly the case with Communist China at the present time. During 1964 and 1965, however, the idea of an anti-United Nations spearheaded by both China and Indonesia gained substantial political currency.

[55] This is especially evident in the case of the current interest in African issues. The proportion of the Organization's effective attention devoted to African problems in recent years has been both very large and growing markedly.

[56] This is by no means to argue that membership for the People's Republic of China is undesirable. The point is simply that many of

fore, it seems likely that the United Nations will be limited to a somewhat peripheral role in many of the key problems of Asian security in the immediate future.[57]

Third, in somewhat broader terms, a significant shift of the underlying axes of political contention in the international system has been growing since the sixties. And these changes are reflected quite clearly in the activities of the United Nations even though the fact that they are still in a stage of "becoming" means that many elements of ambiguity and contradiction are currently evident in the operations of the Organization.[58] A decline in the dominance of the East-West axis of world politics coupled with the growth of a meaningful North-South axis is clearly becoming an influential determinant of UN activities. In general terms, this shift has produced a significant tendency to conceptualize more and more issues in fundamentally North-South terms and increasing pressure for at least tacit coordination on critical issues between the USSR and the USA in the interest of protecting their growing common interests in essentially conservative solutions for various international problems.[59] At the same time, the new salience of the North-South axis is exercising a profound influence on many of the more specific focuses of UN activities, and the idea of utilizing the United Nations as an instrument for change in world politics is acquiring a new prominence. The remaining vestiges of colonialism are being powerfully

the high hopes associated with membership for China are almost certainly unrealistically optimistic.

[57] Some plausible exceptions to this conclusion are discussed at a later point in this essay.

[58] In fact, the current activities of the United Nations often reflect a peculiar and ambiguous mixture of old and new patterns of political attitudes and alignments.

[59] "Conservative" in this context refers to the overlapping interests of the superpowers in taking steps to preserve their positions of predominant influence in the international system. The linked developments referred to in the text tend to set in motion reciprocal pressures. In brief, the more the United Nations becomes an arena for North-South contention the greater are the incentives for Soviet-American coordination and vice versa.

assaulted,[60] and there are obvious signs of interest in the potential of the UN to coordinate attacks on various forms of "neocolonialism." In a related fashion problems arising from racial inequalities are being pressed with increasing virulence and impatience through the United Nations.[61] But above all the Organization is rapidly becoming one of the focal points in the emerging North-South contention arising from problems of nation building, economic welfare, and, in general, the redistribution of economic and political values in the international system.

By the same token, however, these shifts in the underlying axes of international politics are producing interesting changes in great-power diplomacy that are beginning to affect UN operations.[62] The decline of bipolarity and the rise of polycentrism within the principal blocs is producing a political environment with new elements of fluidity. As a result, the United Nations is no longer categorically prohibited from handling many important international problems by the preponderant realities of bipolarity; but for the same reasons the Organization is less of a "sure-fire" springboard for the political designs of the so-called nonaligned states[63] than it was in the fifties when the superpowers could always be played off against each other. Furthermore, the decline of bipolarity and the growing awareness on the part of the superpowers of important overlapping interests is now opening up possibilities for regulatory activities on the part of the United Nations even in the realm of great-power problems. While the dangers of great-

[60] This is particularly evident in the African context with respect to the Portuguese colonies and the successors to the United Kingdom's colonialism in Rhodesia and South Africa.

[61] Rhodesia, South West Africa, and South Africa all provide salient, concrete, and politically powerful vehicles for the pursuit of such interests in the United Nations in the current period.

[62] See Michalak, below, pp. 97-99.

[63] Given the general patterns of change in the international system, it is becoming increasingly unclear whether the postwar notion of nonalignment has any remaining meaning except in the vaguest political terms.

41

power confrontations have by no means disappeared,[64] the fact that the superpowers are increasingly anxious to prevent mutually disadvantageous outcomes places the United Nations in a new position vis-à-vis these powers.[65]

Perhaps most important of all for the UN, however, is the fact that shifts in the underlying axes of world politics are now beginning to create at least a limited interest on the part of the superpowers in utilizing the Organization to pursue some of their overlapping interests.[66] At this point several current trends affecting the position of the UN in the international system start to cross courses. The incipient efforts of the superpowers to coordinate through the United Nations in the interests of a kind of controlled conservatism are both significantly at odds with the desires of the Southern states to utilize the Organization as a pressure lever to achieve drastic changes in the international system, and sharply limited by the new realities of UN politics arising, fundamentally, from the great changes in both the general composition and the interest patterns of the membership. It is quite probable that the next few years will witness a sharpening of North-South contention in the Organization, though there are considerable incentives on specific issues to relapse into older patterns of East-West disagreement.[67]

These trends in great-power diplomacy, combined with the peculiarities of the Asian subsystem, open up another interesting possibility for shifts in UN activities. As Com-

[64] The dangers arising from the 1967 confrontation in the Middle East and the continuing problems of West Berlin and Vietnam are sufficient to demonstrate this point.

[65] For a brief discussion of the consequences of these changes see Young, *Trends in International Peacekeeping*.

[66] The maneuvers through which the superpowers recently sought to make use of the United Nations to drive home their position on the nonproliferation treaty constitute a clear illustration of this point.

[67] The fact that the superpowers have growing incentives to coordinate on *some* important issues does not in any way indicate that the numerous competitive aspects of their relationship will disappear. On many specific issues, therefore, the pressures for a policy of coordination are apt to be tempered by a temptation to play for proximate gains in terms of the East-West competition.

munist China becomes increasingly critical to the maintenance of even a minimal balance of power in Asia, the United States and the Soviet Union may find it attractive to coordinate, through the United Nations, in creating a counterweight to the Chinese pole. This would in fact represent an ironical, partial reversion to activities more or less compatible with the underlying conceptions of 1945, which have grown unfamiliar in the intervening years.[68] Curiously, many of the other Asian states might support such a move at least tacitly,[69] though pained reactions could be expected from those more interested in North-South perspectives (especially the Africans).[70] It is interesting to note that if such a pattern does begin to emerge, it will constitute an important shift away from the traditional regulatory conceptions of the role of the United Nations, and one that will be sharply castigated by actors, such as the African states, interested in movement away from these conceptions in *different* directions.

Fourth, the preceding discussion makes it important to emphasize the extent to which shifts in the membership patterns of the United Nations are affecting its operative balances of political interests. The most critical changes in this area stem ultimately from the rapid expansion of the membership that occurred in response to drastic shifts in the overall international system in the aftermath of World War II, but that were also facilitated by the activities of the Organization itself. The general effect of these changes, of

[68] It would be a reversion to the notion of the United Nations as an effector of great-power agreements. It would not be a straightforward reversion to this notion, however, since the results might often be agreement among the existing *superpowers* to contain a rising *Great* Power.

[69] The ranks of supporters, depending upon the specific nature of the actions in question, might well include the Republic of Korea (South Korea), the Philippines, New Zealand, Australia, Indonesia, Thailand, Malaysia, the Republic of Vietnam (South Vietnam), and, potentially, the Democratic Republic of Vietnam (North Vietnam) and India.

[70] Interestingly, such activities might not be affected in any drastic way by the entry of Communist China into the United Nations.

43

course, has been to speed up the emergence of North-South perspectives within the United Nations and to circumscribe the previously dominant position of the great powers.[71]

There are several more specific shifts, however, that have been significantly accelerated in recent years by the changing patterns of UN membership. Above all, this trend has sharply augmented pressures *within* the United Nations to utilize the Organization as a legislative device in world politics even if this requires UN action deliberately to break the peace, by force if necessary, in the interests of various conceptions of justice or equity.[72] And in fact, despite the impact of the changes in great-power diplomacy discussed above, the increasing influence of these sharply revisionist forces in the United Nations has tended to involve the Organization more and more in the business of political change.[73] In recent years, therefore, a number of political devices have been developed through which to handle activities aimed at political change under the guise of less controversial procedures.[74]

At present, however, the dangers inherent in this arrangement are on the upswing: the revisionist forces are becoming increasingly impatient with the current rate of progress and the great powers are increasingly concerned to prevent any swing toward excessively drastic revision-

[71] While the Great Powers can often exercise considerable control over the outcomes of debates in the United Nations, it has become increasingly difficult in recent years for them to control the allocation of effective attention within the Organization.

[72] Interest in the "peacebreaking" potential of the United Nations in the effort to achieve political change is evident, for example, in current debates concerning such issues as Rhodesia and South Africa.

[73] See Miller, Chapter 4 below.

[74] These devices include: 1) operations set up in such a way as to provide *de facto* sanction for efforts outside the United Nations to achieve political change (e.g., Indonesia in the 1940's); 2) efforts to disguise activities relating to political change under the guise of regulatory actions (e.g., the Congo); and 3) arrangements to give the Secretary-General *carte blanche* authority in specific situations either by passing ambiguous policy resolutions (e.g., the Congo after the death of Dag Hammarskjöld) or by moving to sanction his actions on an *ex post facto* basis (e.g., North Borneo and West Irian).

ism.[75] And this growing instability brings into focus another element of fluidity associated with the changing membership patterns: the contemporary version of the problem of orchestrating relationships between the United Nations and various regional organizations. Whereas orchestration was once primarily (though not solely) a problem of great-power interests in achieving security through collective defense arrangements rather than universal collective security mechanisms, it is now increasingly a problem of satisfying southern demands in the North-South context.[76] At present the critical danger in this connection arises from the glaring weaknesses of regional organizations[77] and the very real possibility that the Southern states, having exacerbated the regulatory problems of the universal Organization by shifting their revisionist endeavors to various regional actors, will be even more frustrated at this level and be tempted to turn to more radical actions in the pursuit of revisionist objectives. Whether the effective result of such shifts would be a breakdown of the current international system or a forceful reimposition of order by the superpowers is difficult to predict. But such developments, no matter which channel they followed, would produce extremely dangerous stresses from the point of view of overall international stability.

Finally, the rapidly shifting nature of the underlying context of world politics and the consequent emergence of a variety of qualitatively new concerns in the international arena also contribute to the prevailing sense of fluidity in both the overall international system and the politics of the

[75] This shift is ofen complicated, however, by the temptation to cheat on projects of great-power coordination outlined earlier in this essay.

[76] In other words, the context in which this problem is most pressing has shifted from the East-West arena to the North-South arena.

[77] The most relevant case in point is the Organization of African Unity (OAU). This constitutes another point of divergence between the African bloc and the Asian group since the Asian experience with regional organizations has so far been even less promising than the African experience.

45

United Nations. There are fundamentally new concerns arising from rapid developments in many areas such as the penetration of space, the exploration of possible uses of the oceans, population growth, urban agglomeration, almost universal efforts at modernization, and so forth. At the same time, virtually all relationships in world politics are sharply affected by the phenomenon of continuous innovation associated with constant, rapid, and accelerating developments in a wide range of both military and nonmilitary technologies. In other words, the emerging *political* flux discussed in the preceding paragraphs is playing itself out in an international system whose fundamental contextual conditions are also changing at an unprecedented rate.

This contextual fluidity in the international system creates both opportunities and pitfalls for the United Nations. The situation by its very nature emphasizes the norm creation and collective legitimization role of the Organization. And the fact that many of the emerging problems are relatively new ones makes them seem more promising areas for UN activity than many of the long-standing and intractable political difficulties confronting the Organization. The United Nations may well be able to play a role in creating regulatory arrangements for new human endeavors before they become deeply embedded in political controversy, or even, in areas such as space exploration, to participate in the development of control regimes designed to remove the area in question from the principal arenas of political contention.[78]

As to the pitfalls: the temptation to move into each new area as a major participant, despite the clear-cut political limitations on the capacities of the Organization in the present international system, raises serious dangers of overcommitment. Though the source of this problem is under-

[78] The space treaty negotiated toward the end of 1966, for example, constitutes an interesting attempt to implement the "removal from contention" notion. For a more extended discussion in which ideas of this kind figure prominently see Cyril Black, Richard Falk, Klaus Knorr, and Oran Young, *Neutralization and World Politics* (Princeton: Princeton University Press, 1968).

standable in terms of the universalist thrust of the underlying ethos of the UN, its potential consequences are sufficiently important in terms of realistic political calculations to warrant pause in many cases. In addition, many of these new problems have a substantial partisan potential in terms of evolving lines of contention in world politics. It is therefore to be expected that the upsurge of interest in roles for the United Nations in at least some new areas will contain a strong admixture of interest in utilizing the Organization for partisan purposes.[79] Though there is no *a priori* reason to condemn partisan efforts along these lines, they have frequently become serious liabilities for the long-term prospects of the United Nations in the past, and there is little reason to suppose that the situation now is very different.

There are virtually no general conclusions to be drawn from this discussion of the current flux in both the international system and the United Nations except to stress the absence of clarity. It is evident that much of the current confusion surrounding the UN stems from the rapidly changing quality of the international system. With respect to the future, however, the indeterminate nature of current trends in world politics makes it extraordinarily difficult to project a probable evolutionary course. Under the circumstances perhaps the most fruitful approach to assessing future changes in the links between the overall international system and the United Nations lies in comparing the implications of several plausible alternative patterns of evolution.

V

Much of the debate concerning ongoing and impending changes in world politics is presently structured in terms of the spectrum between the conceptual poles of bipolarity

[79] These partisan interests were quite evident in the early debates in the United Nations concerning the regulation of outer space. And they are presently increasing with respect to the problems of regulating the exploration and use of the resources of the oceans.

47

and multipolarity.[80] It is important to emphasize, therefore, that this is a very partial and frequently inadequate way to conceptualize the problem. First, while it is true that recent years have witnessed a marked decline in bipolar relationships in the international system, there is little evidence to suggest a sharp movement in the direction of clear-cut multipolarity. If the polar conception of multipolarity encompasses a situation in which there is a relatively large number of independent and significant actors, many of them with global or systemwide interests, and there is a marked tendency toward cross-cutting lines of conflict and rapidly changing patterns of alignment, it is evident that we are still far from full-blown multipolarity.[81] Second, the bipolarity-multipolarity spectrum taps only a limited number of the variables that are important in assessing ongoing and future developments in the international system.

What we need, therefore, is not a complete shift away from this perspective but an effort to formulate a broader range of models with which to conceptualize future developments. The material in the following pages is an attempt to deal with this problem in considering the probable links between the United Nations and a number of plausible changes of major proportions in world politics. The resultant models vary substantially in the extent to which they are compatible with each other, but each focuses on a clearly distinguishable and potentially influential set of possibilities.[82]

[80] For illustrative examples consult Kenneth Waltz, "The Stability of a Bipolar System," *Daedalus*, 93, 3 (Summer 1964), 881-909; Karl Deutsch and J. David Singer, "Multipolar Power Systems and International Stability," *World Politics*, 16, 3 (April 1964), 390-406; R. N. Rosecrance, "Bipolarity, multipolarity, and the future," *Journal of Conflict Resolution*, 10, 3 (September 1966), 314-327; and Ciro Elliott Zoppo, "Nuclear Technology, Multipolarity, and International Stability," *World Politics*, 18, 4 (July 1966), 579-606.

[81] For a fuller discussion of this question see Oran R. Young, "Political Discontinuities in the International System," *World Politics*, 20, 3 (April 1968), 369-392.

[82] Since the models are not mutually exclusive, they do not add up to a logical partition. This would create serious difficulties for some purposes but not for those which underlie the present analysis.

The United Nations in a New Balance System[83]

It is quite possible that in the foreseeable future the international system will evolve increasingly in the direction of an admitted and self-conscious resumption of interest in balance-of-power arrangements and the diplomatic procedures associated with them. Several incipient trends already point in this direction, above all, the continued rise of a small number of additional powers to great-power status in contrast to an unlimited spread of nuclear weapons throughout the system.[84] In addition, movements toward the fragmentation of universal ideologies and increasing fluidity in alliance systems that were previously quite rigid suggest the emergence of new possibilities for balance-of-power diplomacy.[85] And the emerging *political* necessities of maintaining minimal levels of international stability in a world that is both increasingly interdependent and characterized by the existence of nuclear weapons may well produce, in the near future, a variety of pragmatic arrangements for the management of high-level coercion in world politics.

A new balance system would obviously produce certain difficulties for the United Nations. In the first place, it would create a political milieu so sharply at odds with major elements of the underlying mythology of the UN as

[83] See also Michalak's remarks, below, p. 99 and passim.

[84] The actors in world politics appear to be evolving at the present time toward an increasingly complex stratification pattern. Though it is not to be expected that states such as Communist China, Japan, France, and West Germany will reach the level of influence of the superpowers in the foreseeable future, these actors are growing markedly in terms of influence vis-à-vis the lesser states in the system. For further discussion of the diffusion of effective power in the international system as well as these evolving patterns of stratification in world politics see Young, *The Intermediaries*, Chapter 9.

[85] While the role of ideology in general may not be declining, the fragmentation of integrated, worldwide ideological movements alters the impact of ideology on world politics considerably. Similarly, though alliances of various kinds remain important, the differences between rigid alliance systems and more fluid patterns of alliances in terms of their impact on world politics are striking.

to necessitate wide-ranging adaptations in prevailing images and conceptions of its roles.[86] It might well increase both the availability and the efficacy of regulatory mechanisms in the international system outside the UN framework. And it would very probably lead to a significant decline in the norm creation and collective legitimization activities that are so evident in the present period of flux.

At the same time, however, a return to overt balance-of-power politics might well have some advantageous consequences for the United Nations. It would underline sharply the fact that the Organization is only one of a number of relevant actors in world politics, thereby deflating many of the temptations to overcommitment out of the misplaced desire to achieve universal relevance. Even more important is the fact that a new balance system would inevitably be a "balance with a difference" in an international system characterized by global interdependencies and nuclear weapons. Under the circumstances, the "rough and ready" quality of the classical balance of power would almost certainly be incompatible with the achievement of even minimal levels of international stability.[87] The United Nations might therefore move toward the performance of new regulatory functions, playing the roles of moderator and safety-valve in a twentieth century balance system. Finally, developments along these lines would probably heighten the role of the Organization as a forum for political brokerage

[86] Above all, it would mean carving out roles for the United Nations explicitly within a balance system rather than thinking of the activities of the Organization as an alternative to the power politics associated with balance arrangements.

[87] The classical balance-of-power system was "rough and ready" because it sanctioned large-scale hostilities of various kinds, delegated decision-making in the war-peace area almost entirely to individual actors, and accepted the possible destruction of individual actors as relatively normal. Each of these characteristics may be acceptable even in the contemporary world in limited forms. But the necessary limits in all these areas are almost certainly sharper and more extensive in the present nuclear and highly interdependent system than they were in the systems of the seventeenth and eighteenth centuries.

50

in the constant process of cementing and altering alignments attendant upon balance-of-power diplomacy.

The United Nations in a World of Soviet-American Coordination[88]

An important possibility in the foreseeable future, already briefly mentioned, is the prospect of the two superpowers moving increasingly toward limited coordination on the basis of an agreement to secure at least minimal levels of stability in the overall international system. The problem of stability may well take on such importance and political salience that these powers will no longer consider it acceptable simply to assume that international stability will be a natural by-product of the interactions of world politics, or to relegate such questions to the somewhat peripheral arena of the United Nations without further consideration. This is not to argue that the superpowers will coordinate with each other formally or explicitly on a wide range of issues, that they will cease to compete on many important issues in world politics, or that they will systematically attempt to prevent the occurrence of many lesser forms of international coercion. The reference is instead to the prospect of much more limited forms of coordination aimed at preventing an outright breakdown of the existing international system. In the light of this limited conception of coordination, current indications of growing Soviet and American willingness to opt for policies of coordination with each other over policies of alliance cohesion on important concrete issues, such as preventing the spread of nuclear weapons, begin to look significant.

Even such limited forms of superpower coordination, however, would produce a great impact on the position of the United Nations in the international system. It would clearly tend to relieve the Organization of some of the more far-reaching regulatory responsibilities nominally assigned to it in the Charter. And it might well generate increased

[88] See Falk's description of UN System II, below, pp. 216-218.

51

barriers to the utilization of the UN as an instrument for the achievement of political change in the interests of the Southern states, since it must be expected that one of the sources of superpower coordination would be agreement on a relatively conservative attitude toward major changes in the distribution of political values in the international system.[89] On the other hand, the idea of superpower coordination on a limited basis is not foreign to many of the ideas concerning roles for the United Nations originally projected at San Francisco. The superpowers might well find it highly desirable to work through the UN in orchestrating their efforts to handle specific threats to the stability of the international system. And there would in any case be numerous lesser cases of international conflict and coercion in which the competitive interests of the superpowers would probably overshadow their fundamental agreement on the maintenance of international stability, and in which the Organization might, therefore, play a number of independent roles. In addition, developments that would in effect relieve the United Nations of some of its rigidifying fixation with international stability at the strategic level might well free the Organization to play more extensive roles in longer-term projects aimed at creating lasting conditions of stability in the international system, and at satisfying widespread desires in the areas of economic development and political modernization. While effective superpower coordination would clearly limit the roles of the United Nations in some ways, it might also free the Organization to perform other roles with greater efficacy.

The United Nations in a System of Discontinuities

At present it seems less and less adequate to discuss the evolution of the international system in terms of uniform

---

[89] As the major "have" powers in the system, the superpowers must be affected negatively by large-scale changes in the distribution of political values in world politics. Their interests in regulating the use of the United Nations as an instrument for the achievement of

projections covering the entire system rather than in terms of emerging relationships between the major regional subsystems of world politics.[90] While there are a number of global or universal issues and actors in the system, we are increasingly faced with a situation in which individual subsystems are acquiring unique qualities of considerable significance, and in which there are therefore growing discontinuities between the various subsystems. In such a system it is to be expected that the specific relationships between the global actors will vary substantially from one subsystem to another.[91] Moreover, although there are obvious and important interconnections between the subsystems, it cannot be expected that the requirements and problems of managing power will be the same for each of them.

If the international system develops very far in this direction, it will in the first place lead to a growing fragmentation of roles for the United Nations. And in fact a number of growing discontinuities in the patterns of UN activities in the Asian, African, European, and western hemisphere subsystems, alluded to in an earlier section, suggest that this process of fragmentation is already under way. Further developments along these lines would clearly reduce even further the influence of universalist precepts in the underlying mythology concerning roles for the United Nations in world politics. But it is by no means clear that they would reduce the overall impact of UN activities on world politics in more pragmatic terms. Trends of this kind would, however, produce several specific difficulties. First, they might well exacerbate contradictions among the activities of the United Nations which are already noticeable, thereby increasing the possibility of efforts to manipulate the opera-

political change are therefore both overlapping and essentially conservative.

[90] The notion of a system involving extensive political discontinuities is discussed at length in Young, "Political Discontinuities in the International System," *World Politics*, 20, 3 (1968), 369-392.

[91] This is clearly the case already with respect to Soviet-American relationships. For a discussion contrasting their relationships in the European and Asian subsystems consult *ibid.*

tions of the Organization for partisan political purposes. Second, such trends might raise increased barriers to efforts within the framework of the UN to deal meaningfully with some of the remaining issues of global significance (e.g., problems of arms control and disarmament) as the political coalitions within the Organization began to fragment in response to the external fragmentation of world politics. Already, for example, it is difficult for the superpowers to organize the political resources of the United Nations on those issues of global significance on which they have begun, tentatively to be sure, to move toward limited coordination.[92] And the growth of diverging perspectives between the African and Asian members of the Afro-Asian bloc is beginning to hamper the coordination of the Southern states in prosecuting general North-South issues.

The United Nations in a System of Mixed Actors

Though the United Nations is not itself a state, it is predicated to a large extent on a conception of the international system in which states are the fundamental units and in which ideas concerning territoriality, external sovereignty, and juridical equality are extraordinarily influential.[93] Increasingly, however, the realities of world politics appear to be departing from this conception. The territorial state is declining in terms of a number of its functions although, at the same time, nationalism and the nation-state are expanding in influence in some parts of the world.[94] More-

[92] This is evident, for example, even with respect to an issue like the nonproliferation of nuclear weapons where the position of the superpowers is strongly backed by idealistic sentiments. In this connection note especially the contrast between the passage of general resolutions and effective actions.

[93] These ideas are explicitly incorporated in Articles 2 and 4 of the United Nations Charter.

[94] The differences between the concepts of state and nation are frequently overlooked in discussions of such questions. A state is an administrative unit involving central institutions of government and the ability to enter into sovereign relations with other states. A nation, on the other hand, is a group of people bound together by some combination of ethnic similarity, linguistic compatibility, shared tradi-

54

over, a wide range of essentially transnational actors are rising in importance in world politics despite the continued conceptual and juridical predominance of the state. And the various roles of regional and international organizations of the interstate type can no longer be dismissed as essentially peripheral developments that do not affect the basic nature of the international system as a states system. The United Nations, therefore, is now operating more and more in a system of mixed actors that encompasses important patterns of interaction between qualitatively distinguishable types of actors.

The potential impact on the United Nations of developments along these lines is very great.[95] Since an increasingly mixed-actor situation would be both extraordinarily complex and sharply at odds with prevailing images, assumptions, and norms concerning world politics, the roles of the UN as a forum for clarifying discussion and as a creator of norms might well expand even more rapidly. In particular, the need for several coexistent conceptual and normative structures governing the relationships of world politics, together with the complexities arising from various patterns of interpenetration among relevant actors, would generate extensive requirements of adaptation with respect to diplomatic procedures, political norms, and legal arrangements. And here the underlying universalism of the United Nations might well project it into a position of considerable prominence.

In addition, the United Nations would offer a relatively natural forum for diplomatic interaction between the different types of actors in the international system. Developments along these lines, however, would also generate growing pressures for adaptation within the UN itself, since

---

tions, and common culture. A nation-state exists when the state and the nation are geographically coterminous. Though current orthodoxies enshrine the nation-state as the fundamental unit of world politics, political realities now appear to be departing more and more from the conditions envisioned in these orthodoxies.

[95] See Gordenker, below, pp. 179-183.

its structures and procedures presently incorporate a number of the postulates of a state-centered conception of world politics. Among other things there would probably be a steady growth of pressure to alter membership requirements to give a larger role to actors other than states, as well as to consider complex restructurings of various procedural arrangements dealing with questions such as voting.[96]

The United Nations in an Increasingly Interdependent System

One of the most marked trends in world politics stems from the rapid growth of influential interdependencies throughout the international system. Interdependence refers in this context to the extent to which actions or events occurring in one part of the international system affect other parts. Interdependence is therefore the opposite of isolation, and it encompasses the possibility of both positive and negative interdependencies as far as relations between the actors in the system are concerned: the growth of interdependencies may increase the scope and incentive for cooperation between the actors or generate new causes and opportunities for conflict.[97] Both results occur frequently in the contemporary world.

Despite some important exceptions the current growth of interdependencies is characterized by a rather strong thrust toward globalism.[98] Though it is a common mistake

[96] Significant pressures for change in some of these areas are already becoming evident. So far, the most influential pressures of this kind are those supporting various forms of weighted voting.

[97] It is commonly (but mistakenly) argued that the growth of interdependencies in the international system must lead to the strengthening of international community. There is, however, no necessary link of this kind. As indicated in the text, new interdependencies may produce either positive or negative results from the perspective of international community.

[98] The movement toward European integration, for example, constitutes an exception since it tends to foster partial integration even when this requires a reduction of global interdependencies.

56

to overemphasize the image of isolated islands of civilization in describing past periods,[99] there is no doubt that at present levels of systemwide interdependence as well as interdependencies in many subsystems are rising to unprecedented heights.[100] As a result the concept of "one world" will be increasingly relevant in the foreseeable future, though relations between individual units of the international system may be anything but harmonious.

The impact of such developments on the United Nations will depend on the specific nature of rising interdependencies, the balances of interdependencies between the overall system and various subsystems, and the mixture of positive and negative interdependencies. If, for example, the international system evolves in the direction of positive interdependencies and, consequently, underlying international community, traditional regulatory conceptions of the role of the United Nations may be increasingly supplemented and eventually replaced by an emphasis on activities relating to peaceful change and long-term international development. Under such circumstances, the Organization might well become increasingly preoccupied with efforts to launch and direct cooperative projects rather than with desperate attempts to dam the floods of chaos. On the other hand, the picture would be radically different if the continued growth of interdependencies leads primarily to greater and greater scope and incentive for political conflict without producing any compensatory movement toward

[99] For some fascinating comments on the relatively extensive links between "East" and "West" even in ancient times see Bozeman, Parts I and II.

[100] Some writers have stressed the proposition that interdependencies *within* the units of world politics are increasing more rapidly than interdependencies *between* the units. See, for example, Karl Deutsch and Alexander Eckstein, "National Industrialization and the Declining Share of the International Economic Sector, 1890-1959," *World Politics*, 13, 2 (January 1961), 267-299. The point to be emphasized here, however, is that important types of interdependence between units can increase simultaneously with the growth of interdependencies within units.

international harmony.[101] If specific local conflicts were increasingly apt to ripple through the entire system and exacerbate adversary relationships at a variety of levels, for example, the prospects for the United Nations might well become more and more desperate.[102] Efforts to utilize the Organization for the achievement of change or as a tool of partisan politics would no doubt be rife. And the UN would be fortunate to be able to perform constructive tasks even in highly restricted regulatory efforts.

It seems most probable, however, that a complex mixture of trends involving the growth of both positive and negative interdependencies will continue to characterize world politics for the foreseeable future. To a very real extent it is the clear movement toward an increasingly interdependent international system, coupled with the complex mosaic pattern formed by the simultaneous growth of positive and negative interdependencies of varying dimensions, which accounts for the current flux pervading UN operations. This set of developments simultaneously keeps the United Nations relevant to the problems of world politics and prevents it from evolving in any clear-cut direction. It seems probable that the resultant pattern of ambiguity will continue, at least in the immediate future.

It is of course evident that these models are not all mutually exclusive. On the contrary, various combinations of them range all the way from sharp contradiction to probable coexistence. Analytically, the separation of these evolutionary patterns is of considerable utility in the effort to focus clearly on changes in specific variables while holding others constant. At the same time, each of the models represents an extrapolation of the logical implications of

[101] See Falk's description of UN System V, below, pp. 225-227.

[102] Many aspects of the current Vietnam conflict suggest that this pattern is a realistic and potentially dangerous one. In the long run it may well be the more general intangible and symbolic consequences of Vietnam rather than the extensive local problems raised by the conflict which will have the greatest impact on the problems of maintaining stability in the international system.

important trends whose beginnings are already apparent. Though they have no formal predictive value, they are by no means irrelevant fabrications bearing little or no relationship to international realities.

Substantively, a discussion along these lines serves to emphasize ever more clearly the responsiveness of the United Nations to changes in the overall international system. Under the circumstances, contemporary phenomena such as the role fluctuation and the general inchoateness of the Organization are fully understandable. And it is hardly surprising that it is presently impossible to project with certainty the probable patterns of the future evolution of the United Nations.

CHAPTER 2

The United Nations and the League

STANLEY J. MICHALAK, JR.

I. Introduction

This chapter explores some of the relationships between the behavior of universal international organizations in the realm of peace and security and the systemic conditions within which they operate. While much has been written about the League and the United Nations, comparative analyses of these two institutions are exceedingly rare in the literature on international organization.[1] In fact, at a general and theoretical level, little is known about the reciprocal and mutual interactions between each of these organizations and its international system.[2]

[1] The only major systematic comparative study of the League and the United Nations in the area of peace and security is George Liska's, *International Equilibrium* (Cambridge, Mass.: Harvard University Press, 1957).

[2] To be sure there is a plethora of implicit theoretical propositions in the existing literature on international organization. Systematic treatments, however, are rare. In 1949, C. Easton Rothwell wrote an essay, "International Organization and World Politics," *International Organization*, 3 (November 1949), 605-619, in which he called for greater explicit attention to the relationships between all types of international organizations and the systemic contexts in which they exist. His call was not heeded. In 1960, Ernst Haas made a similar plea in his review of the Carnegie series of *National Studies on International Organizations*. See his "The Comparative Study of the United Nations," *World Politics*, 12, 2 (January 1960), 198-322.

With the exception of this collection of essays, the only explicit attempts to grapple with this problem may be found in two articles and a monograph. The articles are: Wolfram Hanreider, "International Organizations and International Systems," *Journal of Conflict Resolution*, 10 (September 1966), 297-313 and Oran Young, "The United Nations and the International System," *International Organization*, 22, 4 (Autumn 1968), 902-922. The monograph is Haas' own: *Collective Security and the International System* (Denver: Social Science

Yet, because the two organizations operated in considerably different settings and behaved differently in important respects, comparative analyses could contribute to our understanding of international organizations in three ways. First, at the theoretical level, such studies would focus thinking explicitly on the question of what types of systemic variables are most crucial in determining different types of organizational behavior. For example, one could explore the types of behavior that international organizations display in a particular type of system, be it bipolar or multipolar. Or existing hypotheses on this question could be tested.

Secondly, such comparative analyses would provide a perspective on existing studies of the work of the League and the United Nations. A wealth of propositions about the roles or functions performed by the United Nations in the postwar international system can be found. Yet, as long as these propositions relate only to the postwar system, it is hard to know to what extent such behavior is unique to this particular system or is a function of factors endemic in any type of international system. To understand the relationship between any international organization and its particular international system, comparative analysis is essential.

Finally, greater understanding about the relationships between international organizations and international systems at a general level may help to provide a theoretical framework for integrating studies of international organization. Such a framework could also illuminate areas in which further study and research are needed.

This chapter will make a start in this direction. First, the major similarities and differences in the behavior of the two organizations will be noted. Next, a set of systemic variables of seeming relevance for the behavior of international

Foundation, University of Denver: 1968). A condensed form of this work may be found in an essay under the same title in R. A. Falk and W. F. Hanreider, eds., *International Law and Organization* (Philadelphia: Lippincott, 1968), pp. 299-344.

UN AND THE LEAGUE

organizations will be described and defined. Third, an attempt will be made to explain the similarities and differences in the behavior of the League and the UN, in terms of the selected set of systemic variables. Finally, several tentative hypotheses will be set forth on the relationships between universal international organizations and international systems in general.

II. Similarities and Differences in the Behavior of the League and the United Nations

Perhaps the most notable similarity in the behavior of the League and the United Nations is that neither organization brought to an end or fundamentally affected the major international conflicts taking place around them. Their founders and champions hoped that these institutions would become the center of world politics, but this has not been the case. Historians of the interwar period focus not so much on Geneva as on Genoa, Locarno, Washington, Stresa, and Munich. In the postwar period, the major parleys affecting international politics have been held not in New York but in Paris, Moscow, Washington, and Geneva. In fact, both institutions failed even to consider a number of important conflicts. Of the 37 disputes involving force or the threat of force which occurred during the interwar period, the League considered only 21, or slightly more than half. The United Nations considered 28, or about three-fourths of those that occurred between 1945 and 1966.[3]

[3] The conflicts analyzed in this essay are those studied by K. J. Holsti in his "Resolving International Conflicts," *The Journal of Conflict Resolution*, 10 (1966), 271-296. Holsti distinguishes between "disputes" and "conflicts." The former are said to arise from accidents and minor provocations while the latter stem from incompatible collective objectives. Holsti identified 80 conflicts occurring from 1919 through 1965 and analyzed 77 of them. Three were rejected for reasons of ambiguity and lack of data. A conflict was defined as "a situation where one or more governments have made

It is also true that both organizations were unable at times to respond beyond the verbal level to blatant breaches of the peace. For the League this was increasingly true through the 1930s when some of Hitler's most flagrant actions, such as the partition of Czechoslovakia, failed even to appear on the organization's agenda. In the postwar period, the United Nations failed to respond beyond the verbal level when Communist China annexed Tibet in 1951, when the Soviet Union intervened in Hungary in 1956, and when the United States similarly intervened in Guatemala in 1954 and the Dominican Republic in 1965.

On the positive side, both organizations have contained and abated serious conflicts. During the first decade of its existence, the League facilitated the resolution of a series of important ethnic and territorial conflicts stemming from the peace treaties. The United Nations, while less success-

---

demands against another state, backed up with the threat of force or where they have taken planned military or confiscatory actions which were a threat to the interests of other states" (272). Given the emphasis on the use or threat of military force in this definition several important issues and crises of concern to the students of international organization are not included by Holsti—e.g. Southwest Africa, apartheid, and the Congo. But I do not think this fact detracts from the basic points made and conclusions drawn by either of us.

The sources of information for each of these conflicts included standard reference and documentary sources as well as diplomatic histories. For conflicts in the interwar period, the major sources were: John I. Knudson, *A History of the League of Nations* (Atlanta: Smith, 1938); Denys P. Myers, *Handbook of the League of Nations* (Boston: World Peace Foundation, 1935); F. P. Walters, *A History of the League of Nations*, 2 vols. (London and New York: Oxford University Press, 1952); and various volumes in the Royal Institute of International Affairs, *Survey of International Affairs* (London: 1925). For conflicts in the postwar period the major sources were: Catherine Teng, *Synopses of United Nations Cases in the Field of Peace and Security*, 1946-1965 (New York: Carnegie Endowment for International Peace, 1960); Royal Institute of International Affairs, *Survey of International Affairs* (London: 1946ff); *United Nations Yearbook* (New York: 1946ff); and Council on Foreign Relations, *The United States in World Affairs* (New York: 1948ff).

For stylistic purposes the terms disputes and conflicts are used interchangeably unless otherwise noted in the text.

ful in producing settlements, has been crucial in restoring and maintaining the peace in Suez, Lebanon, the Congo, Cyprus, and West Irian.

Finally, beyond involvement in specific disputes or crises, both institutions have reflected in their deliberative organs a preoccupation with some of the fundamental international issues of their times, be it disarmament in the interwar period, or the postwar development of the backward areas. On such issues, extended discussion has taken place, judgments have been made, and proposals for dealing with them have been adopted.

Equal, if not more noteworthy than these similarities, are the differences between the two institutions. The most obvious one is the simple fact that while the League ceased functioning after twenty years, the United Nations is still an active organization. Yet the former was more successful in the peaceful settlement of disputes than the latter. Of the 21 conflicts brought before it, the League settled seven completely, in accordance with procedures outlined in the Covenant. Between 1945 and 1966, however, only one dispute has been solved solely within the principles and procedures outlined by the United Nations Charter—the dispute between France and Morocco over Bizerte.[4]

The League and the United Nations also differed both geographically and substantively in the scope of their attention. In regard to matters of peace and security the League was largely a European-oriented organization: while the scope of its obligations was universal, its involvement was not. Of the 21 conflicts that came before it, 15 (more than 70 per cent) were located in Europe, three in Latin America, and one each in Asia, the Near East, and Africa. As Table 1 indicates, this focus reflected the European base of interwar international politics. The United

---

[4] And the solution of this dispute involved considerable risks for the Organization's Secretary-General. See Leon Gordenker, *The UN Secretary-General and the Maintenance of Peace* (New York: Columbia University Press, 1967), pp. 167-171.

Nations, on the other hand, has had a much more global scope: only 25 percent of the conflicts coming before it originated in Europe.

TABLE 1

GEOGRAPHIC LOCUS OF DISPUTES CONSIDERED
BY THE LEAGUE AND THE UNITED NATIONS

Locus	League Disputes	Total Interwar Disputes	United Nations Disputes	Total Postwar Disputes
Europe	15	26	7	9
Latin America	3	4	3	6
Asia	1	1	9	13
Near East	1	5	8	9
Africa	1	1	1	2
North America	0	0	0	0

The substantive scope of the issues considered by each institution also varied considerably. Aside from specific conflicts, the League was largely preoccupied with one problem: the creation of a stable international system in Europe. The United Nations, on the other hand, has confronted a much wider range of problems, such as decolonization, the eradication of racism within nation-states, and the redistribution of wealth and income from industrial to nonindustrial nations. This reflects a widening of substantive concerns far beyond that even envisaged by participants in the League.

A final difference between the two organizations concerns the relationships between their two major organs. Within the League a division took place between the major organs, while during the lifetime of the United Nations, division has largely cut across them. In the interwar period, the Council acted largely as a concert of major powers holding similar underlying doctrines about patterns of authority and decision-making in the international system. The League Assembly, on the other hand, was largely under the influence of the leaders of the smaller states who espoused rather different doctrines. Thus a split existed between these organs.

In the postwar period, there have been sharp differences in the underlying doctrines of the superpowers and, until recently, a bipolar split pervaded the General Assembly as well as the Security Council. The former organ never developed a sense of its own corporate distinctness, in spite of the fact that the General Assembly has supervisory powers over the Trusteeship Council and the Economic and Social Council, corresponding to powers which during the League period were vested with the Council. Also, because of the fixed, rigid positions of each bloc and the leadership and authority exercised by the bloc leaders within the General Assembly, that organ failed to become the preserve of the leaders of the smaller nations, as had happened in the League Assembly.[5] If the current multipolarity continues, however, such a division may occur over the next decade.

III. Some Systemic Variables

Any attempt to explore the relationships between these similarities and differences and "international systems" requires some clarification of the latter term. Myriad factors operate upon an international organization at any one time, so one must necessarily be selective. This paper will therefore focus upon two clusters of variables which many systemic theorists consider to be crucial determinants of any international system: 1) the unit configuration and distribution of power, and 2) the homogeneity or heterogeneity of underlying doctrines of the major powers in each system.[6]

---

[5] See, however, Lande's exploration of the surprising effectiveness of the General Assembly, Chapter 3 below.

[6] See for example: Morton A. Kaplan, *System and Process in International Politics* (New York: Wiley, 1957), chs. 1-5; Raymond Aron, *Peace and War* (Garden City, N.Y.: Doubleday, 1966), chs. IV, V; Richard Rosecrance, *Action and Reaction* (Boston: Little, Brown, 1963), chs. 1, 11, and 12; Stanley Hoffmann, *Contemporary Theory in International Relations* (Englewood Cliffs, N.J.: Prentice-Hall, 1960), 179-183; Haas, *op.cit*; and Young, *op.cit*.

Unit configuration refers to the differentiation of the actors in a system on the basis of size, resources, and power. The distribution of power concerns the power differentials between those states wishing to maintain the existing systemic configuration or systemic status quo and those states wishing to alter in a fundamental sense either the basic systemic configuration or the status quo within it. Systems are stable when nations supporting the status quo have a preponderance of power to deter or regulate action by anti-status quo powers. Unstable systems are those in which the power differential is unclear or uncertain. Transitional systems are those in which the preponderance of power is shifting from the status quo powers to the anti-status quo powers. When this occurs, status quo powers will have to either wage war or acquiesce in major changes in the status quo or the system itself.

Underlying doctrines comprise the conceptions of purpose and authority held by the major members of a given system. Conceptions of purpose refer to views expressed by decision-makers about the substantive ends of international politics. These include conceptions about legitimate or illegitimate goals of nation-state behavior, in terms of both scope and extensiveness and attitudes toward system maintenance. Two questions are most important: 1) whether the territorial aims of the major powers are limited or unlimited, whether they involve change within a system or change of a system, and 2) whether there is general agreement on the substantive areas considered legitimate or appropriate for international action—whether, for example, there is agreement that the nature of regimes is not a legitimate issue for international conflict.

Conceptions of authority refer to the views of decision-makers as to how decisions should be made within the international system in those issue-areas considered legitimate for attention. These include conceptions about the roles which various members of the system should play and the rights and perquisites they should enjoy in the international decision-making process.

67

When there is substantial consensus on legitimacy and authority among the major actors of an international system, the underlying doctrines may be said to be homogeneous. Where this consensus is lacking, they may be termed heterogeneous. Seldom is there complete homogeneity or heterogeneity: reality is never that kind to the abstract models of social scientists. Nor are measurements better than crude. Furthermore, there is often a discrepancy between ideal and actual patterns of behavior. Thus, judgments can only be rough and open to question.

IV. Why the League Ceased to Exist While the United Nations has not

Using the framework outlined above, the behavior of universal international organizations may be seen as having taken place within four systemic contexts:

I. A multipolar, homogeneous system with the preponderance of power residing among the status quo powers (1919-1933).

II. A multipolar, heterogeneous system with the preponderance of power decreasingly residing with the status quo powers (1934-1939).

III. A bipolar, heterogeneous system with the preponderance of power residing with the status quo powers (1945-1962).

IV. A bi-multipolar, heterogeneous system with the preponderance of power residing with the status quo powers (1963-).

The purpose of this section is to examine the relationships between these systemic contexts and the persistence of the League and the United Nations. However, the distinction between sheer persistence of an institution *qua* institution and the particular roles an organization will play within a given systemic context must be borne in mind; for these are two separate questions. Here, the emphasis will be largely on the former; the latter will be dealt with in following sections.

Formally as well as empirically, any international organization designed to protect a given status quo from change by unilateral or multilateral uses of violence will persist only so long as those nations dedicated to the maintenance of that status quo do the following: 1) agree on what aspects of the status quo are vital for general system maintenance; 2) agree on the methods for maintaining those aspects of the status quo; and 3) possess sufficient power to maintain those aspects. The failure of any one of these conditions to exist or materialize will seriously jeopardize the persistence of any international organization in a *de facto* sense if not in a legal one. The analysis will proceed, first, by examining the relationships between these conditions for persistence and the variables selected for analysis within each of the systemic contexts. Some concluding comments will be made about the relationship between systemic variables and organizational survival in general.

During the first systemic context, from 1919 until 1933, only the last of these three conditions was met.[7] As to what

---

[7] The historical analysis in this paper is based on standard works in the field of diplomatic history and international politics. The major sources relied upon for the interwar period were: E. H. Carr, *German-Soviet Relations between Two World Wars, 1919-1939* (Baltimore: Johns Hopkins Press, 1951) and *International Relations Between the Two World Wars, 1919-1939* (New York: Macmillan, 1951); G. M. Carter, *The British Commonwealth and International Security: The Role of the Dominions, 1919-1939* (Toronto: Ryerson Press, 1947); G. A. Craig and F. Gilbert, eds., *The Diplomats 1919-1939* (Princeton: Princeton University Press, 1953); E. Eyck, *A History of the Weimar Republic*, 2 vols. (Cambridge, Mass.: Harvard University Press, 1962, 1963), C. J. Friedrich, *Foreign Policy in the Making: The Search for a New Balance of Power* (New York: Norton, 1938); G. M. Gathorne-Hardy, *A Short History of International Affairs, 1920-1939* (London: Oxford University Press, 1950), W. M. Jordan, *Great Britain, France, and the German Problem, 1918-1939* (London and New York: Oxford University Press, 1943); Royal Institute of International Affairs, *Survey of International Affairs* (London: 1925ff); H. Seton-Watson, *Eastern Europe between the Wars, 1918-*

aspects of the status quo were vital for systemic maintenance and the methods of insuring them, the major status quo powers, Britain and France, were in disagreement. Thus, conflict operated on two axes: 1) between status quo and non-status quo powers, most importantly Germany and the East European revisionists, and 2) among the status quo powers. In fact, the latter conflict engendered a great deal of instability within the system and had a major impact in shaping the behavior of the League, as will be described below. Yet, despite the sharpness of this conflict among the major status quo powers and the feelings of insecurity that resulted from it, two major stabilizing factors were at work in the system. First, German decision-makers had neither the will nor the capacity to seek a revision of Versailles

---

1941 (Cambridge: Cambridge University Press, 1945); A. J. P. Taylor, *The Origins of the Second World War* (New York: Athenaeum, 1962), F. P. Walters, *A History of the League of Nations*, A. Wolfers, *Britain and France between Two Wars: Conflicting Strategies of Peace Since Versailles* (New York: Harcourt Brace, 1940), and A. Zimmern, *The League of Nations and the Rule of Law* (London: Macmillan, 1936).

For the postwar period the following books served as general sources: P. Calvocoressi, *International Politics Since 1945* (New York: Praeger, 1968); Council on Foreign Relations, *The United States in World Affairs* (New York: 1948ff); Louis Halle, *The Cold War as History* (London: Chatto and Windus, 1967); Stanley Hoffmann, *Gulliver's Troubles* (New York: McGraw-Hill, 1968); W. Knapp, *A History of War and Peace* (New York: Oxford University Press, 1967); E. Luard, ed., *The Cold War: A Re-appraisal* (New York: Praeger, 1964); E. Luard, *Conflict and Peace in the Modern International System* (Boston: Little, Brown, 1968); W. W. Rostow, *The United States in the World Arena* (New York: Harper, 1960); and H. V. Seton-Watson, *Neither War nor Peace* (New York: Praeger, rev. ed., 1962).

For the more recent period, 1962 on, the following articles were of special value: Wolfram Hanreider, "The International System: Bipolar or Multibloc," *Journal of Conflict Resolution*, 9, 3 (1965), 299-308; R. N. Rosecrance, "Bipolarity, Multipolarity, and the Future," *Journal of Conflict Resolution*, 10, 3 (1966), 314-327; Oran R. Young, "Political Discontinuities in the International System," *World Politics*, 20 (April 1968), 369-392; and Kenneth N. Waltz, "The Stability of a Bipolar World," *Daedalus*, 93 (Summer 1964), 881-909.

through the threat or use of military force. Britain, France, Italy, and the East European nonrevisionists did possess a preponderance of power which could, if concerted, handle any German military action. And German leaders were well aware of this fact. Their diplomacy consisted largely of seeking gains through moderate demands and keeping the status quo powers in disagreement among themselves.

Secondly, homogeneous underlying doctrines aided in stabilizing the system. None of the major participants sought to change the existing multipolar configuration of power. Despite British skepticism, France sought not hegemony on the continent but what she considered equilibrium. And despite French skepticism, Germany sought not hegemony but greater influence within a basically multipolar structure. France's allies also sought system maintenance. Even Italy, despite the bombast of Mussolini, pursued a status quo policy. In addition to sharing limited aims, these nations also accepted the idea that authoritative decisions of systemic importance were to be made through a process of bargaining and maneuver, and were to be legitimated through a concert of those powers responsible for system maintenance.

In the second systemic context, from 1934 through 1939, these two stabilizing factors disappeared. First, Hitler's accession to power in Germany marked a change to heterogeneity among the underlying doctrines of states. As his demands mounted, it became increasingly apparent that he sought not change within the system but a change *of* the system. Thus, by the end of the decade, the system was split between 1) those states seeking the maintenance of both the systemic configuration and the traditional patterns of decision-making, and 2) those seeking transformation in both areas. On the former side were Britain, France, and what was left of the nonrevisionist states in Eastern Europe. On the latter were Germany, Italy, and the Eastern European revisionists.

As Hitler's policies succeeded, a second and even more

71

crucial destabilizing process ensued: passage of the preponderance of power within the system from those nations seeking system maintenance to those seeking systemic change and transformation. In fact, in 1939 when Britain finally decided to act against any further German expansion, she could look back on five years of diplomacy which had allowed almost all of the weights which might have been employed in support of the status quo to be neutralized, conquered, or added to the side of Germany. These included Italy, Belgium, the Soviet Union, Czechoslovakia, Albania, Austria, Spain, and Portugal. In the East, Poland, Yugoslavia, and Rumania were very weak allies; in the West, only France was arrayed with Britain.

In the interwar period as a whole the absence of the first two conditions outlined above jeopardized the League from its very beginning, while later the loss of the third sounded its death-knell. In fact, the existence of a preponderance of power among the major status quo powers allowed the League to persist as long as it did, while the absence of the first two conditions was largely responsible for much of the behavior of the Organization throughout its life. Ironically, when the first two conditions were finally fulfilled at the end of the 1930s, the third was not. As a result, war on unfavorable terms was the only recourse open for the maintenance of the status quo. And, as we now know, even war failed to maintain or restore the prewar multipolar configuration and distribution of power.

In the third systemic context, from 1945 until 1962, the cold war was, to be sure, an almost all-consuming preoccupation. Yet, pervasive as this conflict may have been in terms of intensity as well as extensity, greater stability characterized this system than the preceding one—because the conditions for systemic stability were largely met. First, a preponderance of power resided with the bloc in support of the status quo. Second, American decision-makers, who controlled the greatest amount of power within the entire system (and even more with its coalition) had a clear view as to what aspects of the status quo were vital for system maintenance: namely, that any increment in communist territorial control would threaten the stability of the system. Finally, the United States was usually prepared and willing to use whatever forms of power it deemed necessary to preserve those aspects of the status quo considered vital. And in almost all such cases, its bloc allies either aided, supported, or acquiesced in such actions.[8]

In the fourth systemic context, the bipolar-cold war focus of the previous system was considerably eroded. First, in terms of configuration and distribution, power had become considerably diffused. Bloc solidarity could be said to operate only in regard to each of the superpowers' European coalitions, and even there it had weakened considerably. In fact, in each camp there were allies who refused to carry the concert beyond Europe.[9] In other areas the superpowers had even less influence, let alone control. And this was true even in regard to allies. Communist China was increasingly acting on its own, seeking the status of a great world power independent of, if not hostile to, the Soviet Union. Castro was increasingly an embarrassment rather than an asset for the Soviets. The United States, which had more allies outside of Europe than did the Soviet Union, faced similar problems. Pakistan moved into a position of neutrality. Japan pursued an independent trading policy in

[8] The major exceptions to this were the extensions of communism to China in 1949 and North Vietnam in 1954. In both cases, however, there was a common element: the perception that no form of American power short of nuclear weapons could prevent the expansion. That is, while every extension of communism was considered as being extremely serious, there was some tempering of idealism with reality. Also, in the latter case, a division within the alliance and especially the hesitance of the British to support an armed engagement in Indochina did much to forestall any forceful action on the part of the status quo coalition.

[9] France, for example, differed with United States foreign policy in Vietnam and in the Middle East during the Arab-Israeli War of 1967. Rumania and other members of the Warsaw Pact balked at Soviet proposals and policies in regard to Castro's Cuba, Communist China, and Israel.

73

regard to Communist China. But for most of the nations of Asia, Africa, and the Middle East, varying degrees of neutrality, if not hostility, toward East-West issues prevailed. Instead of cold war issues, regional conflicts and internal unrest seemed to preoccupy them.

Thus, while territorial conflicts in the previous system usually had consequences for the global distribution of power, such was not the case in this later period. There were instead four classes of conflicts: 1) direct conflicts between the two superpowers clearly involving the systemic distribution of power, such as that over Berlin and Germany; 2) regional conflicts that might or might not affect the global balance, such as the war in Vietnam; 3) conflicts probably affecting only regional balances, such as that between Egypt and Saudi-Arabia over Yemen; and 4) purely local conflicts not even affecting regional balances. The leaders of each superpower in this period faced increasingly difficult and perplexing problems in determining to which of the latter three categories the disputes they dealt with belonged and what the interests of their governments were in regard to them.

At the same time, the effects of elements of heterogeneity were increasingly abated by elements of homogeneity. While neither superpower openly discarded its ideal aims, both seemed more interested in system management than system transformation. Because both nations were secure and relatively prosperous, each desired to maintain its status and security. Also, while neither side could obtain global supremacy or a world in its own image, each could set off a holocaust which could destroy the world. Consequently, while conflict and competition between the two superpowers continued, it increasingly took place within a framework of common interests. It descended into a struggle for power and influence within a system and not for a system.

Between themselves, the superpowers had somewhat institutionalized their relationships: each recognized the

74

other's sphere of influence. In general, the Soviet system ceased to be the seedbed of revolution and guerrilla war, and the United States no longer sought liberation in Eastern Europe. When they clashed, neither side sought to place the other in a humiliating position, and when they collided in one geographic or issue area, common interests in other areas were conspicuously acknowledged.

In acting to maintain stability, both superpowers seemed to prefer the concert type of diplomacy employed in past historical periods. In dealing with major international problems, the Soviet Union had always sought arrangements with the powerful. Increasingly, the United States, too, came to prefer more intimate contacts with her co-equal. The bickering of hostile factions in the General Assembly or even the cacophony of disagreeing allies had become tiresome and displeasing.

While the superpowers moved closer together, the underlying doctrines of the newer states tended to create new elements of heterogeneity in the system.[10] Demands for ending racism through international organizations portended explosive situations which might slip beyond the control of the superpowers. Regional imperial designs of such leaders as Nasser, Castro, and Sukarno also raised serious problems. Thus, the United States and the Soviet Union were faced with substantive issues which they perceived as not legitimate for an international approach or too laden with danger to pursue. In response, the superpowers at-

---

[10] The nature and basis of these newer elements of heterogeneity can be gleaned from the following essays in Linda B. Miller, *Dynamics of World Politics* (Englewood Cliffs, N.J.: Prentice-Hall, 1968): Richard A. Falk, "Revolutionary Nations and the Quality of the International Legal Order," 126-199; Robert L. Friedheim, "The 'Satisfied' and 'Dissatisfied' States Negotiate International Law," 168-187; and Ernst B. Haas, "Dynamic Environment and Static System: Revolutionary Regimes in the United Nations," 188-236. Also, see the following essays in N. J. Padelford and L. M. Goodrich, eds., in *The United Nations in the Balance* (New York: Praeger, 1965): Arthur Lall, "The Asian Nations and the United Nations," 364-389, and John Karefa-Smart, "Africa and the United Nations," 400-409.

tempted to manage the system between them. Yet the more such acts were taken, the greater the heterogeneity between them and the other members of the international system as to legitimate patterns of decision-making. As a result, debates occurred within the system as to what mechanisms were legitimate for making authoritative decisions.

This last system, then, was the most stable of the four. The pervasive systemic conflict which characterized systems II and III was not present, nor was the insecurity which pervaded system I. Nuclear weapons and a stable deterrent system seemed to rule out the possibility of any radical changes in the systemic distribution of power. The general diffusion of power and the rise of complex and intensely emotional regional problems also abated the interest of the superpowers in continuing their competition. For all their activity in the developing areas in the early 1960s neither superpower had significant benefits to display after considerable expenditures of resources. Rather than gaining allies, such activity tended to involve and preoccupy the superpowers with nearly insoluble problems unrelated to the cold war. As a result each perceived a limit to its interests as well as its power in these areas.

Thus, the post-World War II and the post-colonial configuration of power had become accepted and stabilized. Were this to be seriously jeopardized or threatened, the requisites under consideration would again become of increasing importance. However, the problem does not seem to be one which will arise in the foreseeable future; for despite the emotional intensity that underlay the new elements of heterogeneity, such as the desire to end apartheid by any means, those who adhere to these doctrines lack any power sufficient to cause serious systemic disruption.[11]

Given this historical experience, what general statements can be made concerning the relationships between the variables selected for study and the survivability of a universal international organization? First, the distribution of power

[11] See Falk's description of UN System III, below, pp. 218-222.

seems more important to persistence than either its configuration or the degree of homogeneity among underlying doctrines in the system. During the three periods when the preponderance of power resided among the status quo powers, the organization survived, despite differences in configuration and homogeneity-heterogeneity.

Second, given the preponderance of power residing with the status quo powers, a bipolar configuration seems more conducive to survivability than a multipolar one, apparently because the leadership function is more centralized in a bipolar system. However, this assumes that the given superpower will 1) possess the will to act in such a situation and 2) that it will not make errors in judgment that would destroy the system.

Thus, in those three systems where elements of multipolarity have been present, quick and concerted action on the part of the status quo powers was not as common as it was in the bipolar system. Coalitions in which the power among its members is relatively equal seem to lack a propensity for clear and quick concerted action. Governments seem none too willing to accede to the judgments of their equals or near-equals. Why this is so is not clear—perhaps because the weaker members of a bipolar coalition have no choice but to concert with or acquiesce in the decisions of the superpower. Given the great disparity of power within the blocs of a bipolar system, the minor members of a status quo bloc must, when threatened, defer to the decisions and other leadership roles of the superpower. Yet, the opponents of an aggressive Germany had "no choice" save to concert their actions, but they did not.

In any event, the historical data indicate the solidarity among status quo powers is less forthcoming in multipolar systems than in bipolar ones. During the interwar period, France and Britain were at loggerheads on both the nature and the means of handling the German problem. Later, as this problem grew in intensity and seriousness, the four major powers with interests in system maintenance, France,

Britain, Italy, and the Soviet Union, were unable to mold any meaningful concert in support of the status quo. This also seems to be the case in the later postwar period. While both have common and acknowledged interests in system maintenance, the United States and the Soviet Union have had considerable difficulty in acting together in areas of major importance, such as agreeing on measures to halt the spread of nuclear weapons or bringing stability to the Middle East.[12]

V. Why the League Fared Better in the Area of Peaceful Settlement

Universal international organizations address themselves to the problem of peace and security in two basic ways: first, in their handling of specific disputes brought before them by one or more of the parties to the dispute or by some interested party; and second, through considering and attempting, usually in their deliberative bodies, to deal with more general problems affecting the international system such as disarmament, decolonialization, and economic development. The first type of behavior will be dealt with here; the latter will be considered in the next section.

As Table 2 indicates, the League resolved a greater proportion of the conflicts brought before it than has the United Nations. The explanation for this difference resides in the homogeneity of underlying doctrines among the major members of the former. From an examination of those cases in which the League succeeded, three important facts emerge. First, seven of these eight disputes either occurred, or their means of resolution were agreed upon, during the period of homogeneity among the major powers; in fact, all were dealt with before Germany was admitted to the League. Had Germany been a member of the Council, the Organization might have been unable to resolve these disputes and would have experienced the same difficulty

[12] Yet some positive cooperation occurs from time to time.

TABLE 2

General Effectiveness of the League and the United Nations in the Settling of International Conflicts

Type of Settlement	League	United Nations
Settled in accordance with Organizational machinery, procedures, and proposals	Aaland Islands Upper Silesia Burgenland Jaworzina Mosul Greece-Bulgaria Leticia Saar Plebescite	Bizerte
Not settled but peace restored or maintained through the involvement and/or action of the Organization	——	Palestine Kashmir Korean War Suez (1956) Lebanon (1958) Thailand-Cambodia
Settled through some procedures or mechanism outside the Organization but with the Organization playing some facilitative role	——	Indonesia West Irian
Settled through some procedures or mechanism outside the Organization	Tacna-Arica Hungarian Optants Corfu Gran Chaco	Iran Trieste Syria-Lebanon Greek Civil War Great Britain-Egypt Berlin Yugoslavia-USSR Anglo-Iranian Oil Company Laos Cuba, USSR-US Panama-US
Settled by one of the parties contrary to Organizational procedures or proposals	Vilna Carelia Memel Manchuria Ethiopia Rhineland Spanish Civil War Czechoslovakia Finnish War	Hyderabad (1948-49) Guatemala Hungary Goa
No settlement	——	Korean Unification Corfu Channel German Reunification Suez Canal

that characterized the Security Council in the postwar period. Solutions would then have necessarily been sought outside the League.

Second, almost all of these disputes involved minor powers and none involved any issue which significantly affected the distribution of power in Europe. In fact, five of the eight cases were conflicts in which the major powers, in concert, were unable to agree upon a solution. Thus, the League served as a device for bailing out the great powers on issues where they could not agree but had no interest in continuing.[13]

Third, all of these disputes were solved through some nonpolitical or neutral means. Commissions of inquiry were used in the Aaland Islands controversy, Upper Silesia, Jaworzina, Mosul, the Greek-Bulgarian crisis, and Leticia. The secretariat worked on the problems of Burgenland and all parties agreed to the suggestions that were finally made. In the Saar, a plebescite was held. Thus, the League handled disputes between minor states in an effective and impartial manner whenever none of the major powers perceived their interests to be involved.

The failure of the United Nations to do as well stems from three factors. First, the heterogeneity between the superpowers and the pervasiveness of the conflict between them minimized the realm of common interest. Therefore they saw most disputes as having implications for this conflict, and they could not allow the Organization to work toward some nonpolitical solution. Second, in those few instances where the superpowers saw no direct involvement of their interests, the level of hostility and tension among the participants in the dispute made any effort at solution, even by the superpowers, futile. Examples of this are the conflict between the Arabs and Israelis over Palestine in 1948, and that between Pakistan and India over Kashmir. During the early interwar period, moreover, many minor

[13] See Young, above, pp. 21-22, for comment on a similar function performed by the UN.

powers were anxious to see the League succeed and were willing to allow its involvement in their disputes. This commitment was largely lacking in the postwar period.

Third, a number of conflicts have been handled by various regional organizations. Unlike the League, the United Nations has had to exist in a world of such competitors as the OAS and the OAU. Indeed both were explicitly created, in part, to escape the clash of doctrines that occurred when disputes reached the United Nations. As a result, the degree of UN involvement in Africa and Latin America (with the exception of the Congo crisis) has been minimal.

An examination of the remaining cases in Tables 2, 3, and 4 leads to some inferences about 1) the underlying doctrines of the major powers in each system; and 2) the relationships between these doctrines and the nonbehavior or lack of success of the two organizations. That is, they suggest explanations for the major similarities in behavior: a) their failure to affect the major international conflicts of their times, b) their failure even to discuss some of the most important conflicts occurring about them, and c) their failure to resolve many of the conflicts placed before them. We shall consider, first, the interwar period, then the postwar one.

If one considers League noninvolvement as well as involvement, a number of patterns appear. First, disputes and issues of major systemic importance seem to have been reserved for consideration by the major powers outside the League context. Throughout the entire interwar period, in fact, the methods of handling disputes of systemic importance were more attuned to Metternich's ideas regarding the Concert of Europe than to those of Woodrow Wilson concerning collective security. At the outset of the interwar period, this Concert approach was institutionalized in the Conference of Ambassadors, which was later succeeded by quiet, traditional diplomacy as well as by the whole series of *ad hoc* conferences ranging from Locarno to Munich.

As Tables 3 and 4 indicate, most of the aggressive acts of

81

TABLE 3

CONFLICTS NOT CONSIDERED BY THE
LEAGUE OR UNITED NATIONS

League	United Nations
Allied Intervention-USSR	Nicaragua-Costa Rica
Poland-Russia	China-Tibet
Syria-France	Viet Minh-France
Smyrna	Egypt-Jordan-US
Ruhr Occupation	Honduras-Nicaragua
Great Britain-Egypt	Quemoy
Nicaragua-US-Mexico	Berlin (1958)
Black Sea Straits Rearmament	China-India
Teschen	Cuba-US (1961)
Germany-Austria	Berlin (1961)
Germany-Czechoslovakia	Morocco-Algeria
Memel	
Germany-Poland	
USSR-Baltic States	
Ruthenia	

Germany were not considered by the League, and in those few cases that did come before it, involvement was minimal. In the case of Czechoslovakia, the level was that of discussion only. In the Rhineland crisis, the League acted less as an executive body than as a court, deciding whether or not a breach of the Locarno Treaty had been committed. After a decision, action would be up to the Locarno powers and not the Council. In the Spanish Civil War, the degree of involvement was the highest. But a mere reading of Table 4 is somewhat deceptive; for the decision made by the only Council meeting held on the dispute simply urged that outside powers should not intervene and that this should be ensured by the Non-Intervention Committee—which was not a creature of the League, which met in secret, and of which Spain was not a member.

As a result of this play of underlying doctrines, historians now customarily trace the struggle for Europe not through a series of Council or Assembly discussions, but through a series of traditional diplomatic mechanisms such as the

Four Power Pact, the Franco-Italian Pact of 1934, the Stresa Conference, the Franco-Russian Alliance, the Anglo-German Naval Agreement, the Non-Intervention Committee, and Munich, to name some of the major ones. The Ethiopian crisis also underscores this fact. During it, the British and French were almost embarrassed into action through the League; but, all through the crisis, they also worked together and alone to secure a private solution of the settlement.

A second pattern which emerges comprises efforts by the permanent members on the Council to insure that the League did not interfere in the actions taken by one of them without that power's acquiescence. The League was an institution where the small fry were to be called to account; great powers were not to be so humiliated. For example, Britain readily acceded to League involvement in the Mosul because a settlement was desired in London, and the League could depoliticize the situation. However, when Mussolini balked at the League's daring to ask Italy to account for its actions in the Corfu crisis, the major powers took up the issue in the Conference of Ambassadors.[14] Thus, while disputes were treated unequally within the system, so, too, were member-states.

Third, the data reveal tacit conceptions of spheres of influence which were off limits to the League unless it was specifically asked to enter. In the Near East, disputes between France and Syria or Great Britain and Egypt were treated as problems facing only the European power. The Western Hemisphere was also such a sphere. While the League entered this area on several occasions and, in fact, played an important role in the disputes involving Leticia, Tacna-Arica, and the Gran Chaco, every action was considered and taken with great concern for the views and reactions of the United States.

[14] The Conference did deal with the matter, however, on the basis of the principles outlined in the Council Session. See Walters, *op.cit.*, 244-255.

TABLE 4

Degree of Involvement in Conflicts Brought Before League and United Nations

Degree of Involvement	League	United Nations
Discussed only	Czechoslovakia	Syria-Lebanon Great Britain-Egypt Hyderabad Berlin (1948) Anglo-Iranian Oil Company Guatemala Goa Cuba-US-USSR Panama-US
Discussed and referred to disputing parties to settle on their own or referred dispute to somebody outside Organizational context	Rhineland	Iran West Irian Bizerte
Discussed and called for investigation and/or referred to another Organizational body or set up own body for keeping peace, observing, insulating, mediating, or proposing a solution	Tacna-Arica Carelia Corfu	Indonesia Greek Civil War Corfu Channel German Reunification Lebanon Laos Thailand-Cambodia

Made pronouncements on substantive issues in the conflict and/or method to be used in settlement	Aaland Islands
	Vilna
	Upper Silesia
	Burgenland
	Hungarian
	    Optants
	Jaworzina
	Memel
	Mosul
	Greece-Bulgaria
	Manchuria
	Leticia
	Saar
	Spanish Civil
	    War
	Finnish War
		Trieste
		Korean
		    Reunification
		Palestine
		Kashmir
		Yugoslavia-USSR
		Suez Canal
		Suez (1956)
		Hungary

Sought to enforce adherence to either its proposed method of settlement or substantive proposals	Gran Chaco Ethiopia	Korean War

Fourth, each of those disputes, ending in settlement by one of the parties in a manner contrary to the principles of the Organization, involved 1) the quick use of force resulting in a *fait accompli*, and 2) a disinclination on the part of the major members of the Organization to use counterforce because none of their own interests were directly threatened. In the Vilna incident, this disinclination was underscored by the fact that Poland was the keystone of France's alliance system in Eastern Europe. In Memel, the Lithuanians used force against the Germans, as the Poles had done against them in Vilna. In the Carelia case, hesitancy resulted largely from the fact that the Soviet Union had presented the world with a *fait accompli*. In all three disputes, the Council did not move beyond persuasion.

The Manchurian crisis of 1931 to 1933 also illustrates this point. Were the League to have attempted sanctions or other enforcement action against the Japanese, the major burden in any such effort would have fallen almost solely on Britain, whose leaders were hesitant to act for several reasons. First, there was the question of what the United States would do if League action were undertaken. Since the beginning of the interwar period British statesmen had been careful of jeopardizing American good will. Second, the area coveted by Japan in no way threatened any British interest in China or in Asia; the Japanese action seemed clearly limited. Third, China's claim to the territory in dispute could be seen as questionable because of the internal disarray within that country. Finally, great internal troubles were plaguing Britain at the time—on the day of the Japanese invasion, Britain had gone off the gold standard. Thus, it appeared that any forceful operation would involve great risks with few possible gains, either for Britain or for those living in the disputed territory.

During the entire interwar period, then, the underlying doctrines of the major powers were not congruent with the universal requirements and principles of behavior prescribed in the League Covenant. There was no commitment

85

to a global scope of obligations. There was no commitment to the literal guarantees regarding territorial integrity in the Covenant. And there was no commitment to an obligatory response.

British policy-makers saw the League mainly as a place where European powers could meet to handle minor European disputes and problems of mutual concern. They made it clear again and again that they perceived the Covenant as under no circumstances imposing any obligation upon them to act in an automatic way. Problems with systemic implications were to be handled by the major powers concerned, but outside the League framework. These basic tenets were shared by France, Italy, Japan, and Germany.[15] The United States also largely accepted this code in Asia, while reserving a free hand in the Americas and ignoring the security problems of Europe.

Ironically, of the major powers in Europe, only the Soviet Union, after she became a League member in 1933, persistently and consistently called for the upholding of the obligations of the Covenant. But Soviet good faith was never really tested, for two reasons: the Soviet state was considered a pariah, and its exposition of the doctrine of the Covenant was too alien to prevailing underlying doctrines to be adopted.

Most of these patterns of behavior persisted in the post-World War II period and similarly affected the behavior of the United Nations. Disputes which involved systemic or important regional balances were largely handled outside the UN, although there was one important difference from the interwar period. While the Soviet Union favored a tra-

---

[15] It is true that France, unable to gain the security she sought through traditional efforts, did seek a strengthening of the universal obligations of the League. This she did, however, for particular reasons—to obtain through a universal pledge the British guarantee she could not otherwise get. In so acting, French decision-makers had no intentions of obligating themselves to responding to breaches of peace in Asia, Africa, the Middle East, Latin America, or even Europe.

ditional diplomatic approach to major problems, the United States did not, except as a last resort; it sought always to begin with the international organization mechanism. Thus, in the early years of the United Nations, during the administrations of Truman and Stalin, disputes went through a three-step process: 1) submission of the dispute by the United States or one of its allies to the United Nations; 2) stalemate or noncompliance with the proposed settlement; and 3) further handling through unilateral or multilateral acts and conferences.

But this difference did not last for long. By the middle 1950s, disputes having systemic implications were increasingly handled outside the Organization. In fact, after the Suez crisis of 1956, Secretary of State Dulles explicitly stated that issues involving the two blocs could not and should not be handled by the United Nations.[16] Thus, there arose a dichotomy between those problems involving the Soviet Union which would be handled through unilateral or multilateral efforts outside the world organization and those not involving the cold war which would be left largely to the United Nations.

At the same time, in disputes between the major powers the UN, unlike the League, did serve in three capacities. First, it provided a forum for the airing of points at issue between the contending bloc and superpowers. Second, the Organization served as a mechanism for facilitating agreements between the superpowers.[17] In the Cuban missile crisis, the Organization was expected to provide an inspection and legitimating function, although this was prevented by the negative response of Castro.[18] Finally, the Organiza-

[16] See his statement before the Senate Foreign Relations Committee in support of the Eisenhower Doctrine: U.S. Senate, Committee on Foreign Relations. *Hearings on S.J. Res. and H.J. Res. 117* (*The President's Proposal on the Middle East*). Pts. 1 and 2. (Washington: 1957), pp. 52-54.

[17] See Falk's Description of UN System II, below, pp. 216-218.

[18] For a concise discussion of this function, see I. L. Claude, *The Changing United Nations* (New York: Random House, 1967), ch. 4.

tion did play a role in the Middle East and in the Congo, insulating and containing conflicts between the superpowers or their clients.

Spheres of influence also limited the involvement and success of the United Nations. American interventions in Latin America were either not considered, as in the Cuban invasion of 1961, or merely discussed, as in the Guatemalan case of 1954. Other disputes not involving force, such as that between Panama and the United States, were kept largely outside the UN framework through the preemptive utilization of the OAS. Organizational involvement in the Soviet invasion of Hungary and the Chinese annexation of Tibet also did not go beyond the verbal level.

Third, disputes not involving the interests of those who would bear the burden of enforcement likewise resulted in only a verbal response. The use of force by India in Hyderabad and in Goa were merely discussed by the Organization. Similar but less successful uses of force resulted, at times, in the restoration of peace, such as in the Kashmir crisis, but usually in no settlement.

Finally, the only pattern which has not carried over from the League period is that of not considering a major power's behavior without its consent. The superpowers have not extended this precept to each other. In fact, each has enjoyed embarrassing its opponent in the forum of the United Nations whenever possible. This form of behavior has been especially intense and prevalent in conflicts in which one superpower is involved and the other has decided that it cannot respond in other than a verbal way. In such instances, as in the Hungarian and Guatemalan cases, the United Nations was used by each power to the fullest of its verbal capacity.

This particular pattern of behavior did not exist during the interwar period, because of the absence of a sharp doctrinal conflict when all the major powers were members of the League (1926-1933), and because the underlying doctrines did not encompass international public opinion as either a practical or a legitimate arbiter of national policy. However, one may still speculate as to what would have happened had the Axis powers not left the League and had used its forums to propound their grievances and doctrines. Would not the pattern have been different? And what would have been its implications for the behavior of the League?

VI. WHY THE FOCI OF THE LEAGUE AND THE UNITED NATIONS DIFFERED

The foci of these two organizations differed both geographically and substantively. The reason for the geographical difference stems largely from the differences in the configurations of power and the underlying doctrines extant in each system. The reasons for the substantive differences are related largely to the nature of the conflicts which ensued from these configurations of power and underlying doctrines.

The League was largely a European organization for three reasons. First, the mere existence of nation-states was largely a phenomenon of Europe and the Western Hemisphere. As Table 5 indicates, roughly three-fourths of the members of the League came from these areas. Statistically speaking, therefore, the prospects for conflicts among local powers in these same areas were small, and, as indicated above, most of them were considered off limits to the League.

Second, American isolation and attitudes toward the League curtailed both the degree and amount of Organizational involvement in the Western Hemisphere; furthermore, many Latin Americans accepted the point of view that the League should largely stay out of conflicts arising in that hemisphere. Their difference with the United States was over the issue of unilateralism versus multilateralism. But for most Latin countries, membership in the League was valued largely for the status it conferred and whatever

TABLE 5

MEMBERSHIP PATTERNS OF THE LEAGUE AND
THE UNITED NATIONS

	Europe	Latin America	Asia	Near East	Africa	Oceana	North America
League: Original Members	16	17	4	1	2	2	1
League: Total Members	28	21	5	4	3	2	1
United Nations: Original Members	15	20	3	6	3	2	2
United Nations: Total Members (1966)	29	24	16	10	40	2	2

advantages could be gained from economic, social, and cultural cooperation.

Finally, and most importantly, the major powers in the League, the permanent members, were predominantly Europeans who conceived of the Organization primarily as an adjunct to European diplomacy, and with a limited role even in Europe. Instead of submitting themselves to the universal obligations and doctrines of the League, they turned it into an instrument of their particular form of concert diplomacy.

During the post-World War II period, the global involvement of the United Nations has developed largely through the creation of new members through decolonialization. Almost all the areas of Africa, Asia, and the Middle East that had been dependencies in the League period have become independent and eager participants in the international system. The membership of the United Nations has thus changed vastly—so much, in fact, that the Organization at its inception resembled the League in membership patterns more than it resembled itself in 1966.

A second reason for this change stems from the fact that Europe has ceased to be the center of world politics. With World War II the European *system* was gone. In its place were two blocs between which conflict was carefully managed and within which, restrained and contained. In short, European politics had become frozen; action occurred where the power and influence of the great powers was least and where, therefore, the requisite of independence for conflict existed.

While the differences in geographic scope between the two organizations can be accounted for largely on the basis of configurations of power, the variance in substantive matters may be found in the nature of the systemic struggles and the degrees of heterogeneity in each system. In its preoccupation with the creation of a stable security system, the League reflected the instability existing in Europe. At the base of this instability lay two questions: the future role of Germany in the European system, and the resolution of the Franco-German problem.

French leaders, having twice suffered defeat at the hands of Germany, saw their security as residing in the reduction of Germany to minor status and the maintenance of France as the predominant power on the continent. At the same time, German elites sought to reverse what they considered to be the most unjust aspects of the Versailles treaty and ultimately, to restore Germany to a status of "equality" with France and Britain. The two nations were at loggerheads: what was security to France was injustice and inequality for Germany; what was equity and equality for Germany meant utter insecurity for France.

The feelings of France would have been greatly assuaged had her views on security problems been supported by her wartime allies, but such was not the case. In fact, a series of events seemed to reverse the decision reached on the bat-

91

tlefield in World War I. First, the United States refused to undertake any responsibilities for maintaining the postwar status quo, either through the proposed Anglo-American treaty of reassurance or through active participation in the League. Consequently, only France and Britain remained to police the postwar settlements. But they alone had been unable to defeat Germany decisively in the war. If they were to have a falling out and Germany were to regain a position of military and economic strength, at best they would face stalemate, or, more likely, revision of the Versailles treaty on Germany's terms, or war.

French leaders estimated their situation as increasingly insecure as the latter possibilities became distinct probabilities with the emergence of a second factor: the hesitancy of Great Britain to make a firm pledge to guarantee the European settlement, either by signing the Anglo-American treaty after the defection of the United States, or by taking other measures which would have satisfied the French. Several reasons accounted for Britain's behavior. First, there was the traditional British hesitancy to make commitments on the continent in times of peace. Second, this point of view was reinforced by the strong opposition of the Dominions to any "European preoccupation" in British diplomacy. Third, Britain faced a serious economic crisis at home, a solution to which seemed to lie in the rapid economic recovery of Germany. Fourth, in the early postwar period, British policy-makers downgraded fears about German power and suggested that France was the greater threat on the continent, an apprehension fed by the efforts of French leaders to hinder German reconstruction. Finally, lack of British support for French views may also have arisen from the fact that victory had erased Britain's major fears about Germany—the threat posed by the latter's navy and her active entrance into the competition for empire outside Europe.

These differences appeared at the very first meeting of the Assembly when the Canadian delegate called for the repeal of Article 10, the clause of the Covenant which called upon each member to respect and preserve the territorial integrity and political independence of all other members. In reaction to this position of minimizing obligations, which was supported by Britain and the Dominions, there were states, mainly continental and led by France, which sought to strengthen the Covenant and create an airtight security system. Between these two groups were a number of states led by the Scandinavians, who sought what might be called a compromise solution, an airtight system of obligatory arbitration.

Within the first systemic context, then, the key to understanding the politics of the Assembly in the realm of peace and security lay in a series of proposals designed to satisfy the needs of the continental and Scandinavian groups. These include the Draft Treaty of Mutual Assistance of 1923, the Geneva Protocol of 1924, the Nansen plan for compulsory arbitration, and the General Act for the Peaceful Settlement of International Disputes, both of 1927.

The more ambitious of these proposals never succeeded, and the League failed to solve the problems of security or disarmament; in fact, the debates on this issue tended to feed the instability felt within the system. The more the League engaged in inconclusive debate and failed to solve the security problem, the more insecure nations became. The more insecure governments became, the more they drew the Organization into the problem of security.

In the second systemic context, 1934-1939, debate over schemes for solving the problem of security ceased. Things had gone too far. France had given up her efforts to obtain security through the League, and those smaller powers that perceived the disintegration of the Versailles system knew there was little that they could do about it. Thus, the majority of the members of the Assembly watched in anguish: their fate lay in the hands of the great powers who now chose to deal with systemic problems outside the Organizational framework.

93

Yet even had the League solved this problem of security, it is doubtful that it would have made major strides into other substantive areas—because the underlying doctrines of the period narrowly construed the range of legitimate issues for international consideration. While vast studies were made during the League period in the realm of economic, technical, and cultural cooperation, such programs as existed were largely anodynes. Proposals for decolonialization or an international redistribution of national wealth were simply beyond the ken of most League participants.

During the first post-World War II period, the preoccupation of the United Nations was not so much with stability, for that existed outside the Organization, as with debating the legitimacy of the positions taken by bloc members on the issues between them. Thus, because there did exist a stable balance of power, the United Nations was never preoccupied with questions of systemic security. The Security Council quickly became stalemated through a lack of unanimity among its permanent members, and disputes passed to the Assembly; there large majorities legitimated Western positions on not only specific disputes but also a series of more general issues ranging from human rights to the control of armaments. While there were some exceptions, it is not inaccurate to say that during its first ten years the Assembly served mainly as a legitimator of Western bloc positions on cold war and other issues.[19]

The focus of the United Nations began to change with decolonialization, the change in Soviet attitudes toward the newly independent states after the death of Stalin, and the break of the membership deadlock in 1955. Both the West, by adding greater weight to its majority strength in the Assembly, and the Soviet Union, by redressing somewhat or transforming this distribution of power, may have hoped

[19] See, for example H. R. Alker, Jr. and B. M. Russet, *World Politics in the General Assembly* (New Haven, Conn.: Yale University Press, 1965), and H. F. Haviland, Jr., *The Political Role of the General Assembly* (New York: Carnegie Endowment for International Peace, 1951).

to gain the support of the new members for their cold war positions. Such hopes were vain. As the geographic distribution of the membership changed, so, too, did the interests and concerns of the Organization.

Instead of reaping support for particular positions on Europe and other postwar issues, the superpowers soon found the new majority often uninterested in, if not hostile to, any extensive consideration of cold war issues. Consequently, the deliberations of the General Assembly increasingly moved into such issues as decolonialization, the redistribution of resources from industrial to nonindustrial nations, a radical revision of traditional international law, and even the eradication of racism within nation-states.

Although these new elements of heterogeneity may have increased the issue-load on both the system and the Organization, they did have the effect of turning the United Nations into a stronger catalyst of change than was the League.[20] Had the new members not been admitted or had not been allowed to press their claims in the Assembly, it is doubtful that decolonialization would have come as quickly as it did, especially in Africa. In short, the Organization increasingly has come to serve as a vehicle for the articulation, aggregation, and mobilization of new conceptions of purpose and authority. It has become a forum for nations which rejected not only the European system of international politics but American conceptions of world order and international organization as well.

Even more important is the fact that the newer states were successful in having some of their demands accepted by the "older" members of the Organization. The multilateral approach to aiding economic development is a case in point. At first neither superpower nor most of its allies favored any of the schemes for multilateral aid. Increasingly, however, all sides have given ground, so that multi-

[20] See, for example H. K. Jacobson, "The United Nations and Colonialism: A Tentative Appraisal," *International Organization*, 16 (Winter 1962), 37-56, Claude, *op.cit.*, Chapter 3, and the essay by Haas cited in note 9.

95

lateral programs are now commonly accepted, and an element of homogeneity of doctrines in regard to the legitimacy of this problem as well as one of the mechanisms for its solution has been established.[21]

Thus, the United Nations was afforded luxuries that could not be indulged in by the League. During the interwar period, the balance of power was never so stable and the cohesion of blocs not so clear. To be sure, France waged political warfare with the British in the Assembly, but she was never able to capture the Organization. In fact, even had the unanimity rule not been in existence, any victories in terms of resolutions adopted would not have served her needs. This was so because what France wanted was not so much the legitimation of her views but their acceptance by the British; and this differs considerably from what the Western powers sought from the United Nations.

VII. Why the Political Axis of the League Lay between the Major Organs While the Axis of the United Nations Cut across the Major Organs

During the interwar period, the homogeneity in doctrines among the major powers made the Council the focal center of the Organization, where the major powers worked together to deal with those disputes which they allowed to be handled through the Council mechanism. At the same time, this very vibrance and effectiveness of the Council led to the growth of a sense of corporate separateness within the Assembly. As the Council was operated more in terms of the traditional conceptions of European diplomacy than according to the letter of the Covenant, the members of the Assembly increasingly began to operate in the form of a supervisory or watchdog committee.

A rivalry thus developed between the two organs. The Council sought to keep in its hands as much power, perqui-

---

[21] For a cogent discussion of this process see the essay by Haas cited in note 9.

sites, and discretion as was possible. The Assembly, on the other hand, became increasingly dominated by the leaders of small states who used it as a vehicle for continually reminding the Council members of the purposes, ideals, and obligations imposed upon them in the Covenant. The general debates of each Assembly, for example, usually focused upon one major problem, such as Corfu in 1924 and the Disarmament Conference in 1931.[22] In this way, the representatives of smaller states carefully scrutinized the behavior of the major powers on fundamental issues of peace and security. Also, in its regular business, the committees of the Assembly carefully reviewed the work of the Council in regard to mandates and minorities. In short, the Council was under constant scrutiny in all respects. The members of the Assembly, by and large, conceived themselves as trustees of the Covenant. The actual impact and influence of these activities upon the behavior of the great powers, however, has never been researched in any depth.

Such a differentiation did not develop during the postwar period, largely because of the bipolar configuration of power and the heterogeneity of underlying doctrines. In a multipolar system the inherent dichotomy between large and small states and their respective interests can find expression. Thus, when an international organization is created, the cohesion and articulation of these differences is greatly facilitated. In a tight bipolar system the axis of differentiation lies elsewhere; there is a sharp dichotomy between blocs whose members find no bonds between them. Also, because of the considerable intrabloc solidarity which usually exists in a bipolar system, there is very little open diversity on political issues among bloc members. Instead,

---

[22] For an introduction to the relations between the major organs during the life of the League see M. E. Burton, *The Assembly of the League of Nations* (Chicago: University of Chicago Press, 1941), T. P. Conwell-Evans, *The League Council in Action* (London: Oxford University Press, 1929), and F. Morley, *The Society of Nations* (Washington, D.C.: Brookings Institution, 1932), Chapters x, xi, xiii, xiv, xv.

the two blocs compete in every organ of the institution with the larger bloc "winning" the legitimation of the Organization as a result of its more powerful voting position. And so it was in the United Nations.

The entrance of nonbloc members into such a situation may result in the emergence of new substantive concerns unrelated to the original bloc issues. If so, bloc discipline may decrease somewhat as issues arise which do not seem relevant to the major conflicts separating the blocs. As these trends continue, considerable fluidity can result in the assembly of an organization. In the United Nations this has been the case, although more so in regard to the Western bloc than the Soviet bloc. In fact, the decrease in hostility among the superpowers and the rise of new substantive non-cold war issues have led to a revival of the Security Council in recent years.[23] This development, as indicated above, is based on two factors: 1) the perception among the superpowers that they have a common interest in their management of non-cold war problems, and 2) their realization that they cannot influence greatly, let alone control, the resolutions of the General Assembly.

This latter development stems from the fact that the smaller states, albeit largely the underdeveloped ones, have steadily been developing a sense of corporate solidarity and distinctness. While this first manifested itself outside the United Nations at UNCTAD I in 1964, third-world solidarity has been increasingly growing within the General Assembly while the United States has become concomitantly more and more isolated and on the defensive. At an April, 1970, meeting of sixty nonaligned nations in Dar es Salaam, in fact, Marshal Tito called upon the delegates to present a united front at the Twenty-Fifth General Assembly and break the "domination" of the superpowers.

[23] For changes in the foci of the Assembly see the work by Alker and Russet cited above. On the revival of the Security Council see K. S. Peterson, "The Business of the United Nations Security Council: History (1946-1963) and Prospects," *Journal of Politics*, 27 (November 1965), 818-838.

If these trends continue, if multipolarity and fluidity persist, we may see a pattern similar to that of the early League period develop within the United Nations.[24] On the one hand, the superpowers and other permanent members of the Council would seek to resolve nonsystemic disputes among themselves in the way the permanent members of the League did. On the other hand, there would be a vocal Assembly, critical of Council hesitancy to take "just" and perhaps forceful steps on such issues, and, very probably, adopting resolutions embodying their criticisms in order to put pressure on Council members.

At this point it is interesting to speculate on the issue of Communist China in this scenario. If she were admitted only to the Assembly, China would probably attempt to take on the role of aggregator and leader of a largely proletariat Assembly against an affluent Council. Were she to be admitted to both Council and Assembly, the common interests among the superpowers would remain in regard to non-cold war issues but their control in the Council would be ended. In this case, there might be a return to an ideological but verbal and inconclusive struggle in the Assembly. Or perhaps the superpowers might lose interest in the Organization and remain members in name only.

In any case, the sharp division of an international system on the basis of conceptions of purpose and authority instead of gradations of power can have a considerable impact upon an international organization. Where ideologies are a significant element in systemic conflict, political divisions cut across organs of international institutions. Where ideological differences among the major actors of an international system are less important, divisions will occur between organs.

VIII. Conclusions

The purpose of this chapter was to relate some of the major similarities and differences in the behavior of the United

[24] See Young, above, pp. 41-44.

Nations and the League to the systemic contexts within which they operated. To assert that the behavior of an international organization depends much more upon what takes place outside it than what may appear in its formal-legal documents has, of course, become banal. But banality aside, our knowledge in this area is minimal at a general and theoretical level.

What can be said about the relation between international organizations and international systems in general? While this analysis has been of necessity rudimentary and brief, the following hypotheses are offered for consideration. If they clarify thought, provoke questions or doubt, or spur further research, they will have served their purpose.

1) The behavior and roles played by an international organization will be shaped more by the underlying doctrines of its major, more powerful members than by the role functions or political processes outlined in its constitutional documents.

2) Unless its major members both support the general systemic status quo and possess a preponderance of power to maintain it, any international organization designed to maintain that status quo is doomed to failure.

3) Even if such powers do possess a preponderance of power, the prestige and effectiveness of the international organization will be jeopardized if a) these powers disagree upon what is vital for the maintenance of the given status quo, b) do agree upon what is vital but lack the will to use their preponderance of power, or c) prefer to handle disputes and tensions through channels other than those of the international organization.

4) At the same time, the greater the agreement upon the nature and maintenance of the status quo, the greater the tendency for the great powers to handle international disputes in their semi-exclusive bodies, i.e. councils. Thus, under these conditions, the organization will serve as a legitimator and implementer of great-power agreements.

As this occurs, the major organs of the institution will tend to develop a sense of corporate identity and distinctiveness.

5) Even when there is considerable consensus among the major members on the nature of the systemic status quo and its maintenance, the organization may still not respond with counterforce to all breaches of the peace; for those nations who will bear the major burdens of any enforcement action will not heavily engage themselves in sanctions or military actions where costs and risks may be high and returns in terms of their own national interests would be minimal.

6) When an international system divides into blocs or coalitions, stalemate in the exclusive decision-making body will lead to an attempt by the larger coalition to use a more inclusive organ (i.e., assembly) as a legitimator of its particular coalition policy. When power in the international system becomes fragmented or atomized, the international organization, lacking leadership, will move toward disarray and impotence.

7) The role of small states in international organizations will tend to vary with the relationships among the major powers in the organization.

In a tight bipolar system, they will acquiesce in or serve as defenders of their respective bloc positions.

In a loose bipolar system, bloc members will serve in the roles mentioned above. Nonbloc members will 1) attempt to avoid taking substantive positions on the issues between the blocs, 2) attempt to abate conflict among blocs by containing the areas of conflict through insulation, and 3) attempt to move the organization into substantive areas other than issues of bloc conflict.

In a system of substantial consensus among the great powers and willingness to play oligarchical decision-making roles, the smaller powers will tend to coalesce and provide a kind of watchdog or supervisory function. Also, they will attempt to move the satisfied powers into doing

101

something about system-wide tensions or problems other than that of maintaining order.

This chapter has sought to show that the type of polarity, the nature of underlying doctrines, and the degree of doctrinal homogeneity among the major powers can go far to explain and predict general patterns of organizational behavior. Certainly, the general statements made in the preceding pages should be subjected to further research as well as refinement. However, if they have attracted attention to an area virtually untouched in the increasing theoretical literature on international organizations they will have served their purpose.

Before concluding, three suggestions for further inquiry will be made. First, a more comprehensive analysis of the relations between systemic contexts and the behavior of the League and the United Nations in handling international disputes seems eminently worthwhile. The sample of conflicts examined in this paper is quite small and the analysis necessarily brief. Much more could be done. Depending upon one's criteria of counting, the League considered between 39 and 83 separate conflicts of interest among its members, while Catherine Teng has included 71 conflicts in her *Synopses of Cases Before the United Nations.*[25] Certainly, an examination of all these disputes would do much to refine and to expand upon the conclusions set forth here.

Second, the relationship between systemic contexts and the different roles played by member states within these Organizations is virtually unexplored. We know almost

[25] In *Essential Facts about the League* (Geneva: League of Nations Secretariat, 1937), 47 "political questions" are discussed, not including the Russo-Finnish War which occurred after this compilation. Quincy Wright, p. 1430, lists 66 political disputes as having come before the League, although he combines eighteen cases involving railway controversies in the Austro-Hungarian successor states into one case, thus yielding a total of 83 cases. J. T. Shotwell and M. Salvin discussed 37 disputes in their "Comprehensive Survey of Security Disputes before the Council" in their *Lessons on Security and Disarmament* (New York: King Crown's Press, 1949), pp. 45-81.

nothing about the nature, types, and development of roles within international organizations, as the hypotheses listed above indicate. While the literature is filled with assertions about the "power" of the small states in the League, this subject remains largely uninvestigated in terms of extended scholarly study. Comparative analyses of the role behavior of different types of states within different types of systemic contexts could contribute significantly to our understanding of the limits and possibilities of universal international organizations.

Finally, theoretical consideration might be given to the relationships between systemic contexts and regional international organizations. Almost nothing has been done in this area. In fact, even the impressionistic type of research that might yield starting hypotheses similar to those listed above for universal international systems is yet to come. Such an undertaking, of course, would not be an easy task because attempts to apply systemic constructs to regional areas have been few. Yet, such analyses might be helpful in unravelling the interplay between universal and regional organizations and thereby contribute to our understanding of both.

Beyond the theoretical and academic contributions that might be made by increasing studies of systemic variables and organizational behavior, there are some practical considerations that should not be overlooked. As the international system becomes increasingly multipolar, comparisons between the behavior of the multipolar enveloped League and the, until recently, bipolar enclosed United Nations become exceedingly important. Given the continuing détente between the United States and the Soviet Union, their increasing homogeneity of doctrines, and their polarization from the Third World, the experience of the early League Council may have a great deal to contribute to policymakers, American and Soviet, who might want to use the United Nations as a means of minimizing unilateral ventures in conflicts of little relation to their immediate interests.

103

During its first decade, the League operated in a manner quite alien to the conceptions of Woodrow Wilson because those who found themselves in charge of the Organization knew no system other than the traditional, multipolar one of European diplomacy. Yet in the light of history, these years may be viewed as a golden age of universal international organizations. By serving as an adjunct of major-power diplomacy and by not having placed before it problems it could not solve, the League performed more successfully during that period than either organization has done since then.

Clearly the hopes of some American policy-makers of transforming the nature of international politics during the early postwar period are now recognized for the utopian dreams that they were. But the leadership of the Soviet Union has given up its equally utopian ideas for transforming the international order. As both now grope for institutional modes and forms to manage and maintain international peace the United Nations stands as an institution of opportunity. If the leaders of the superpowers have the historical insight and wisdom to use the United Nations in the manner in which the League was used during the 1920s, the current world organization might experience a renaissance. In fact, it might serve, for the first time, in the manner that Franklin Roosevelt had hoped it would in the days before his death. Instead of being a forum for Soviet-American conflict, it could become a reflection of their cohesion and concert.

SEVERAL years ago Louis Hartz argued that the American study of politics has been shaped more by the public or social problems with which it has been preoccupied than by any academic inquiries into the proper "scope" and "methods" of political science.[26] Now that the bipolarity of the

[26] See his comments which were transcribed and edited by James C. Charlesworth in A Design for Political Science: Scope, Objectives, and Methods (Philadelphia: The American Academy of Political and Social Science, December, 1966), pp. 24-27, 45-56, 49-50.

postwar international system is gone, students of international politics and organization will be forced to return to history in order to evaluate and analyze the behavior of states. With the exception of the work of James Barros,[27] scholarly studies on the work of the League have been almost nonexistent over the last two decades. But now that multipolarity has been thrust upon us, scholars may be forced into the type of comparative historical research that has so long been neglected.

[27] See his: *The Aland Islands Question* (New Haven: Yale University Press, 1968), *Betrayal from Within* (New Haven: Yale University Press, 1969), and "The Greek-Bulgarian Incident of 1925," in J. Larus, ed., *From Collective Security to Preventive Diplomacy* (New York: Wiley, 1965), pp. 57-91.

CHAPTER 3

An Inquiry into the Successes
and Failures of the United Nations
General Assembly

GABRIELLA ROSNER LANDE*

What factors have weighed heavily for or against the success of the United Nations General Assembly in its efforts to promote the aims of the Charter and resolve or adjust the important political and security problems brought before it? Even a cursory examination of the Assembly's record is overdue: "There is general awareness of the failures of the United Nations, but less consciousness of its pacificatory successes, and still less recognition of the possibilities that it has prevented some controversies from growing big enough to bring it either blame for failure to solve them or credit for success in so doing."[1] More importantly, perhaps, an analysis of the outcomes of Assembly decisions should yield a number of patterns and clues significant for an evaluation of the possibilities of the United Nations' growing into an increasingly effective organization.[2]

In dealing with the many political questions brought to its attention, the world body has recommended or requested in the form of resolutions specific action of its Member States and, frequently, has set forth particular objectives. Hence, the success of the General Assembly may be judged in the light of 1) the compliance with and implementation of its resolutions by the Member States, espe-

* The author is grateful to the Center of International Studies, Princeton University, for research support.
[1] Inis L. Claude, Jr., *Swords into Plowshares* (New York: Random House, 1961), 209.
[2] In this connection see Falk, Chapter 6 below.

cially the parties directly concerned; and 2) the effectiveness of the resolutions in promoting not only the specific objectives set out, but also the general purposes of the UN, particularly the maintenance of peace and security and friendly relations among nations.[3]

Compliance may be assessed by evaluating whether the principal parties concerned, the collective membership, or both, have indeed carried out the General Assembly's requests and recommendations. Effectiveness may be rated not only on the achievement of specific objectives, but also on the broader basis of whether the Assembly's action has influenced the policies of the statesmen concerned and the settlement of the question at hand. It may, *inter alia*, have constrained extremist positions, helped to reduce tensions, contributed to a resumption or adoption of direct negotiations, influenced the terms eventually reached by the parties to a dispute, provided a face-saving mechanism or special inducement to speed up a settlement, helped to localize a conflict or prevent its exacerbation.[4] A measure of success can be "the improvement of foreign policies": that they may "at least fall within the lower limits of international tolerability and at most conform to the higher requirements of international acceptability."[5]

Compliance with and cooperation in making effective the

[3] See Leland M. Goodrich and Anne P. Simons, *The United Nations and the Maintenance of International Peace and Security* (Washington: Brookings Institution, 1955), pp. 250-259.

[4] The specific effect of a resolution upon national policy and behavior is, of course, singularly difficult to analyze because, apart from the empirical question of determining the pressures and influences upon particular governments that may have come from the General Assembly itself, there is the question of whether in the absence of Assembly action the course taken would have been substantially different. One must rely on a series of views from the national statesmen concerned, accounts of outside observers, and clues available in both national parliamentary debates and UN discussions. The weight of the evidence will often indicate when a resolution has had a strong influence. At the very least, determination of certain patterns of effect may be made when there is agreement between the intent of the resolution and the actions of the states in question.

[5] Claude, *op.cit.*, p. 311.

107

General Assembly's decisions are, of course, not solely dependent upon the efforts of the Organization; a host of considerations may enter into the calculation of national decision-makers in formulating their policy positions on given issues.[6] However, my inquiry concerns itself exclusively with the salient intra-UN factors which may induce or deter deference to the Assembly's political acts. It is decidedly preliminary and tentative, restricted in scope and intended merely to suggest patterns and lines of further exploration.[7] Moreover, the limited number of cases studied allows no firm statistical conclusions, only trends and indications. The outcome of 29 resolutions concerning important political questions brought to the Assembly between 1946 and 1962 are assessed in relation to five broad categories of variables, in an effort to suggest the relative importance of each of these variables in the achievement of the Assembly's goals:

1) The time at and circumstances under which the resolution was adopted;
2) The nature of the resolution and the fundamental issues to which it pertains;
3) The methods and procedures recommended in the resolution to help reach its purposes;
4) The characteristics of the vote taken on the resolution;
5) The attitudes and expectations of Members in regard to the resolution.

THE RECORD is decidedly mixed.[8] Of the resolutions appraised, the number which proved successful or partially

[6] See Roger Fisher, "Bringing Law to Bear on Governments," *Harvard Law Review*, 74 (April 1961), 1134-35; Gabriella Rosner Lande, "The Effect of the Resolutions of the United Nations General Assembly," *World Politics*, 19 (October 1966), 83-105.

[7] This chapter represents a pilot study for a more comprehensive and detailed work. See the forthcoming book by the author on the United Nations General Assembly.

[8] See charts appended below.

successful with respect to both implementation and effect surpassed by a small margin those which were abjured and had little or no consequence.

Based on the material under review, a very strong correlation can be found between the outcomes of compliance and effectiveness: if not implemented, the probability that a resolution will be ineffective is 79 per cent; if implemented, the probability of fruitful effect is 87 per cent.

The successful operation of the General Assembly therefore seems to be a function of Member States' cooperation in respecting Assembly decisions.[9] But the indication that the implementation and effectiveness of resolutions are so emphatically correlated likewise suggests that the collective judgment of the world forum in dealing with the problems before it is for the most part responsible and wise. Contrary to the opinion of many, collective judgment does seem to be a suitable mechanism for international problem-solving. Since Member States in the United Nations system represent both subject and organ, the cooperative process between the Organization and its Members is mutually dependent and mutually reinforcing—that is, the character and action of the UN surely bear a direct relation to cooperation among its Members, but the Organization itself heightens their cooperation in various ways and affects their behavior.

The attitudes and expectations of the majority of Members seem to be an important dimension of this process. Significant, too, appears to be the enumeration by the collective membership of specific terms for resolving or moderating a controversy. Little evidence could be found in the present survey that a recommendation of specific UN implementary measures substantially influences the success or failure of the Assembly's efforts. Unfortunately, the determination of time-dependent effects was not possible in the decisions reviewed, because of their limited number.

[9] Michalak, Chapter 2 above, indicates several modes of cooperating in the history of the League of Nations and the United Nations.

SINCE the United Nations has exhibited a dynamic quality responsive to changes in the international scene and to the changing attitudes and purposes of its Members, one might expect not only that its decisions will mirror these changes, but also that their effect will vary with the years and with changes in the state of the outside world. A dissection of various time periods, however, does not indicate that one period of the General Assembly's work has proved substantially more fruitful than another.[10]

One might also wonder whether specific circumstances attending the issues with which the Assembly has dealt affect their denouement significantly. Our study considers four such conditions: a) crisis or chronic circumstances: the former are subsumed under Young's definition of events that flare up or jell rapidly and suddenly, raising "the impact of destabilizing forces in the general international system or any of its subsystems substantially above normal (i.e. average) levels and . . .[increasing] the likelihood of violence occurring in the system"; the latter are noted when "stresses and strains on the international system . . . build up slowly and have a cumulative effect."[11] b) The presence or absence of military strife: a contentious matter on the Assembly's agenda may or may not involve armed hostilities or open warfare between two or more parties. c) The presence or absence of internal unrest:[12] a number of situations with which the Assembly has dealt have been plagued by

[10] Our very sparse data give some indication of rather happy results during the years 1958-1962. In a wider study, nonstatistical attention might be given to the evolution of state behavior as the national statesmen "learn" from the UN encounter. National aims and expectations may be reconstituted and Members may take into account what is considered legitimate by the international community, or what the effect can be of UN pressures and interventions. See Ernst B. Haas, "The Comparative Study of the United Nations," *World Politics*, 12 (January 1960), 304-310. Haas's schematization has been extremely useful in formulating a number of the variables considered here.

[11] Oran R. Young, *The Intermediaries* (Princeton: Princeton University Press, 1967), pp. 10-11.

[12] For an extended discussion of the relation of the UN to conflict caused by internal unrest, see Miller, Chapter 4 below.

conditions of civil disturbances or open civil conflict, guerrilla activity, or unrest and disquiet among national civic groups protesting their dependent status. d) Great-power agreement or disagreement in the Security Council: a question upon which the Assembly takes action may or may not have received prior attention by the Security Council; most business which comes before both organs reaches the General Assembly as a result of failure of the great powers in the Security Council to agree on appropriate action.

The record shows that the first and third factors have no appreciable bearing upon an auspicious conclusion to the Assembly's endeavors. The probability of a resolution's implementation in cases of acute crisis is almost exactly the same as in long-standing ones; likewise, the divergence in outcome between resolutions on issues attended by internal unrest or by civic quiescence is infinitesimal. These indications are rather surprising, since it might well be expected that the urgency and danger of critical and highly disturbed situations would provide particular impetus to implementation and solution.

The General Assembly has, however, achieved its purpose somewhat more frequently in cases involving military action than in those where there was no such action. The probability of compliance with a resolution in the former instance is 60 per cent; in the latter instance, 44 per cent: Member States are more often than not willing to abide by the decisions of the world forum when the issue is beset with armed conflict. Nonetheless, the generally low evidence of compliance would indicate that one of the cardinal purposes of the General Assembly—to restore international peace and halt military hostilities—has been effected only partially in the cases under review.

Another surprising supposition supported by the data is that prior disagreement by the great powers in the Security Council on a desirable course of action seems to have a positive effect on its ultimate upshot: when disagreement on an issue has been recorded in the Council, the probability of implementation of an Assembly resolution on that issue is somewhat higher than when no appreciable prior friction has existed. The factors working toward success here are mysterious. Does great power dissension in the Security Council provoke the Members of the General Assembly to search with extraordinary care among various alternatives for those terms of solution to a problem which will yield the most profitable results?[13] Does the political process operating in the General Assembly help to reconcile great power differences?[14] Are attitudes and expectations reconstituted in the plenary body?[15]

THE GENERAL nature of a resolution, and the nature of the problem or the functional area to which a specific resolution pertains, are further dimensions of interest with possible connection to the response the resolution elicits from Member States. Hence, decisions of the General Assembly may be scrutinized with respect to whether or not they concern themselves with substantive issues, expressing the Assembly's views on concrete matters, recommending or extending approval to the terms or basis of settlement of a given case, suggesting the solution considered most desirable. One may consider whether the resolution recommends particular UN procedures, methods, or measures deemed necessary to solve the difficulty and implement the objective. And noteworthy in this connection is whether the resolution does or does not pass judgment on the merits of the positions of the parties, whether it "takes sides" or remains completely impartial.

According to the research undertaken, one finds:

a) A resolution enumerating specific terms of settlement is more than twice as likely to be implemented and effective as is one that does not.

[13] The effect of the Assembly's delineation of terms is considered in the following section.
[14] For further material on the effect of great power support, see below, pp. 118-119.
[15] See below, pp. 120-122.

112

b) A resolution enumerating specific UN procedures, measures, or machinery to help settle the question under consideration is about equally likely to be implemented as one that is silent on this count, either leaving a choice of implementary devices to the parties concerned or recommending direct negotiation without benefit of UN instrumentalities.

c) A resolution which deals with the merits of the case is slightly less likely to be implemented than a resolution that strictly avoids a policy position favorable to one side or another.

The national representatives in the General Assembly have certainly not proved reluctant to define a stand or take a sharp decision, often declaring themselves in their resolutions on the objectives to be gained, or the matters to be negotiated, or even the specific solution to be upheld. It is sometimes contended that "the big conference is at its best in insisting upon, and providing facilities other than its own platform for the promotion of, pacific settlement."[16] Our analysis, on the contrary, points to another possibility: the Assembly's advisement of the specific terms, as distinct from procedures or facilities of settlement, may be extremely rewarding in promoting the UN's purpose.

Moreover, although the United Nations has sometimes been criticized for espousing the cause of one side while attempting to bring about a settlement acceptable to both (thus in the view of some critics disqualifying it as a third-party conciliator), there is insufficient evidence that such a stance is detrimental.

Looking now into the nature of the controversies confronting the General Assembly, it is reasonable to ask whether its resolutions dealing with one type of dispute or situation have been more useful than those dealing with another. We will consider three types of political problems to which Assembly decisions have been directed: a) situations that have not developed into actual disputes between states

16 Claude, *op.cit.*, p. 206.

or assumed the form of immediate threats to peace but which might lead to international friction or give rise to a dispute; b) disputes between nations which endanger, or the continuance of which might endanger, international peace and security; c) threats to or actual breaches of the peace.[17] Put in terms of the major political functions that the United Nations can be called upon to perform, one can distinguish resolutions concerning a) peaceful change; b) pacific settlement of disputes; c) collective action in the maintenance or restoration of international peace and security.

The audit undertaken suggests that resolutions concerning threats to and breaches of the peace have a somewhat greater probability of implementation and effectiveness than those pertaining to situations or disputes. In 64 per cent of the resolutions in category c) the Assembly gained its end, as compared to 37 per cent and 43 per cent in categories a) and b).

One might, furthermore, relate functional areas or "issue" distinctions among resolutions to their varying outcomes. Most fundamentally, the resolutions may refer to questions involving a) violations of territorial integrity or of political independence; b) colonialism, self-determination, or the nature of the government of a state; c) the cold war; d) territorial claims; or e) human rights and fundamental freedoms. But a suggestive pattern of outcome here is extremely difficult to discern: the resolutions of the General Assembly most frequently fall into several of these categories, and a judgment on the exclusively characteristic issue involved presents thorny problems of interpretation. Even speculations on these matters therefore require further scrutiny.

THE NATURE of the various policies, methods, and means used by the General Assembly to give effect to its resolutions and the response of Members to these methods are

[17] For a discussion of terms, see Goodrich and Simons, *op.cit.*, pp. 225-232, 354-360.

also significant in evaluating the whys and wherefores of the Assembly's successes and failures. Which methods have proven particularly effective in resolving disputes and promoting compliance?

In terms of broad policy, the Assembly may adopt, on the one hand, what Stanley Hoffmann calls a policy of "pure coercion": through injunctions, threats, or instruments of collective action, it may seek to oblige transgressor states to surrender any gains acquired in violation of the Charter, and may try to place a return to law above an accommodation by concession. On the other hand, Assembly resolutions may reflect a policy of "pure conciliation": in such a case "it treats all parties to a dispute as equals and tries to reach a compromise through accommodation without any pressure being put on either side."[18] And there is, of course, a third policy, the middle road between the paths of pure coercion and pure conciliation.

When evaluated in these terms, it is the third policy which has prospered. In our survey, all but one of the General Assembly's actions which may be loosely called a judicious mixture of coercion and conciliation has successfully prevailed. A strictly coercionary approach has a mere 42 per cent probability of a happy aftermath, a purely conciliatory course of action about the same. The material under review is clear on these points. However, it gives little indication of the ingredients of the right mixture. It is mainly in the vaguer realm of general policy, rather than in specific measures or procedures employed by the Assembly to help implement its resolutions, that any significant factor appears pointing toward worthwhile results.

a) In its efforts to follow a conciliatory policy with the hope of thereby relieving tension between contestants and gently prodding them to compose their differences by methods of their own choice, the Assembly has sometimes

[18] Stanley Hoffmann, "Sisyphus and the Avalanche: The United Nations, Egypt and Hungary," *International Organization*, 11 (Summer 1957), 452.

utilized formal statements in the name of the United Nations. It may merely indicate its concern with the disagreement in question, declare itself confident or hopeful that a just solution will be quickly found in conformity with the principles of the United Nations Charter, or express satisfaction that the course of events is proceeding toward a peaceful solution.

b) The Assembly, becoming a degree more specific, but again in a spirit of pacification and conciliation, may deem it desirable in a particular instance to issue a general appeal for a settlement, ask the parties concerned to take the necessary steps for implementation of the resolution, request disputants to negotiate their differences directly or with the assistance of extra-UN instrumentalities.

c) Frequently, the Assembly may decide to deal with a problem or help the parties in arriving at an agreement by engaging the services of the Secretary-General, a special representative of the General Assembly, or an international committee or commission. Such an organ or subsidiary organ may be given a mandate to: i) investigate, observe compliance, report developments; ii) represent the interests of the United Nations, take the steps deemed appropriate (without the guideline of specific instructions) to achieve the Assembly's objectives, and assist the government responsible for compliance with the terms of a resolution; iii) consult specifically with and advise the parties, mediate, use good offices, or exercise wider powers of administration, even government.

d) Following a more compelling tactic, especially when faced with the need to avert or end armed hostilities between disputants, the General Assembly has often brought into play procedures known as provisional measures, in which Member States are asked to refrain from or cease particular actions: desist from intervention in the affairs of another state, discontinue assistance to a transgressor, halt military maneuvers, withdraw armed forces, and so on.

e) If other means have failed to settle a dispute or if hostilities are actually in progress, the Assembly may advocate the use of stronger measures of collective action—political, diplomatic or economic, paramilitary or military. Political measures might include a formal determination of the existence of a threat to the peace, breach of the peace, or act of aggression; collective denunciation; threat of further action, possibly by the Security Council. Diplomatic measures might involve a recommendation for severance of diplomatic relations; the withholding of accreditation or recognition; the denial of membership in the United Nations or its Specialized Agencies. A wide variety of economic and financial measures might conceivably be applied, but, in the resolutions here considered, we find only the partial blocking of commodity trade. The General Assembly has never recommended the application of coercionary collective military measures against a state, although its resolutions during the Korean War sustained Security Council action to this end. International paramilitary or police forces have been created or supported by the Assembly to help implement UN objectives in disturbed areas.

Although the General Assembly, then, has been extremely resourceful in creating and employing a wide variety of measures and combination of procedures to induce acceptance and fulfillment of its purposes, few indicators regarding their comparative efficacy issue from the data. Not unexpectedly, when the General Assembly has provided teeth for its resolutions in the form of economic and paramilitary sanctions, the record of compliance with its recommendations is good. The probability of success in such instances is 80 per cent. But the margin of success between the various other measures listed above is narrow.

It is curiously difficult, in the group of decisions here

117

examined, to discern a trend toward particularly fortunate results when the Assembly has enlisted the services of a committee, commission, special representative, or the Secretary-General to assist in the resolutions' implementation—despite a rather general acceptance by scholars and Assembly delegates of the intrinsic worth of these methods. In such instances the resolutions received compliance and effect no more frequently than when other implementary measures were employed. Resolutions asking UN organs or subsidiary organs to undertake good offices, mediation, conciliation, or to consult with and advise the parties concerned in an effort to reach a settlement of a question, were shown to have a 61 per cent chance of effectiveness. The probability of implementation of resolutions which created or utilized UN organs to observe compliance, report developments, or investigate conditions in a troubled situation was 47 per cent. And finally, resolutions which gave such bodies a broader and vaguer mandate—to assist Member Governments in implementing the terms of a resolution, to represent the United Nations in achieving its objective in the particular case, to take the steps deemed appropriate to fulfill the Assembly's aims—came out well in only 41 per cent of the decisions reviewed.

Another rather curious indication suggested by a review of the methods and means utilized by the General Assembly to implement its resolutions is that collective denunciation by the membership—the castigation of a lawbreaker or aggressor, the condemnation of certain policies or actions of a Member State—has not produced as many failures as some national representatives in debate would lead one to suppose, although the use of this tactic does not appear particularly successful.

THREE factors measuring the quantity, intensity, and quality of the community support behind a resolution are considered in our survey in an effort to determine their import: a) the size of the vote; b) the presence or absence of great-power support; and c) the ease or difficulty experienced in mustering the requisite two-thirds vote to pass a resolution. The response by interested states to resolutions receiving extended support can certainly be expected to differ from the response to resolutions backed by a bare majority. It is also reasonable to ask whether approval by the more powerful states in the Assembly increases the possibility that a resolution will be implemented and effective. Dag Hammarskjöld, in his statements on the principles and practice of preventive diplomacy, indicated that decisions of the United Nations in the political and security field would not be effectual in the absence of agreement between the superpowers. Does the record uphold his judgment?

a) Resolutions receiving either unanimous support or a favorable majority of 85 per cent or more of the total vote have a 70 per cent probability of implementation, as compared to a 37 per cent probability in decisions receiving less than 85 per cent of the total vote. Twice as many decisions approved by 80 per cent or more of the membership attained their objective, as compared with decisions approved by a smaller percentage of the national representatives.

b) Great-power support, abstention, or absence appear indeed to foster the attainment of the General Assembly's goals: 71 per cent of such resolutions proved effective, whereas only 33 per cent did so in the face of opposition by one or more permanent members of the Security Council.

c) Whether or not the necessary majority vote for a resolution is easily rallied, and whether it is preceded by little or much contentiousness, seem to have little to do with a resolution's fruitful aftermath.[19]

Of the three factors examined, it is only the outcome of the last that can be said to be unanticipated.

[19] For a discussion of related points, see below, pp. 120-122.

CLOSELY allied to the dimension of the vote is the question of the expectations entertained and the satisfaction or disappointment experienced by national decision-makers in respect to a resolution. These feelings may in turn bear upon the effect given to a particular resolution and to subsequent decisions. The effect seems to be intimately affiliated with a government's general anticipation of helpful action by the world organization.

Although a detailed analysis of these attitudes is a project too extensive to undertake in our study, a summary of opinion may be gleaned by noting the attitudes toward the resolutions under consideration,[20] both of the parties particularly concerned and of the composite majority. "In the Assembly, we should bear in mind an infallible rule in the interpretation of laws: namely, that the formula adopted is independent of those who vote for it and should be regarded as the result of the general feeling of the Organization."[21] Is the resolution in question widely viewed as an important and credible decision that bids fair to contribute to a settlement of the quarrel at hand? Is it seen mainly as a weak or unrealistic palliative unlikely to achieve its aims? Is the resolution given approval by the majority with considerable satisfaction and enthusiastic, strong support or is action taken despite dissatisfaction, even widespread misgivings? Are one or more of the principal parties, independent of their vote, strongly opposed to the content of the resolution?

More particularly, one may note whether the discussions and debates on a specific question reveal consistent agreement among the majority of UN Members regarding the terms and type of action favored in a particular instance, and the necessary measures to be recommended. Apart from the views of those delegates directly concerned with

[20] The author's evaluation was made mainly on the basis of United Nations debates, supplemented by pertinent memoirs, extra-UN statements by national spokesmen, and secondary case studies.

[21] The delegate of Uruguay, General Assembly, *Official Records*, Plenary, 11th Session (1956-1957), 654th meeting, 15 February 1957, 1110.

the question, the proceedings prior to a resolution's adoption may reveal greatly divergent points of view, considerable friction between opposing sides, or vastly contrasting policy positions. The member representatives in each instance may explore fairly thoroughly the various alternatives of UN action and seriously attempt to find a solution acceptable to the parties concerned, or such effort may be minimal. They may be clear, or confused and uncertain, as shown in the course of debate and in the substance they write into the resolution itself, as to their specific intentions, what they hope to accomplish, and what they expect from concerted action.

The factor, among these dimensions, which seems most telling in support of the General Assembly's efficacy is a major effort by members to explore thoroughly a variety of courses of action—to determine which might best ease the tensions between the opposing parties and enlist some measure of cooperation from all concerned. Based on our information, a resolution has a 78 per cent probability of implementation when such an effort has been made, and only 26 per cent when it has not.

The delegates' own estimate of credibility and expectation of compliance is reliable: when such expectation is high, actual implementation is likewise high. In those cases under consideration where the prevailing view was negative, only 31 per cent of the resolutions were implemented, as opposed to 77 per cent in those cases where the delegates expected positive action.

The attitudes toward the resolution of the principal parties concerned are naturally a strong factor influencing its aftermath. When one or more of the major interested states is vehemently opposed to an Assembly decision, the result is usually, though not always, unrewarding. In eighteen resolutions where such opposition occurred, six received implementation, twelve did not; resolutions which were approved or only mildly opposed by the parties concerned were 82 per cent implemented.

A factor which appears to some extent to inhibit fruitful

results is a confused or ambiguous conception on the part of the UN delegates of their objectives or of the methods by which the objectives may be reached. When this conception is not clear, the relative possibility that compliance with a resolution will follow is 42 per cent; when precise and unequivocal, 59 per cent. Furthermore, an Assembly decision with which the great majority of delegates are satisfied and to which they lend enthusiastic support has a better chance of a worthwhile sequel than one receiving indifferent or grudging approval, though the difference between outcomes in this respect is perhaps not as marked as might be expected. The size of the vote appears to be the more significant determinant.

Whether or not, during debate prior to a vote, there have been marked differences among the representatives of the Member States on the terms to be recommended for solution of a given problem, or on the type of change required in a particular situation, does not seem to affect the outcome appreciably. And where such differences exist in regard to the UN measures whereby the Assembly would facilitate implementation, only a few more resolutions fail than when there is appreciable agreement. One might note, however, that there may be some justification for a presumption that General Assembly resolutions which are the result of compromise and considerable give-and-take, fare much better than resolutions which represent a spontaneous or a manipulated majority consensus. This appears particularly true when the pattern of compromise emerges "on the basis of deliberately or inadvertently upgrading the common interests of the parties," thus coming closest "to peaceful change procedures typical of a political community."[22]

THE WISDOM and judgment of a collective assembly of national statesmen, their capacity to see clearly the many

[22] For further discussion, see Ernst B. Haas, *Beyond the Nation-State: Functionalism and International Organization* (Stanford: Stanford University Press, 1964), p. 14.

facets of complex political situations, and, above all, their ability to find suitable resolutions for difficult international problems, have often been challenged. With no resources of compulsion directly available, a large association of rival groups probes and analyzes and debates, sometimes most acrimoniously, frequently with stubborn partisanship, the proper course of action to avert or remove intricate and perplexing disorders in international relations. In such circumstances, one is likely to doubt the utility of such a body in upholding the purposes for which the United Nations was established.

Nonetheless, the evidence points to decided capability in these realms. National representatives in the General Assembly frequently apply themselves diligently to the search for answers. And when they specify with precision, even with detail, the terms they consider necessary for promoting peaceful and friendly relations among nations or for settling an international dispute, when their trust in the credibility of the implementation of these terms is stout and their expectations clear, and when they uphold their position by a vote in strength, their probability of success is high—success in relieving the tension surrounding a dispute, in inducing protagonists to come to terms, to cease hostilities, and to accept the provisions recommended for a settlement. The Assembly has an inherent power, and is capable of immense influence, not often wielded or generally recognized; in a still misunderstood and rather mysterious way this society is its own best friend.

LIST OF RESOLUTIONS

1. *Spain*:
   R. 39 (I), Dec. 12, 1946: "Relations of Members of the United Nations with Spain."
2. *Greece I*:
   R. 109 (II), Oct. 21, 1947: "Threats to the Political Independence and Territorial Integrity of Greece."
3. *Korean Independence I*:
   R. 112 (II), Nov. 14, 1947: "The Problem of the Independence of Korea."

4. *Palestine Partition*:
   R. 181 (II), Nov. 29, 1947: "The Future Government of Palestine."
5. *Greece II*:
   R. 193 (III), Nov. 27, 1948: "Threats to the Political Independence and Territorial Integrity of Greece."
6. *Korean Independence II*:
   R. 195 (III), Dec. 12, 1948: "The Problem of the Independence of Korea."
7. *Korean Independence III*:
   R. 293 (IV), Oct. 21, 1949: "The Problem of the Independence of Korea."
8. *Greece III*:
   R. 288 (IV), Nov. 18, 1949: "Threats to the Political Independence and Territorial Integrity of Greece."
9. *Italian Colonies*:*
   R. 289 (IV), Nov. 21, 1949
   R. 390 (V), Dec. 2, 1950: "The Disposal of the Former Italian Colonies."
10. *Korean War I*:
    R. 376 (V), Oct. 7, 1950: "The Problem of the Independence of Korea."
11. *Korean War II*:
    R. 384 (V), Dec. 14, 1950: "Intervention of the Central People's Government of the People's Republic of China in Korea."
12. *Korean War III*:
    R. 498 (V), Feb. 1, 1951: "Intervention of the . . . People's Republic of China in Korea."
13. *Korean War IV*:
    R. 500 (V), May 18, 1951: "Intervention of the . . . People's Republic of China in Korea."
14. *Germany*:
    R. 510 (VI), Dec. 20, 1951: "Appointment of an Impartial International Commission under United Nations supervision to carry out a simultaneous investigation in the Federal Republic of Germany, in Berlin and in the Soviet Zone of Germany in order to determine whether existing conditions there make it possible to hold genuinely free elections throughout these areas."
15. *Morocco I*:
    R. 612 (VII), Dec. 19, 1952: "Violations by France in Morocco of the principles of the United Nations Charter and the Declaration of Human Rights."
16. *Morocco II*:
    R. 812 (IX), Dec. 17, 1954: "Violations by France in Morocco. . . ."

* These resolutions are treated as a single case since they form a composite picture when analyzed in respect to their nature, implementary measures, voting record, and the attitudes entertained toward them.

17. *Morocco III:*
   R. 911 (X), Dec. 3, 1955: "Violations by France in Morocco. . . ."
18. *W. Irian I:*
   R. 915 (X), Dec. 16, 1955: "The Question of West Irian (West New Guinea)."
19. *Suez I:*

R. 997 (ES-I), Nov. 2, 1956:	"Question considered by the
R. 998 (ES-I), Nov. 4, 1956:	first emergency special session
R. 999 (ES-I), Nov. 4, 1956:	of the General Assembly from
R. 1000 (ES-I), Nov. 5, 1956:	4 to 10 November, 1956."
R. 1001 (ES-I), Nov. 7, 1956:	

   R. 1120 (XI), Nov. 24, 1956: "Intervention by Israel and by France and the United Kingdom in Egypt."
20. *Hungary I:*

R. 1004 (ES-II), Nov. 4, 1956:	"Ques. considered by the 2d
R. 1005 (ES-II), Nov. 9, 1956:	emerg. spec. sess. . . . Nov.
R. 1127 (XI), Nov. 21, 1956:	4-10, 1956" "The Question of
R. 1128 (XI), Nov. 21, 1956:	Hungary."
R. 1130 (XI), Dec. 4, 1956:	

21. *Hungary II:*
   R. 1131 (XI), Dec. 12, 1956: "The Question of Hungary."
22. *Hungary III:*
   R. 1132 (XI), Jan. 10, 1957: "The Question of Hungary."
   R. 1133 (XI), Sept. 14, 1957:
23. *Suez II:*

R. 1123 (XI), Jan. 19, 1957:	"Intervention by Israel and by
R. 1124 (XI), Feb. 2, 1957:	France and the United King-
R. 1125 (XI), Feb. 2, 1957:	dom in Egypt."

24. *Algeria I:*
   R. 1012 (XI), Feb. 15, 1957: "The Question of Algeria."
   R. 1184 (XII), Dec. 10, 1957:
25. *Lebanon and Jordan:*
   R. 1237 (ES-III), Aug. 21, 1958: "The Situation in Lebanon and Jordan."
26. *Hungary IV:*
   R. 1312 (XIII), Dec. 12, 1958: "The Question of Hungary."
   R. 1454 (XIV), Dec. 9, 1959:
   R. 1741 (XVI), Dec. 20, 1961:
27. *Algeria II:*
   R. 1573 (XV), Dec. 19, 1960: "The Question of Algeria."
28. *Algeria III:*
   R. 1724 (XVI) Dec. 20, 1961: "The Question of Algeria."
29. *W. Irian II:*
   R. 1572 (XVIII), Sept. 21, 1962: "The Question of West Irian (West New Guinea)."

* These resolutions are treated as a single case since they form a composite picture when analyzed in respect to their nature, implementary measures, voting record, and the attitudes entertained toward them.

Categorization and Effectiveness of General Assembly Resolutions

Resolutions	Spain Dec. 1946	Greece I Oct. 1947	Korean Independence I Nov. 1947	Palestine Nov. 1947	Greece II Nov. 1948	Korean Independence II Dec. 1948	Korean Independence III Oct. 1949	Greece III Nov. 1949	Italian Colonies 1949 1950	Korean War I Oct. 1950	Ko... D...
Implementation	Ⓘ	≠	Ⓘ	≠	Ⓘ	≠	≠	I	I	≠	
Effectiveness	E̸	E̸	E̸	Ⓔ	Ⓔ	E̸	E̸	E	E	E̸	Ⓔ
Time and Circumstances: Crisis conditions		≠E̸			ⒾⒺ					≠E̸	≠
Time and Circumstances: Chronic conditions	ⒾE̸		ⒾE̸	≠Ⓔ		≠E̸	≠E̸	IE	IE		
Time and Circumstances: Military strife		≠E̸			ⒾⒺ			IE		≠E̸	≠
Time and Circumstances: No military strife	ⒾE̸		ⒾE̸	≠Ⓔ		≠E̸	≠E̸		IE		
Time and Circumstances: Internal unrest		≠E̸	ⒾE̸	≠Ⓔ	ⒾⒺ	≠E̸	≠E̸	IE	IE		
Time and Circumstances: No internal unrest	ⒾE̸									≠E̸	≠
Time and Circumstances: Non-consideration or agreement in Security Council			ⒾE̸	≠Ⓔ		≠E̸	≠E̸		IE		
Time and Circumstances: Disagreement in Security Council	ⒾE̸	≠E̸			ⒾⒺ			IE		≠E̸	≠
Nature of Resln.: Terms specified	ⒾE̸	≠E̸	ⒾE̸	≠Ⓔ	ⒾⒺ	≠E̸	≠E̸	IE	IE	≠E̸	
Nature of Resln.: Terms not specified											≠
Nature of Resln.: UN measures specified	ⒾE̸	≠E̸	ⒾE̸	ⒾⒺ	ⒾⒺ	≠E̸	≠E̸	IE	IE	≠E̸	≠
Nature of Resln.: UN measures not specified											
Nature of Resln.: Partial	ⒾE̸		ⒾE̸	≠Ⓔ	ⒾⒺ	≠E̸	≠E̸	IE		≠E̸	
Nature of Resln.: Impartial		≠E̸							IE		≠
Nature of Resln.: Situations	ⒾE̸		ⒾE̸	≠Ⓔ		≠E̸	≠E̸		IE		
Nature of Resln.: Disputes		≠E̸									
Nature of Resln.: Threats to, breaches of the peace					ⒾⒺ				IE	≠E̸	≠
Nature of Resln.: Violations territorial/political independence		≠E̸			ⒾⒺ				IE	≠E̸	≠
Nature of Resln.: Colonialism, self-determination, government of state	ⒾE̸		ⒾE̸	≠Ⓔ		≠E̸	≠E̸		IE		
Nature of Resln.: Cold War		≠E̸	ⒾE̸		ⒾⒺ	≠E̸	≠E̸	IE	IE	≠E̸	≠
Nature of Resln.: Territorial claims					≠Ⓔ				IE		
Nature of Resln.: Human Rights	ⒾE̸										
Method: Coercion	ⒾE̸	≠E̸		≠Ⓔ	ⒾⒺ				IE	≠E̸	
Method: Conciliation			ⒾE̸			≠E̸	≠E̸		IE		
Method: Mix: Coercion / Conciliation											≠
Method: Expression of confidence, hope, concern											≠
Method: Call to cooperate, take steps extra — UN											

1. For number and title of resolution, see appended list.

2. I : Implemented.
   Ⓘ : Partially implemented.
   ✗ : Not implemented.

3. E : Effective.
   Ⓔ : Partially effective
   E̸ : Not effective.

4. For explanation or definition of variables, see text.

	Korean War IV	Germany I	Morocco I	Morocco II	Morocco III	West Irian I	Suez I	Hungary I	Hungary II	Hungary III	Suez II	Algeria I	Lebanon Jordan	Hungary IV	Algeria II	Algeria III	West Irian II
	Nov 1951	Dec. 1951	Dec. 1952	Dec. 1954	Dec. 1955	Dec. 1955	Nov. 1956	Nov. 1956	Dec. 1956	Jan., Sept. 1957	Jan., Feb. 1957	Feb., Dec. 1957	Aug. 1958	1958 1959 1961	Dec. 1960	Dec. 1961	Sept. 1962
	I	≠	≠	(I)	I	≠	(I)	≠	≠	≠	I	≠	I	≠	(I)	I	I
	E	≠	≠	(E)	E	≠	E	≠	≠	≠	E	(E)	E	≠	(E)	E	E
	IE						(I)E	≠≠	≠≠	≠≠	IE		IE				
		≠≠	≠≠	(I)(E)	IE	≠≠						≠(E)		≠≠	(I)(E)	IE	IE
	IE				IE		(I)E	≠≠	≠≠			≠(E)	IE		(I)(E)	IE	IE
		≠≠	≠≠	(I)(E)	IE	≠≠					≠≠	IE		≠≠			
		≠≠		(I)(E)	IE			≠≠	≠≠	≠≠		≠(E)	IE	≠≠	(I)(E)	IE	IE
	IE	≠≠			≠≠	(I)E					IE						
		≠≠	≠≠			≠≠						≠(E)			(I)(E)	IE	IE
	IE		(I)(E)	IE		(I)E	≠≠	≠≠	≠≠	IE		IE	≠≠			
	IE					(I)E	≠≠	≠≠	≠≠	IE		IE	≠≠	(I)(E)	IE	IE
		≠≠	≠≠	(I)(E)	IE	≠≠						≠(E)				
	IE	≠≠				(I)E	≠≠	≠≠	≠≠	IE		IE	≠≠			IE
			≠≠	(I)(E)	IE	≠≠						≠(E)			(I)(E)	IE
	IE	≠≠					≠≠	≠≠	≠≠				≠≠	(I)(E)	IE
		≠≠	(I)(E)	IE	≠≠	(I)E				IE	≠(E)	IE			IE
	≠≠				≠≠	(I)E							≠≠		
		≠≠	(I)(E)	IE	≠≠					≠(E)			IE
	IE				(I)E	≠≠	≠≠	≠≠	≠≠	IE		IE	(I)(E)	IE
	IE				(I)E	≠≠	≠≠	≠≠	IE		IE	≠≠		
		≠≠	≠≠	(I)(E)	IE	≠≠		≠≠	≠≠	≠≠		≠(E)		≠≠	(I)(E)	IE	IE
	IE	≠≠			(I)E	≠≠	≠≠	≠≠	IE		IE	≠≠		
				≠≠	(I)E				IE			IE
		≠≠	(I)(E)	IE	≠≠		≠≠	≠≠	≠≠			≠≠	IE
	IE					≠≠	≠≠	≠≠			≠≠	IE
		≠≠	≠≠	(I)(E)	IE	≠≠			≠(E)			IE
				(I)E				IE	IE	(I)(E)	IE	IE
		≠≠	(I)(E)	IE	≠≠			≠(E)		(I)(E)	IE
		≠≠						I(E)	IE	(I)(E)	IE

	Spain	Greece I	Korean Independence I	Palestine	Greece II	Korean Independence II	Korean Independence III	Greece III	Italian Colonies	Korean War I	Korean War II
Method: Refrain, cease, do particular acts	⊕ ∉	≠ ∉	⊕ ∉	≠ Ⓔ	⊕Ⓔ	≠ ∉	≠ ∉	Ⅰ Ⲉ	Ⅰ Ⲉ	≠ ∉	≠Ⓔ
Method: Committee / Commission / Secretary—General		≠ ∉	⊕ ∉	≠ Ⓔ	⊕Ⓔ	≠ ∉	≠ ∉	Ⅰ Ⲉ	Ⅰ Ⲉ	≠ ∉	≠Ⓔ
Method: Collective Measures	⊕ ∉			≠ Ⓔ	⊕Ⓔ			Ⅰ Ⲉ		≠ ∉	≠Ⓔ
Method: Committee/commission: investigate, observe		≠ ∉	⊕ ∉	≠ Ⓔ	⊕Ⓔ	≠ ∉	≠ ∉	Ⅰ Ⲉ	Ⅰ Ⲉ	≠ ∉	≠Ⓔ
Method: Committee/commission: assist government, represent UN		≠ ∉		≠ Ⓔ	⊕Ⓔ		≠ ∉	Ⅰ Ⲉ	Ⅰ Ⲉ	≠ ∉	≠ Ⓔ
Method: Committee/Commission: good offices, mediation, conciliation		≠ ∉	⊕ ∉	≠Ⓔ	⊕Ⓔ	≠ ∉	≠ ∉	Ⅰ Ⲉ	Ⅰ Ⲉ		≠Ⓔ
Method: Collective Measures: political	⊕ ∉			≠Ⓔ	⊕Ⓔ			Ⅰ Ⲉ			
Method: Collective Measures: diplomatic, economic	⊕ ∉							Ⅰ Ⲉ			
Method: Collective Measures: military, para-military										≠ ∉	≠Ⓔ
Vote: above 85%		⊕ ∉		⊕Ⓔ	≠ ∉			Ⅰ Ⲉ			≠Ⓔ
Vote: below 85%	⊕ ∉	≠ ∉		≠Ⓔ			≠ ∉		Ⅰ Ⲉ	≠ ∉	
Vote: above 80%		⊕ ∉		⊕Ⓔ	≠ ∉	≠ ∉	Ⅰ Ⲉ	Ⅰ Ⲉ	≠ ∉	≠Ⓔ	
Vote: below 80%	⊕ ∉	≠ ∉		≠Ⓔ							
Vote: support or abstention all great powers	⊕ ∉		⊕ ∉	≠Ⓔ					Ⅰ Ⲉ		
Vote: non-support all great powers		≠ ∉			⊕Ⓔ	≠ ∉	≠ ∉	Ⅰ Ⲉ		≠ ∉	≠Ⓔ
Vote: majority not difficult to muster		⊕ ∉			⊕Ⓔ	≠ ∉	≠ ∉	Ⅰ Ⲉ	Ⅰ Ⲉ	≠ ∉	≠Ⓔ
Vote: majority difficult to muster	⊕ ∉	≠ ∉		≠Ⓔ							
Attitudes: credible decision, hope of implementation								Ⅰ Ⲉ	Ⅰ Ⲉ	≠ ∉	
Attitudes: little hope of implementation	⊕ ∉	≠ ∉	⊕ ∉	≠ Ⓔ	⊕Ⓔ	≠ ∉	≠ ∉				≠Ⓔ
Attitudes: satisfaction, strong support					⊕Ⓔ			Ⅰ Ⲉ	Ⅰ Ⲉ	≠ ∉	≠Ⓔ
Attitudes: misgivings, weak support	⊕ ∉	≠ ∉	⊕ ∉	≠Ⓔ		≠ ∉	≠ ∉				
Attitudes: party opposed	⊕ ∉	≠ ∉	⊕ ∉	≠Ⓔ	⊕Ⓔ	≠ ∉	≠ ∉	Ⅰ Ⲉ		≠ ∉	≠Ⓔ
Attitudes: party agreed, mildly opposed									Ⅰ Ⲉ		
Attitudes: agreement on terms	⊕ ∉		⊕ ∉		⊕Ⓔ		≠ ∉	Ⅰ Ⲉ		≠ ∉	⊕Ⓔ
Attitudes: disagreement on terms		≠ ∉		≠Ⓔ		≠ ∉			Ⅰ Ⲉ		
Attitudes: agreement on methods			⊕ ∉		⊕Ⓔ		≠ ∉	Ⅰ Ⲉ		≠ ∉	≠Ⓔ
Attitudes: disagreement on methods	⊕ ∉	≠ ∉		≠Ⓔ		≠ ∉			Ⅰ Ⲉ		
Attitudes: alternatives explored				≠Ⓔ	⊕Ⓔ			Ⅰ Ⲉ	Ⅰ Ⲉ		
Attitudes: alternatives not explored	⊕ ∉	≠ ∉	⊕ ∉			≠ ∉	≠ ∉			≠ ∉	≠Ⓔ
Attitudes: expectations clear					⊕Ⓔ			Ⅰ Ⲉ	Ⅰ Ⲉ	≠ ∉	≠Ⓔ
Attitudes: expectations not clear	⊕ ∉	≠ ∉	⊕ ∉	≠Ⓔ		≠ ∉	≠ ∉				

	Korean War IV	Germany	Morocco I	Morocco II	Morocco III	West Irian I	Suez I	Hungary I	Hungary II	Hungary III	Suez II	Algeria I	Lebanon Jordan	Hungary IV	Algeria II	Algeria III	West Irian II
	I∈						⊕∈	≠∅	≠∅	≠∅	I∈		I∈	≠∅	⊕∈	I∈	
	I∈	≠∅					⊕∈	≠∅	≠∅	≠∅	I∈		I∈	≠∅			I∈
	I∈						⊕∈	≠∅	≠∅	≠∅	I∈		I∈	≠∅	⊕∈		I∈
	I∈	≠∅					⊕∈	≠∅		≠∅	I∈		I∈	≠∅			
		≠∅					⊕∈	≠∅	≠∅	≠∅	I∈		I∈	≠∅			I∈
	I∈												I∈				I∈
								≠∅	≠∅	≠∅					≠∅	Ⓔ∈	
	I∈																
	I∈						⊕∈				I∈		I∈				I∈
	I∈			⊕∈	I∈	≠∅					I∈	≠Ⓔ	I∈				I∈
		≠∅	≠∅				⊕∈	≠∅	≠∅	≠∅				≠∅	Ⓔ∈	I∈	
	I∈			Ⓔ∈	I∈	≠∅					I∈	≠Ⓔ	I∈				I∈
		≠∅	≠∅				⊕∈	≠∅	≠∅	≠∅				≠∅	⊕∈	I∈	
	I∈		≠∅	⊕∈	I∈	≠∅						≠Ⓔ	I∈		⊕∈	I∈	I∈
		≠∅					⊕∈	≠∅	≠∅	≠∅	I∈			≠∅			
		≠∅		⊕∈	I∈	≠∅	⊕∈		≠∅	≠∅	I∈	≠Ⓔ	I∈	≠∅		I∈	I∈
	I∈		≠∅					≠∅							⊕∈		
	I∈			⊕∈	I∈		⊕∈	≠∅			I∈	≠Ⓔ	I∈			I∈	I∈
		≠∅	≠∅			≠∅			≠∅	≠∅				≠∅	Ⓔ∈		
				⊕∈	I∈		⊕∈	≠∅	≠∅	≠∅	I∈	≠Ⓔ	I∈	≠∅		I∈	I∈
	I∈	≠∅	≠∅			≠∅									⊕∈		
	I∈	≠∅	≠∅						≠∅	≠∅	≠∅			≠∅			
				⊕∈	I∈	≠∅	⊕∈				I∈	≠Ⓔ	I∈		⊕∈	I∈	I∈
					I∈	≠∅			≠∅	≠∅	≠∅			I∈	≠∅		I∈	I∈
	I∈	≠∅	≠∅	Ⓔ∈			⊕∈				I∈	≠Ⓔ			⊕∈		
					I∈	≠∅	⊕∈		≠∅	≠∅	I∈		I∈	≠∅		I∈	I∈
	I∈	≠∅	≠∅	⊕∈				≠∅				≠Ⓔ			⊕∈		
		≠∅	⊕∈	I∈		⊕∈					I∈	≠Ⓔ	I∈		⊕∈	I∈	I∈
	I∈	≠∅			≠∅		≠∅	≠∅	≠∅					≠∅			
				I∈	⊕∈			≠∅	≠∅		≠Ⓔ	I∈	≠∅		I∈	I∈	
	I∈	≠∅	≠∅	⊕∈		≠∅		≠∅			I∈				⊕∈		

CHAPTER 4

International Organization and Internal Conflicts: Some Emerging Patterns of Response

LINDA B. MILLER

I. INTRODUCTION

What types of internal conflict are likely to characterize the international system of the next decade? What kinds of responses may be expected from the United Nations and from regional organizations? If our knowledge of why various types of internal conflict occur in the polities of "advanced" and "modernizing" countries were more complete, less tentative answers to these questions would be warranted. Similarly, if existing paradigms of modernization or theories of violence commanded wider acceptance,[1] we could assay the prospects for the participation of international organizations with greater confidence. Despite these epistemological problems, there is value in clarifying the changing significance of internal conflicts in the contemporary system.

In the scholarly world, definitional skirmishing continues over the use of terms like "local disorder," "intrastate violence" and "internal war." In the political world, the violence that erupts within individual geopolitical units displays little respect for scholars' categories. Among theorists and policy-makers there is increasing understanding that the lengthy procession of coups, insurrections or factional struggles for governmental power in the 1950s and 1960s reflected major tensions in world politics—especially

[1] A useful review of recent literature is provided in Henry Bienen, *Violence and Social Change* (Chicago: University of Chicago Press, 1968), Chapters 2 and 3.

130

military and ideological vestiges of the cold war, or social and economic remnants of decolonization. There is also increasing awareness that the international regulation of internal conflicts has been rendered difficult by political and legal factors that limit the effectiveness of the United Nations and regional organizations.

My perspective, in attempting to look at the future patterns of response of international organizations to internal conflicts, is well summarized by Ernst Haas: "contingent forecasting based on articulate assumptions, established trends, and probable logical connections between these."[2] My first assumption is that current trends could alter the status of internal conflicts in world politics in the 1970s, although the prevalent types may resemble those of the previous two decades. My second assumption is that the extensive experience of international organizations (both quasi-universal and sub-global groupings) with varieties of internal conflict since 1946 has yielded patterns of response that may help to shape the emerging political order. A critical examination of these assumptions and their implications forms the substance of this essay.

The tasks assumed by international organizations in the amelioration of contemporary internal conflicts have revealed the dual status of these institutions as both "instruments" and "actors" in world politics. Responsibilities for the maintenance of international peace and security and the pacific settlement of disputes have provided these organizations with a raison d'être in intrastate conflicts, yet their mandates, memberships, resources, and jurisdictions have remained restricted. Thus "task expansion" has occurred during a period of "role fluctuation."[3]

Since the effective control of force has remained on the national level, the self-restraint of third parties and their

[2] Ernst B. Haas, "Collective Security and the Future International System," in Richard A. Falk and Wolfram Hanreider, eds., *International Law and Organization* (Philadelphia: J. P. Lippincott, 1968), p. 299.
[3] See Young, above, pp. 13-14.

131

perceptions of the hazards or benefits created by intrastate conflict have influenced the character of UN and regional reactions. Not surprisingly, a general pattern of *ad hoc* responses has emerged to 1) colonial wars, 2) internal conflicts involving a breakdown of law and order, and 3) proxy wars and internal conflicts involving charges of external aggression or subversion.[4] Each type of conflict has revealed distinctive features in origin and evolution, and the responses of international organizations have varied in efficacy and authority. The extent to which these organizations adapt their procedures and scope to the dynamic international environment of the 1970s will determine the impact of their future roles and functions.[5]

II. The Changing Environment of International Politics

If we postulate "incremental" rather than "revolutionary" change[6] for the international system of the 1970s and perhaps the 1980s, the salient roles recently played by international organizations in internal conflicts would seem assured. But the relevance of these roles, especially if we seek to differentiate peacekeeping, peacemaking, peacebuilding, conciliation, mediation, and enforcement,[7] is affected by the structure of the external political milieu in which these organizations must act. An analysis of possible shifts in the global political environment is therefore a necessary prelude to a discussion of "alternative futures" for international institutions in the control of internal conflicts.

[4] This pattern is analyzed in detail in Linda B. Miller, *World Order and Local Disorder: The United Nations and Internal Conflicts* (Princeton: Princeton University Press, 1967), Chapters 2-4.

[5] For some distinctions in the definition of "roles" and "functions" of international organizations, consult Falk, below, pp. 190-198.

[6] Haas, *op.cit.*, pp. 300ff.

[7] See David Forsythe, "United Nations Intervention in Conflict Situations Revisited," *International Organization*, 23 (Winter 1969), 131-139.

Our perceptions of "fluidity" or "flux" in world politics have not produced convincing theories of *transitions* in the structure or content of international systems. Instead, we have partial approaches to the issue of change—some stress the idea of "levels" or "layers" in the international system;[8] others emphasize the concepts of "congruence" or "discontinuity" among "subsystems."[9] The prevailing eclecticism of these approaches makes questionable "the validity of both abstract models of international relations that ascribe stability to particular diplomatic-strategic configurations and state-centered theories that downgrade the impact of transnational forces or non-state actors."[10]

Nevertheless, despite the inadequacy of our theories, it is evident that changes in the role of the nation-state and in the role of military force continue to affect patterns of response to internal conflicts. As a result of ideological and technological "permeability," national sovereignty is more closely guarded but its privileges are less consequential.[11] Inhibitions on the use of nuclear weapons enable threats of force to serve as surrogates for acts of violence, thereby helping to transform traditional relationships among members of the international system; the range of acceptable types of conflict has been altered and the imprecision of hierarchies of states accentuated. While efforts of the present superpowers to "define the rules" of interstate politics persist,[12] the reluctance of middle-rank or smaller states to adhere to these "rules" increases. The US and USSR, the potential "co-managers" of the international system, strive to solidify their partially collaborative relationship vis-à-vis

[8] See, for example, Stanley Hoffmann, *Gulliver's Troubles* (New York: McGraw-Hill, 1968), Part 1.

[9] Oran R. Young, "Political Discontinuities in the International System," *World Politics*, 20 (April 1968), 369-392.

[10] Linda B. Miller, "America, Europe and the International System," *World Politics*, 21 (January 1969), 317.

[11] See Pierre Hassner, "The Nation-State in the Nuclear Age," *Survey*, 67 (April 1968), 5.

[12] Ciro Elliott Zoppo, "Nuclear Technology, Multipolarity, and International Stability," *World Politics*, 18 (July 1966), 589.

challengers to their nuclear primacy. A tendency for American and Soviet leaders to share complementary biases against destabilizing change is strengthened, despite the military and economic asymmetries between the two countries.

The superpowers' preferences for a status quo permitting minor adjustments of interests but preserving the structure of the international system have stimulated the use of internal conflicts as vehicles for expressing the "limited adversary" relationship of the United States and the Soviet Union. External intervention and counterintervention became the convenient mode for states whose leaders viewed internal conflicts as a means of extending national influence at the expense of global or regional competitors. The lack of substantive rules of conduct in civil strife has encouraged unregulated interventions. Indeed, since these conflicts have raged in the less-developed countries of Latin America, Asia, the Middle East, and Africa where few, if any, stakes could justify the use of nuclear weapons, interventionary behavior has stressed economic and propaganda techniques, as well as conventional military forces.

A separation, perhaps inevitable, between the objectives of scholars and policy-makers emerged from the politics of intervention in internal conflicts, as practiced and interpreted in the 1950s and 1960s. Few scholars would disagree with Richard A. Falk, who has insisted that "civil strife constitutes the major challenge to those convinced that decisions to use military power in world affairs should not be matters of national discretion."[13] Yet policy-makers have resisted the acceptance of "legal" restraints that might serve as predictable guides for state behavior. To be sure, the *idea* that the legitimacy of particular interventions might be judged on the basis of respect for "general community consent" rather than "*ad hoc* political majorities of the mo-

---

[13] Richard A. Falk, "The International Regulation of Internal Violence in the Developing Countries," American Society of International Law, *Proceedings* (April 1966), 59.

ment" has gained ground. A graduated "scale of legitimacy" has appeal in a nuclear world, especially in view of the threat of proliferation. Unilateral interventions in internal conflicts would rank lower on such a scale than regional interventions, which, in turn, would rank lower than multilateral interventions by the UN.[14] If our concern is to illuminate the legacy of the last two decades for the 1970s, we must conclude that processes for the accommodation or resolution of conflicts (especially review procedures or legitimacy scales) have lagged behind the development of interventionary techniques, both military and nonmilitary.[15] A predilection for negotiated settlements has developed, although this preference may not be shared by state actors like China whose influence in world politics may grow in the 1970s. Nevertheless its existence, revealing the beginnings of shared conceptions of permissible ways to terminate interventions, provides at least a fragile basis for the evolution of more impressive transnational restraints.

The failure to move beyond this fragile basis is a consequence of the prevailing priorities in a number of policy-making bureaucracies. The political epoch in which the trends and assumptions of the 1950s and 1960s matured was marked by priorities that emphasized the primacy of international politics in the domestic settings of both industrialized and less-developed states. This order of priorities enabled policy-makers to: 1) cite the pressures of the external milieu as an adequate justification for the neglect of cleavages within their own societies, and 2) assess the importance of individual outbreaks of civil strife in modernizing countries chiefly in accordance with racial, ideological, anticolonial, or security perspectives. While it is by no means clear that the dominant-subordinate relationship between international and domestic priorities will be thor-

[14] For a critique of this proposal, consult Miller, *World Order and Local Disorder*, Chapter 5.
[15] For a discussion of the processes of conflict-resolution in the General Assembly, see Lande, Chapter 3 above.

135

oughly reversed in the 1970s, a readjustment did take place in a number of advanced and modernizing societies in the latter half of the 1960s. France, Britain, India, Ghana, and America are notable examples of this tendency.

It would be premature to conclude that this reversal or readjustment will necessarily lead to predictable reconsiderations of the status of internal conflicts in world politics. But a widespread rejection of the preeminence of international politics, if it fostered a global milieu of "competitive domestic stresses and strains and transnational demonstration effects,"[16] could yield new criteria for the conduct and control of intervention in civil strife, even in the continued absence of agreed definitions of "aggression," "subversion," or "self-defense." New criteria, reflecting a desire on the part of the superpowers and others to disengage from the turbulence of "third-world" politics in the 1970s, might embody changed perceptions of the "autonomy" or "inevitability" of civil strife in the process of modernization, and hence the value of third-party interventions.[17]

Ramifications of the new criteria that might evolve are at present speculative. If the leaders of governments that are potential "intervenors" come to regard the outcomes of future internal conflicts as less vital to security requirements or to ideological struggles, "benign" forms of competition, based on tacit agreements, could prevail. External manipulation of weaker, poorly-integrated states could diminish in intensity, or be confined to actions less demanding than full-scale military operations, in conformity with the expectations of third-party domestic elites who would fear the "overcommitment" of intervention on a massive scale. A rejuvenated nineteenth century European concert[18] might be tried, especially if a "benevolent duopoly" of the present

[16] Miller, "America, Europe and the International System," p. 327.
[17] On this point, see Falk's discussion of UN System III, below, pp. 218-222.
[18] This conception has been advanced by F. H. Hinsley in "On the Present State and Future Development of the International System," *World Politics*, 20 (July 1968), 705-720.

superpowers seemed unpalatable to other state actors. But a "concert of powers" for the 1970s, although in theory attractive, in practice could prove to be an unrealistic goal in the aftermath of a post-Vietnam reaction in America and Western Europe—a reaction that rejects the employment of supposedly "usable power," the US subnuclear military instrument, in future postcolonial internal conflicts.[19] A reconsideration of interventionary behavior under conditions of an altered relationship between domestic and international concerns could produce a superficial "moderation" of overt conflict in international politics. This "moderation" might impart a false sense of stability if security tasks were to become divorced from other tasks,[20] or if national concerns became an excuse for ignoring the gulf between developed and less developed states. Serious threats to the structure of the global system could therefore develop in the 1970s if a deterioration in rank orders of states were to accelerate and if the formation of regional or functional balances within subsystems were to fail.

Renewed emphasis on domestic objectives and strategies might facilitate the formation of a "multihierarchical" international system,[21] with a prominent place for existing regional or global institutions in the control of intrastate conflict, especially the prevention of competitive interventions. This essentially negative role would focus on the containment of violence within accepted boundaries, while bilateral or multilateral economic and diplomatic pressures were mounted to encourage all parties to negotiate. The compatibility of functions between regional and global institutions in individual cases would evolve pragmatically, as political constellations within these organizations permitted. If possible, the assumption of responsibility for securing specific settlements should rest with local participants, whose political solutions would be rooted in their

[19] Miller, "America, Europe and the International System," p. 329.
[20] Haas, *op.cit.*, pp. 299-344.
[21] See Hoffmann, *op.cit.*, Part I.

137

own national histories. International institutions might then perform less controversial tasks.

How might the interests and energies of those whose commitment to a multihierarchical system would be necessary for its formation and maintenance be aroused and sustained? Paradoxically, the influence that the present superpowers might exert is limited by their collaborative activities (like the non-proliferation treaty) that appear to consolidate the present distribution of power in their favor. A preoccupation with purely national problems or parochial approaches to world order on the part of European and non-European middle-rank powers could preclude positive contributions to new hierarchies or to new criteria for the containment of lesser levels of civil violence and coercion. For the small states, especially the newly independent UN members, intragroup tensions or intercontinental or intraregional competitiveness[22] might augment fragmentation and prevent effective participation in the new issues a multihierarchical system would generate. It is clear that "there may exist an impressive discontinuity between convergent interests in a multihierarchical system and collective influences that could promote its establishment."[23]

III. The Changing Environment of International Organizations

The obstacles to the promotion of a multihierarchical international system indicate that a radical transformation in the roles or functions of international organizations in civil strife is unlikely. Thus the record of the 1950s and 1960s will remain pertinent, even if third-party perceptions of the status of internal conflicts in world politics should change. In the present decade, then, we can expect that contro-

[22] This point is discussed at length in Linda B. Miller, "The New States and the International Society," *Annals* of the American Academy of Political and Social Science (Fall 1969).

[23] Miller, "America, Europe and the International System," p. 331.

versial foreign policy, economic, ethnic, or racial issues will
continue to spark internal violence, especially in those new
states where, at best, there exists a tentative national consensus about the means or ends of government, or the
legitimacy of ruling regimes. Similarly, we can also antici-
pate that, as in the past, different kinds of internal violence
will create different international concerns. Conflicts that
subside quickly or remain confined within national boundaries will therefore attract little global attention, while pro-
tracted disorders that threaten to spill over territorial
boundaries may stimulate at least regional interests in the
prevention of escalation. We may also expect that most
states will continue to reject advance commitments, for
themselves or for organizations to which they belong, in
cases of civil strife.

Since both regional and global organizations are arenas
in which competing governmental interests are dramatized,
only when these interests converge will a consensus develop
on appropriate responses to internal violence. If, for reasons
suggested earlier, a number of governments with previous
interests in civil strife adopt a position of aloofness from internal conflicts, a trend toward less ambitious international
responses to such disorders could emerge. Future patterns
of response to internal conflicts involving a breakdown of
law and order, or to proxy wars, could include attempts to
isolate the conflict or to foster negotiations, but would exclude efforts to interpose UN forces between disputants.
Therefore, diminished participation on the part of international institutions, in contrast to the Congo and Cyprus conflicts, could become typical in this decade.

In the 1970s, as earlier, the motivations of incumbents,
insurgents, or third parties who wish to involve the UN or
regional organizations in civil strife might include a desire
to restore authority, to end foreign intervention in support
of rebels, or to marshal international opinion against potential adversaries. Similarly, those who would involve international organizations in such conflicts will have to consider:

139

1) whether the range of functions such organizations could perform—investigation, observation, peacekeeping—would be used to facilitate a lasting solution to the conflict or merely to restore a disadvantageous status quo, and 2) whether the activities of regional and global institutions would be contradictory or complementary in the perform-ance of political or diplomatic tasks.[24] Because the activities of international organizations, peculiarly susceptible to shifts in the *external* political milieu, also reflect variations in the *internal* atmosphere, it is necessary to assess the experience of the 1950s and 1960s in the light of the prevail-ing mood within the United Nations and regional organiza-tions today.

The evident priorities of the majority of UN members, the developing states, influence not only responses to in-ternal conflicts *per se*, but also the Organization's reactions to other problems raised by nation-building and insur-gency. A mood of frustration and disillusionment with in-ternational organizations flourished in the latter half of the 1960s, in part because the expectations of the new states for rapid social and economic betterment were excessive and unrealistic.[25] This disappointment has expressed itself in potentially damaging ways: "the African states . . . have succeeded in narrowing the effective scope of issues con-sidered by the United Nations. Problems and concerns other than colonialism and economic development, such as human rights, international law, and disarmament, which have been dealt with traditionally by the United Nations, have either been redefined by the African states in such a way as to complement their primary goals or else have been largely ignored by them."[26]

[24] Relationships between regional and global approaches to inter-nal conflicts are explored in Linda B. Miller, "Regional Organiza-tion and the Regulation of Internal Conflict," *World Politics*, 19 (July 1967), 582-600.
[25] For a discussion of the tensions created by these expectations, see Gordenker, Chapter 5 below.
[26] David A. Kay, "The Impact of the African States on the U.N.," *International Organization*, 23 (Winter 1969), 44-45.

LINDA B. MILLER

As an outgrowth of the narrowed scope of discussion, the bargaining process within the United Nations and regional organizations, a process that fosters compromises and trade-offs, has itself become the dominant focus of political interaction: "Success or failure in the United Nations is increasingly judged by the criteria of parliamentary diplomacy—votes won or lost, amendments adopted or defeated, and successful or unsuccessful parliamentary stratagems—rather than by any contribution made to the control or resolution of the problems at hand."[27] Given these criteria, the attainment of "collective legitimization" via regional or global institutions in cases of civil strife is not necessarily beneficial. Rather, such legitimization may be "inversely related to the degree to which the Organization is customarily used by member-states to implement their traditionally defined national interests rather than to seek consensus, resolve conflict, or build international order."[28]

The earlier enthusiasms of many leaders of the new states for responsible and responsive international reactions to civil strife have dissipated, as the difficulties inherent in their achievement have mounted. Within the group of new states, complete independence for all African and Asian territories could not be attained before postcolonial tensions arrived to plague their leaders. Additional expectations were stimulated as the first-generation leadership sought to consolidate the shaky gains of independence. These postcolonial tensions, often expressed in internal conflicts, revealed an array of loyalties to tribes or entities other than the state. The plethora of internal conflicts in the 1950s and 1960s placed complex demands on the political councils of the UN and later the OAU (to a lesser extent the more "hegemonic" OAS), as these organizations were expected to condemn "internal" threats in the form of separatist or secessionist movements, or to replace the metropoles as suppliers of military assistance in the event of uprisings against

[27] *Ibid.*, p. 40.
[28] Jerome Slater, "The Limits of Legitimization in International Organizations: The OAS and the Dominican Crisis," *International Organization*, 23 (Winter 1969), 71.

141

the central authorities. Since the international organizations have been asked to intervene diplomatically or militarily, and, at the same time, to regulate the interventionary behavior of other actors in internal conflicts, their inadequacies have been demonstrated. With few exceptions they have, at best, encouraged member-states' self-restraint by adoption of innocuous resolutions. When the international organizations have become committed to particular outcomes in the variety of intrastate or interstate conflicts in the modernizing areas, their capacities to affect events in subsequent controversies have been circumscribed.

As these conflicts have preoccupied leaders of the new states within and beyond the councils of international organizations, the apparent uniformity of demands placed on the more advanced states has not masked the development of splits within the group of new states. In the United Nations, the limits of cooperation between the Latin American states and the Africans and Asians have sharpened,[29] and the separate concerns of Asian and African states have become apparent as the Africans have sought to use their numerical superiority against the Asians in bargaining contexts where voting is preeminent. A further note of unpredictability has been introduced into these relationships with the elaboration of theories of intervention that may be used to justify manipulation of the internal affairs of other countries. Egypt's rationale for its intervention in Yemen or Algeria's defense of anti-Israel actions exemplify this tendency.[30] The absence of a hierarchy of legitimacy to guide the actions of "third-world" policy-makers vis-à-vis each other stands in striking contrast to the norms often adduced to guide their actions vis-à-vis Rhodesia, South Africa, or

[29] For useful examples, see David A. Kay, "The Politics of Decolonization: The New Nations and the United Nations Political Process," *International Organization*, 21 (Autumn 1967), 786-811.

[30] Some interesting differences between African and Arab conceptions of permissible norms of "interference" in other states are assessed in I. William Zartman, "Intervention Among Developing States," *Journal of International Affairs*, 22, 2 (1968), 188-197.

Portugal. As a result, the regional organizations identified with the modernizing "subsystems" have fared poorly as instruments of peaceful change (with the possible exception of the OAU's role in helping to settle African border disputes).[31]

Fluctuations in the leadership of the new states augment other frustrations. Although the poses of "self-assertion" employed to conceal the previously mentioned cleavages in domestic polities have by no means disappeared from the international scene with the downfall of Nkrumah and Sukarno, their fate has proved instructive for aspiring leaders who would pursue ephemeral international prestige at the expense of social problems at home. The cost of such neglect now exceeds the routine charges of corruption or bureaucratic bungling.[32] The rash of military coups that toppled numerous African leaders in 1965-1966 doomed the grandiose designs for pan-African unity that would transcend either the artificial boundaries bequeathed by the colonial powers or the suspicions engendered by rival transnational movements.

Thus far, the capacity of new states to press for compulsory action in the fields of international peace and security, and economic and social development, especially their insistence on linking these issue-areas, has depended upon the maintenance of well-established trade-off patterns. The future evolution of these patterns begins to seem uncertain. Interfunctional and interregional bargaining could become more restricted and issue-areas could become more autonomous in the next twenty years.[33] In any case, in the 1970s, the success of legislative techniques may well be measured by the compliance of other states with specific

[31] Miller, "Regional Organization and the Regulation of Internal Conflict," pp. 585ff.

[32] Some interesting propositions about the functions of corruption in the politics of development are advanced in J. S. Nye, Jr., "Corruption and Political Development: A Cost-Benefit Analysis," *American Political Science Review*, 61 (June 1967), 417-427.

[33] Haas, *op.cit.*, p. 340.

143

resolutions, not only by the tactical behavior of various groups in the bargaining processes of international organizations—especially since "the bargaining concerns only an exchange of verbal commitments, thereby accentuating the problems associated with failures of implementation and calling dramatic attention to the disjunction between implementing capabilities within and outside the Organization."[34]

The new states could experience additional difficulties in achieving satisfactory responses to their demands in the 1970s, in part because their capacity to play off Soviet and American policy-makers to advantage has declined. Equally important is a growing resentment on the part of the advanced states at the attempts of new states to use international entities to impose "obligations" on the developed states. The efforts to "legislate" within the councils of international organizations express the new states' desire to link questions of international peace and security with economic and social development. The new states' rejection of *ad hoc* procedures in both fields reveals a lack of confidence in the developed states' willingness to correct inequities.

The accomplishments of the new states in linking the two spheres and in using international organizations as legislative bodies are uneven. Both efforts attest to the obvious fact that the demands of the new states for some visible signs of change are not satisfied by simply keeping issues before the councils of regional or general international organizations. In the international peace and security issues the sanctionist approach to Rhodesia, after a circuitous policy of UN investigation, debate, and resolution is illustrative.[35] Even in circumstances of policy agreement, the African states, alone or with other new states, continue to lack sufficient power to "impose" a settlement on Portugal, South Africa, or Rhodesia. The pattern of settlement in similar cases, especially colonial wars like Algeria or An-

[34] Falk, below, pp. 197-198.
[35] See J. Leo Cefkin, "The Rhodesian Question at the United Nations," *International Organization*, 22 (Summer 1968), 649-669.

gola, indicates a bilateral framework for eventual solutions rather than a multilateral or regional one. But there are benefits in UN or OAU presentations that stress violations of human rights and the compatibility of regional and global concerns. Since the new states' leaders know that the possibilities of mandatory actions in such politically delicate situations are minimal, their advocacy of strong interventionary positions carries with it few responsibilities.

Although there may be little reason to expect consistent Western compliance with sanctions against countries like Rhodesia, Portugal, or South Africa, the process of escalating diplomatic or economic pressures against such regimes in itself has gained support as a surrogate for more direct forms of action. Of course, there are very definite limits to the effectiveness of such an approach. It has scant application in conflicts involving the superpowers, for example, Vietnam, and it could in time provoke additional frustrations if it appears to yield few effective measures against regimes the new states have discredited. Yet it does reveal an acceptance of the fact that 1) "a judgment of censure is one way to use the political arenas of the United Nations in a setting in which other modes of adverse response might seem both too dangerous and too costly,"[36] and that 2) "the learning experience provided by the Congo Operation has induced a sense of modesty about what might be expected from the United Nations in a situation where the scale and stakes of the conflict are sufficiently great as to undermine the stability of the initiating consensus."[37]

Although majorities in the international organizations concerned have expressed definite preferences for change favorable to "insurgents" in Rhodesia and South Africa, the value of the African states' preoccupation with the potential conflicts of Southern Africa is unclear:

Since texts that do not owe their origin to some other and more salient issue area are unlikely to succeed in pene-

[36] Falk, below, p. 202.   [37] *Ibid.*, p. 201.

trating the international environment, the legitimacy now closely associated with certain rights in the decolonization nexus is not destined to last. Even though racial discrimination and the suppression of voluntary organizations are certain to recur, we must be skeptical of their salience in triggering concern or U.N. action. The experience of the ILO suggests that only reconciliation polities of recent origin and certain modernizing oligarchies tend to be responsive to international criticism, primarily in order to demonstrate their respectability. Because the future international system is likely to be inhabited by a very large number of authoritarian polities we cannot rely on the continuation of the pattern of responsiveness. Neither an autonomous expansion of the human rights task nor the possibility of trade-offs with security concerns can be foreseen.[38]

In terms of compliance, a trend toward the autonomy of issue-areas could diminish the significance of the new states' efforts to impose obligations on the developed states, even if it would not diffuse the energies they now expend in securing "legislative" outcomes in international institutions. Moreover, such a trend could produce an alteration in the new states' perceptions of useful legal norms, in civil strife and in other types of conflicts. American and other scholars have clarified the "strategic" approach of many new states toward international law, a combination of "ideological repudiation" and "pragmatic manipulation,"[39] that permits leaders of these states to be *both* "revisionist" and "conservative," depending on the particular set of norms in question. For example, while leaders of the new states have demanded a reinforcement of traditional norms of nonintervention in *their* affairs, they have insisted on the validity of uses of force to end racist policies they find re-

[38] Haas, *op.cit.*, p. 340.

[39] The tension between these two attitudes is discussed in Richard A. Falk, "The New States and International Legal Order," Hague *Recueil des Cours* (1966), Vol. ii.

pugnant. Despite the "radical" positions advanced by a number of new states in international conferences,[40] their daily conduct of international relations reveals a high degree of compliance with established custom or treaty law.

Rejecting the conception of an international system structured to favor states possessing impressive military establishments, the new states have expected the "progressive development" of international law to correct pre-independence rank orders that served to condemn them to the lowest place in the hierarchy. Thus the new states are interested in using legal norms in internal conflicts not only as instruments for restraining national behavior, but also as techniques for mobilizing political support and communicating claims and counterclaims to the developed states. Of necessity, they have approached international organizations as arenas in which the creation of "new" norms occupies a conspicuous position. The capacity of the leaders of new states to employ international law imaginatively in these less conventional ways will be tested if a growing autonomy of issue-areas precludes the links that have permitted them to correlate various types of demands vis-à-vis the developed states in the realm of intrastate violence and beyond.

Even if the new states' complex demands for "justice" and "development" are couched in less vehement terms, it is likely that the international organizations will enjoy but contingent authority in either the peace and security or the economic and social issues in the 1970s. Despite the legislative efforts of the new states in recent years, the resistance of the advanced countries to such efforts prevents these institutions from extending their authority beyond limits that a minority of middle-rank or larger states will accept. The process of ascertaining these uncertain limits may be expected to produce added friction between impatient lead-

[40] Some interesting examples drawn from the two Law of the Sea conferences are presented in Robert L. Friedheim, "The 'Satisfied' and 'Dissatisfied' States Negotiate International Law," *World Politics*, 17 (October 1965), 20-41.

147

ers of the new states (however moderate their approach may seem in comparison with their "first-generation" predecessors) and leaders of advanced countries in the next decade. For this reason, it is by no means evident that a better balance will be struck between national and international approaches to the problems of peace or development stimulated by internal conflicts, a balance more compatible with the complex requirements of global or regional order in the 1970s.

IV. CONCLUSION

My analysis of the changing environments of international politics and international organizations has emphasized some shifts that may affect the future pattern of response to internal conflicts. I have argued that since the perceptions of third-party states, rather than objective tests, have been and are likely to remain significant in determining the classification of internal conflicts and hence the likelihood of interventions, tendencies toward the evolution of new criteria for the conduct and control of civil strife deserve scholarly attention. International organizations in the 1970s, as in the previous two decades, are apt to be poorly equipped to meet the challenges of persistent internal conflicts in the modernizing areas. While the coincident interest of global and regional organizations will remain the maximization of diplomatic or other pressures that will dissuade the superpowers and smaller revisionist powers from a cycle of counterinterventions, this task could be facilitated if national policy-makers, preoccupied with their own domestic problems, exercise greater self-restraint in reacting to outbreaks of civil strife beyond their borders.

The emerging political order, shaped in part by the institutionalization of *ad hoc* international responses to internal conflicts, will permit international organizations to act as centers of occasional debate, conciliation, and negotiation but rarely, if, at all, as initiators or administrators of large-scale field operations that require either a prolonged consensus in the Security Council and General Assembly or established trade-off patterns and linkages between issue-areas. Moreover, the continued lack of review procedures, whereby member-states might subject claims or counter-claims to serious scrutiny, hinders the acceptance of UN or regional precedents as "community authorized norms" which, in practice, might enjoy a greater legitimacy than unilateral standards of conduct in civil strife.

A stable system of neatly-balanced state, regional and global actors efficiently performing tasks for each other in internal conflicts and related issue-areas, is an excessively anthropomorphic vision that does not accord with technological, economic, or political realities. In the 1970s, for entities entering a phase of their development in which the accent may come to fall on "state" rather than upon "new," the vital question could be: how can what has already been accomplished in the transition to self-rule be preserved and protected from within and without? For other states, an equally important question could be: how may regional organizations and the United Nations become more effective instruments of modernization, perhaps exercising a preventive role in internal conflicts?

For the immediate future, two less dramatic but ambitious questions should preoccupy theorists and policy-makers: in view of the structural and political disabilities which preclude the establishment of "rules" for the participation of international organizations in internal conflicts, are there ways in which the capacity of these institutions to encourage third-party self-restraint may be strengthened? In view of the often disappointing efforts to "build the record" of international organizations, efforts that may lead to a postponement of settlements, are there ways in which the smaller and middle-rank states may exercise greater influence on parties to negotiate internal conflicts?

Without persuasive answers to these questions it would appear that "the organized international community can

149

only mobilize effective power to act, and only then selectively, in a peace-keeping capacity; the enforcement of legislative claims [will continue to be] sporadic even in those areas where a value consensus of principal states does obtain."[41]

[41] Richard A. Falk and Cyril E. Black, eds., *The Future of the International Legal Order.* Vol. I, *Trends and Patterns* (Princeton: Princeton University Press, 1969), Introduction, p. x.

CHAPTER 5

The United Nations and Economic and Social Change

LEON GORDENKER

What the United Nations and associated organizations now are doing in the economic and social field produces substantial but varied political results. Furthermore, the ramifications of their programs could conceivably grow in intensity and range to become an important determinant of future economic and social development within states.[1] This chapter will sketch some of the implications of present practices both for the United Nations and for national development programs and will suggest some possibilities of future evolution. It will also point out opportunities for future research.

I. The Political Nature of Economic and Social Activities

Only a few years ago, the suggestion that economic and social activities had anything but a "nonpolitical" character might have been regarded as heresy by those acquainted with international organizations. Beginning before the First World War and still appearing in vestigial form, the belief that functional activities had a special purity was so firmly held as to constitute a myth. It had a tenuous basis in reality and by the end of the Second World War had acquired an

[1] Two recent reports for international organizations presage a campaign to increase the role of multilateral aid in development. See Lester B. Pearson (Chairman), Commission on International Development, *Partners in Development* (New York: Praeger, 1969), esp. Chapter 11; and Sir Robert Jackson, *A Study of the Capacity of the United Nations Development System*, 2 vols. (Geneva: United Nations, 1969), esp. Vol. 1, 18-24.

attractive superstructure, to which frequent additions were made, in the functionalist theory.[2]

The origin and viability of the myth of nonpolitical activity derives in part from a narrow definition of politics. By regarding politics in the international realm as confined to those conflicts in which a probable or fairly imminent use of military forces is involved, everything else can be seen as nonpolitical. Thus, the United Nations Security Council or the Council of the League Nations deal by definition with political matters, for they exist to treat matters of international security. Whatever else the international organizations do is therefore nonpolitical.

This simplistic dichotomy fits fairly well with a conventional view of the origins of the earliest international organizations. Such institutions as the International Telegraphic Union, the Universal Postal Union or the Commission Europeéne du Danube meet obvious needs. They have nothing to do with security. Their scope is limited to specialized, technical subject matter. They are therefore nonpolitical.

If even a slightly more sophisticated definition of politics is applied to such organizations, as well as to the wide range of economic and social activities now undertaken by multilateral bodies, the outcome is quite different. If international politics is viewed as the striving by states within a system to actualize competing claims and demands, even the narrow technical organizations fall under the political rubric. The United Nations system provides an institutional setting within which to enunciate, define, and pursue such values. Thus, the only difference between the handling of security problems and those of the general welfare is that

[2] See David Mitrany, *A Working Peace System* (London: Royal Institute of International Affairs, 1946); Ernst B. Haas, *Beyond the Nation-State* (Stanford: Stanford University Press, 1964), and I. L. Claude, Jr., *Swords into Plowshares* (New York: Random House, 3rd edn., 1964), Chapter 17. Haas refutes the theory that politics are separable from functional activities and Claude's discussion briefly points out the main criticisms of the functionalist doctrine.

in the latter the organization proceeds on the assumption that in no circumstance will force be used to reach settlements.

The norm of nonforceful state behavior, which is the keystone of every international organization,[3] implies further assumptions. One is that conflicting claims can in fact be settled, that conflicting interests can be adjusted.[4] To settle such claims, methods are provided ranging from jural decisions to secret negotiations. A further assumption, therefore, is that the provision of institutionalized means of settling claims promotes their settlement. A final assumption is that only governments advance the claims, even if their satisfaction benefits only private persons.

So long as an element of conflict of interests is admitted, however, the international organizations must be seen as means for handling political issues. The programs which grow out of consideration of political issues, therefore, must be political, in the sense that they deal with competing claims. The political content of international organization activities has three main and connected aspects. The decision-making process within the organization, allocating resources, setting priorities, proposing norms, involves conflict and is political. Second, member governments set policies to achieve their aims within international organizations. And, finally, the administrative process that international organizations set in motion, involving both international and national civil servants and organs, is also political. This chapter will give special attention to the last aspect but will also include comments on the first two.

[3] International organizations in the sense of the term used here exclude alliances which employ an organizational superstructure for the purpose of creating or directing force against an enemy identified in advance.

[4] ". . . multilateral efforts to promote development are predicated upon the notion that the national interests of the participating governments, though not identical, overlap sufficiently to permit each nation to benefit in its own peculiar way from cooperation with others." Robert E. Asher, "International Agencies and Economic Development: An Overview," *International Organization*, 22, 1 (Winter 1968), 434.

Aside from this conceptual basis for considering the international organizations operating in the economic and social field as political, the historical context in which they emerged and developed indicates their political nature.[5] The International Labor Organization represented a response by essentially conservative politicians to the demands of European socialists for stronger attention to problems of social justice. The First World War and the revolution in Russia heightened the effect of the pleas of the left wing, which aimed at extensive social change to produce social justice. An organization responding to such demands, even in a mild way, could only be viewed as political.[6]

The League of Nations increasingly undertook economic and social programs and operations until, by 1939, when the security functions of the organization had withered in the heat of the oncoming war, its members were ready to reorient its work radically in the direction of more nonsecurity activities.[7] It could hardly be claimed that a reorganization of an avowedly political organization to intensify certain allegedly nonpolitical activities in place of others had no political content. The intention of the reorganization was to approach the problem of peace from a different direction—but it was an approach to the same obviously political problem.

The United Nations Charter gave explicit recognition to the theory that international security requires general well-being and the solutions of economic and social problems.[8]

[5] Conventional, common sense definitions of politics as maneuver and dealing in the public realm would also apply to the historical development of the international bodies in question.

[6] "The [ILO] had been set up avowedly in recognition of the workers' sacrifices during the war. Its constitution had been so framed as to give them a direct voice in all its decisions." E. J. Phelan, *Yes and Albert Thomas* (London: Cresset Press, 1949), p. 6. See also the massive work by James T. Shotwell, *The Origins of the International Labour Organization* (New York: Columbia University Press, 1934), p. 55, and for historical material on the development of the transnational labor movement, passim.

[7] F. P. Walters, *A History of the League of Nations* (London: Oxford University Press, 1960), Chapter 60.

[8] United Nations Charter, Article 55.

154

Several of the new generation of international organizations also explicitly connected their specialized work with the creation of conditions prerequisite to peace.[9] Although this theory is not elaborated in the Charter, the United Nations is nevertheless enjoined to promote higher standards of living and economic development, solutions of international economic and social problems, and universal respect for human rights. Achievement of these goals is regarded as instrumental in the attainment of peaceful relations among states. If they be not political, certainly they relate directly to a political goal.

Furthermore, the economic and social cooperation projected in the United Nations Charter fits exactly into one or the other of the two main ideological approaches employed in world politics and domestic systems. The search for peace through economic and social change can easily be linked to socialist and Marxist thought. And contemporary democratic ideological statements also usually propound economic development and well-being as a precondition of peaceful international relations.

In addition to this ideological—and thus clearly political —implication of the Charter, the provisions on human rights cannot be separated from outstanding and controversial policy issues within many countries. Such human rights as freedom of speech and freedom of assembly have a long history of formulation and reformulation; they rank among the venerable political goals of every democracy and have repeatedly been employed in contemporary revolutionary contexts, beginning with the Declaration on the Rights of Man in the French Revolution. But the introduction of such concepts of freedom in many present-day states is regarded

[9] The constitutional documents of the International Atomic Energy Agency, the International Development Association, the UN Educational, Scientific and Cultural Organization and the World Health Organization specifically link the maintenance of peace with underlying social, economic, and cultural well-being. Similar statements appear in the Charter of the Organization of American States. The Food and Agriculture Organization of the United Nations and the International Civil Aviation Organization formally undertake to support the United Nations in efforts to maintain the peace.

by their governments as a threat to national security. Such subject matter must be regarded as political.[10]

In other countries, notably the highly-developed states of the North Atlantic area, some of the original goals of the Charter and some additional ones suggested in the elaboration of the Charter provisions, remain controversial. The successive drafts of covenants on human rights, as well as the Universal Declaration of Human Rights of 1948, list such goals as the right to work and the right to education, but these substantial overlays on the earlier procedural goals have not yet been fully accepted. In the United States, for example, not only the subject matter but also the use of governmental institutions to maintain economic and social standards arouses the opposition of some elements of the population who object to any kind of governmental activity, or at least much extension of governmental activity, to foster economic development and social well-being (but the number of such opponents has probably declined sharply during the last twenty years). From a national standpoint, however, the instrumental goals of the Charter and their substantive expansion must be seen as political inasmuch as they involve controversy over governmental policies.

Furthermore, the development of an increasing number of operational programs and of projects that must be carried out not at some international headquarters, but within the territory of member states, also has political implications. These programs largely relate to economic development and social modernization and take such concrete forms as the provision of an advisor on economic planning, the survey of a river valley in preparation for further development, the securing of a loan from an international agency that insists on certain conditions, or the establishment of a

[10] Among the several states in which freedom of assembly and expression are forbidden are the Soviet Union and South Africa, both of which have been the subject of United Nations pressure. Such incidents as the Soviet invasion of Czechoslovakia also tend to bring human rights considerations into play in international politics.

training institute for lower management personnel. The very subjects of economic development and social change relate to the most important political decisions—or lack of them—that any government can make. The less-developed countries, where most of the operational programs are carried out, treat such decisions as central to their existence, present and future. It follows that for the governments of such countries the international organization programs must be regarded as political.

For the highly-developed countries, too, the operational programs present political issues. The clearest of these relates to the degree of support to be given international agencies which carry on the new programs. At least two kinds of decisions may be involved. The first relates to the emphasis to be given international agency programs in comparison with any bilateral programs: decision on this issue requires an appreciation of relations with recipient countries and with possible rivals in making available assistance intended to have a determinative effect on the political orientation of recipients. No one who has scanned the debates in the United States Congress for comments on the intention of foreign aid programs needs further evidence of the political nature of this issue.[11]

The second relates to the actual level of support, and its financing by highly-developed states. Contributions for the programs of international organizations are, of course, collected almost entirely from governments, which obviously have limited resources. Presumably, therefore, any contri-

[11] A good example can be found in Senator Jacob Javits' speech on 31 July 1968, when he said that "the leverage which is inherent in a United Nations effort as contrasted with a national effort on the part of the United States in many countries . . . makes it very shortsighted for us . . . not to try to push forward, thus forming a multilateral base for reducing other elements of our foreign aid program. . . ." U.S. Congress, *Congressional Record-Senate*, S 9882, 31 July 1968. On the same day, Senator F. E. Moss (Utah) remarked that ". . . we are still the most powerful country in the world, and we are still the leader of the democratic world, and the future stability of this small globe on which we all must live will be sacrificed if the rich do not help the poor" (S 9866).

157

bution to an international agency will reduce the finances available for some other activity demanded by a domestic group, and the level of contribution could in some instances affect the level of taxation by a given national government on its citizens. It is self-evident that allocation of governmental financial resources and taxation are matters of pre-eminent political importance, and there is no avoiding their relationship to the international organization programs.

II. Some Effects on Members

The conceivable effects on member governments of the economic and social programs undertaken by international agencies range from abstract injunctions intended to set the stage for national approaches to problems to exclusively concrete and narrow ones. An activity at the abstract pole may be illustrated by a generalized resolution adopted in the United Nations General Assembly, urging members to adopt a given economic course. For example, the General Assembly has repeatedly asked members to cooperate in the UN Development Decade, using such platitudinous phrases as: "[The General Assembly] urges Member States to consider taking appropriate steps to intensify national and international efforts to formulate and implement a dynamic international policy for economic and social development of the developing countries to be pursued during the next decade."[12] Reports and documents introduced in the General Assembly helped to give this resolution some meaning, setting a goal, for example, of a minimum annual growth rate of aggregate national income of 5 per cent in each developing country at the end of the 1960s.[13]

The outcome on any given national policy of any specific

[12] UN General Assembly Resolution 2305 (XXII), 13 December 1967.

[13] UN General Assembly Resolution 1710 (XVI), 19 December 1961. For the Second Development Decade, beginning in 1971, the General Assembly raised the goal to 6 per cent per year and specified the desirable rate of expansion in various economic sectors. UN General Assembly Resolution 2626 (XXV).

undertaking by an international organization in the economic and social field depends on an enormous number of variables.[14] But the means by which those activities, whether they tend to the abstract or the concrete, are brought to bear on member governments may be confidently described.

The introduction of a generalized resolution in the General Assembly can, by itself, activate the attention of governments, especially if they have not previously been consulted about its text and its aims. In some cases, through membership in the Economic and Social Council or in a more specialized committee or agency, governments will have already reacted to the proposal. Others that have not done so may be obliged to take an "official" position on a resolution which is formally intended to be regarded seriously and which, in fact, may help to affect ultimate policy. For some representatives, such a resolution will require reference to their capitals; others may have general instructions which permit them to determine for themselves how they will vote. In such a case, however, a delegate's attitude will affect his government, since he will probably feel obliged to defend it if opposition arises in his own capital.

The act of referring to the capital for instructions, especially if a recommendation as to the desired response accompanies the reference, may have the effect of sensitizing national government servants to the possibility of adopting or opposing a policy which they had not previously contemplated. It may cause some controversy within the government, for example, between the foreign ministry which seeks influence in the United Nations and the economics ministry which questions the wisdom of the particular resolution. Finally, in some states, private interest groups may take positions on the pending resolution and seek to exert influence on the government. In any case, such a resolution mobilizes supporters and opponents and thus builds a con-

[14] Lande's chapter also recognizes these complexities in the intra-United Nations process. See Chapter 3 above.

stituency for the policy proposed in the international organization.

Once the resolution is adopted, its contents are transmitted to member governments for consideration and action. In some instances, the United Nations Secretariat may have instructions to procure reports from governments on the execution of the resolution. If this process proceeded as planned, a given foreign ministry, upon receiving the resolution, would send it to the head of government or to the appropriate ministries. These would consider it carefully, react to it, and presumably take steps to adopt the recommended policies. In cases where the government's representative to the General Assembly actually voted in favor of the resolution, it would be taken for granted that the policies recommended had government approval.

In fact, field research[15] indicates that this process may from beginning to end suffer serious breakdowns. During the General Assembly, delegates who have no specific instructions with regard to an abstract or general resolution may favor it or oppose it without in any significant sense committing their governments, which have in fact never considered the policy recommended. Even if the delegate in New York has significant influence in the home government, he may not wish to use his position to back a recommendation of this sort. And if he does, he will simply begin an examination of the policy, rather than intervene at the final stage of decision which follows lengthy preliminary examination of the resolution.

In three African governments, Malawi, Tanzania, and Zambia—all of which take strong positions favoring international organization efforts toward economic development and modernization—almost no evidence could be found of careful consideration of broad resolutions adopted in the

[15] The research referred to here was carried out in Malawi, Tanzania, and Zambia during 1965-1966 and reviewed there in 1969-1970. It was made possible by generous assistance from the Center of International Studies, Princeton University, the Social Science Research Council, and the Rockefeller Foundation.

economic field. In fact, the foreign office personnel were so few in number and had so many problems that they could hardly give even minimal attention to communications received from UN headquarters on so-called nonpolitical subjects. Repeated questioning in economic and planning offices failed to disclose more than the most superficial knowledge of United Nations policy resolutions. Furthermore, the speeches made by delegates of the three countries in the General Assembly debate on economic questions consisted of monotonous repetition of a few banalities: the need to provide development assistance, to pay attention to the developing world, and to cooperate with developing countries to ease their economic lot in a world dominated by the developed states.

The more highly-developed countries appear to follow the theoretical procedure more closely in their reactions to United Nations resolutions. Their representatives give assiduous attention to such resolutions at every stage, and in the Economic and Social Council the comments bear the marks of bureaucratic consideration and judgment, perhaps in part stimulated by the generalized demands of less-developed nations. Among the highly-developed countries, the United States in 1968 maintained at UN headquarters an ambassador with duties especially in the economic development field; the fact that he had formerly held a high post in the UN Secretariat, where he helped to develop technical assistance and preinvestment programs, argues that the American government at least wished to follow the preparatory stages of resolutions closely, in order to be fully informed at the final stage when the resolution is adopted. The evidence furnished by Hadwen and Kaufman indicates that a similar procedure applies even in some of the smaller highly-developed countries.[16] Finally, the larger delegations always include officers with special knowledge of the economic and social area.

[16] J. G. Hadwen and J. Kaufman, *How United Nations Decisions Are Made* (New York: Oceana, 1962).

Because the spokesmen of the highly-developed countries in the United Nations come to the General Assembly with freshly prepared statements of policy related to specific issues and because of the studied quality of their stances in the Economic and Social Council, it may be inferred that close consideration is given by their governments to generalized resolutions which may establish principles and claims. In some cases, this is encouraged by formal legal requirements, such as that calling for the establishment of a UNESCO National Commission in each member country.[17] In the United States this commission includes many influential members and meets regularly to advise the government; papers must be prepared and positions taken. More generally, it may be assumed that the Bureau of International Organization Affairs of the Department of State, which has a section devoted to economic and social activities, takes an active role in at least informing other departments about current problems. It is also known that the Department of State is involved in the selection and briefing of delegations, composed primarily of nondiplomatic service personnel, for specialized agency meetings. Nevertheless, relatively little is known about the precise pattern of reactions in the highly-developed countries to generalized United Nations resolutions relevant to economic and social matters.

At the other end of the concrete-abstract continuum of international organization activities can be found the specific project which involves furnishing manpower, materials, or training for a fixed period in relation to a definite program of a member government.[18] Formally, such projects are initiated by a government which forwards a request to the international organization offering assistance,

[17] UNESCO Constitution, Article 7.

[18] In this connection, see the useful account and comments by Walter R. Sharp, "International Bureaucracies and Political Development," in Joseph LaPalombara, ed., *Bureaucracy and Political Development* (Princeton: Princeton University Press, 1963), pp. 456-469.

ensures that the request falls within the policy guidelines of the donor, and receives the requested assistance on the basis of the proposal's merit. In fact, however, the field research noted above has found more deviation from than conformity to this model.

While recipient governments must approve any request for technical assistance from an international organization, usually through the United Nations Development Programme, the idea for the project may be injected at any step of the interlocking relationships between government and organization. Indeed specific projects almost always fall within general guidelines determined not by the government but by deliberative organs of international organizations. These organs never escape the heavy influence of their secretariats, which have advantages of expertness on both subject matter and procedure and continuous contact with programs. To note secretariat influence and the actual centralization of decisions as to priority of assistance does not, however, mean that the projects are useless for developmental purposes or that they are imposed on governments. It does mean that assistance from international organization sources will not be given for projects considered unusually novel, risky, or excluded in terms of accepted policies.

The pre-investment projects supported by the United Nations Development Programme (UNDP) illustrate the effect of international organization guidelines. From the foundation of the UN Special Fund, its managers decided to concentrate on surveys and training enterprises. By 1967, Tanzania was host to ten projects within its own boundaries and four more for the East African region. Each of these involved either a survey, such as that for the irrigation development of the Wami-Pangani River basin, or had a training aspect, as in the National Institute for Productivity, or the program for training secondary-school science teachers. Some of the pre-investment ventures had dual purposes, as the Industrial Studies and Development

Centre. None of them fell outside the guidelines of the Tanzanian national plan, but taken together or individually they neither covered all the projects required for the plan nor did they provide any of the direct investment needed to carry it out. It is possible that one or several of the pre-investment projects may eventually lead to loans from the International Development Association or the International Bank for Reconstruction and Development, especially since these institutions have begun to show interest in the agricultural and educational sectors of national economies. Nevertheless, by 1969, none of these projects had led directly to World Bank loans.

By providing its own guidelines, therefore, the UNDP in effect offered to the Tanzanian government options by which it could get some assistance. At the same time, it signaled the government, if it were serious in seeking outside support for its development effort, to look to other sources for other kinds of aid. On the evidence of the list of projects supported in Tanzania, UNDP did not overstep its own guidelines. If it were assumed that other sources would in fact provide aid for the sectors left uncovered by UNDP, and would provide investment funds, the UNDP influence would rank only as procedural. It would induce the government to arrange its aid requests so that only those projects which UNDP would accept were requested from it. On the other hand, if the aggregate of aid fell short of needs, or if the donors set their own guidelines as well, it follows that the UNDP projects would represent a substantive influence: Tanzania could not follow its own priorities by juggling its aid requests among various sources. Actually, it either had to give priority to what UNDP had to offer or accept nothing at all.

Although international organization guidelines may coincide with recipient government priorities at one period, they may fail to do so later, when changed perceptions among governmental personnel result in the adoption of new emphases. UNDP has supported survey and training

164

projects, but a number of high officials of Malawi, Tanzania, and Zambia stated in interviews that this sort of project was too detached from "action." Although "action" was hardly well-defined, it is clear that the officials wanted concrete results in terms of increased production or of benefits which would be obvious to their people.

The history of one large-scale project in Zambia illustrates this change of priorities. Before Zambia became independent, the UN Special Fund joined with the Northern Rhodesian government in a multipurpose survey of the Kafue River basin, in order to understand better the uses that could be made of the water. Both additional electrical power and a steady supply of water for irrigation conceivably could be derived from the river. After independence and especially after the Rhodesian rebellion, the Kafue was viewed in governmental circles as potentially helping to free Zambia from dependence on the Kariba Dam across the Zambesi River. Financed by the International Bank, the Kariba Dam is owned jointly by Rhodesia and Zambia, but the power station lies on the south bank, entirely within the control of the Rhodesian government.

Yet, near the end of its five-year schedule, the Kafue survey proved increasingly unsatisfactory to the Zambian government. The survey had been designed in a conservative engineering framework: it aimed at the collection of data in an almost academic manner. It was not intended to produce demonstration effects or finished plans for the exploitation of the river; such plans might be based on the data, but further work would clearly be required. The possibilities that the survey rested on perfectly sound engineering principles appeared irrelevant to leading government figures, whose priorities were vastly different from those of the earlier Federation of Rhodesia and Nyasaland. What the government wanted now was "action, not surveys." Yet the project meant that more than $500,000 in local funds was tied up in work the value of which was now in doubt.

The insistence on "action" led to a successful government

165

proposal, framed with help from the UNDP office in Zambia, for a follow-up project. Although minor in proportion to the whole potential of the valley, it at least had the concrete form of a 200-acre irrigation demonstration farm, some institutional training programs and rural development operations. The project came into operation, however, only in 1969, a year and a half after the completion of the survey. The government contribution of $1,000,000 in kind (against a UNDP contribution of $1,600,000) was nearly twice what it had paid into the survey project. Meantime, other work in the Kafue Valley, such as the construction of power plants, received support from other than UN sources and did not necessarily link with long-term plans for the development of the valley. Thus, the priorities set at the beginning of the multipurpose survey had by 1970 almost completely changed. UNDP still had some involvement with the development of the Kafue River, but it was now hardly the leading agency and, in many respects, its tiny but rather costly (in UNDP terms) project represented a final attempt to justify the survey in changed circumstances.

Within the UNDP framework such concrete projects in the pre-investment category must be regarded as large-scale. The smallest concrete projects involve the furnishing of a technical advisor for a limited period, usually a year but sometimes only a few weeks. The variety in this category of aid greatly exceeds that of pre-investment projects, although both are assumed to maintain relevance to economic development. As a result, governments may approach technical assistance aid in a more flexible way than pre-investment projects. Yet UNDP does not furnish any kind of advisor for whom a job specification can be improvised: it does not supply military advisors, for example. Over the years since 1949, when technical assistance began formally to emerge as a UN activity, practice has enshrined a certain specialization. The United Nations itself, for instance, furnishes advisors on public administration, while under UNDP, the Food and Agriculture Organization of the United Nations (FAO) supplies a wide variety of technicians in the agricultural field. Thus, the specialties of the agencies cooperating in UNDP in themselves imply certain guidelines and emphases. The government seeking a favorable response to its request for aid frames its specifications accordingly.

The process of framing a request for technical assistance or for a pre-investment project always involves consultations with resident officials of international organizations. All countries receiving important amounts (in terms of the United Nations program) of international aid now have a UNDP Resident Representative, through whom most requests for technical aid and all pre-investment requests must be forwarded. It is his responsibility to communicate to the government the amount of aid it is likely to receive in the biennial planning periods, and he must see that the requests are technically in good enough order to receive further consideration; he therefore has considerable influence on the government.

This influence may take several forms. The most common type exercised in the three observed African governments appears to be that of defining the terms of reference for an advisor, and drafting or helping to draft the request after a government official has identified the problem. In this case, the expertness and experience of the Resident Representative serves in effect as an adjunct to the governmental bureaucracy. But in the interaction which invariably results from an advisory relationship, the international official may subtly shape the nature of the project, either to conform with the known formal and nonformal guidelines of UNDP and the specialized agencies, or to implement to his own ideas about "coordination" and a "country program."

Some of the Resident Representatives interviewed expressed the hope that they could "coordinate" requests for technical assistance in such a way as to fit with bilateral programs and maximize the effect of all of them. One of them took coordination to mean that the UNDP projects

167

would be linked conceptually so that they had a discernible impact on the government's progress toward economic development. Another Resident Representative saw it as making as coherent a program as possible of all outside aid, whether bilateral or international. But another, who had direct access to the highest circles of government in all three countries, showed no willingness to project a conceptual scheme for the operations in his purview. Instead he expected that UNDP aid would be proffered as far as possible within the formal guidelines to meet the expressed needs of the government, without concern for making a pattern of the projects.

It is noteworthy that at the time of the Rhodesian declaration of independence this "service" approach to requests from the government dominated all other considerations. The Zambian government clearly found itself in a threatened and unpredictable situation which could not fail to upset its economic planning. Officials of the United Nations and the specialized agencies came to the rescue, made suggestions as to technical assistance that might be available on an emergency basis, and arranged for projects then sited in Rhodesia to be brought to Zambia. One energetic, well-informed international official commented at the time that the crisis also provided an opportunity to expand the assistance to Zambia generally, and that this was a major accomplishment for any functionary.

Although the Rhodesian crisis stimulated the international officials to make suggestions of aid to their national governmental counterparts, this kind of influence also takes place in non-crisis situations. From my observation of the three African countries, such suggestions appear less likely to come from the UNDP Resident Representative than from high-ranking visitors with assignments akin to those of an inspector. A stream of such visitors from headquarters of international agencies flows through the recipient government capitals. Some confine themselves mainly to consultative conversations, to ascertain whether any problems exist and how they can be solved; others positively attempt to induce government ministers to commit themselves to programs currently of interest to the international agency in question. Once such a commitment is obtained, the visiting official may suggest that a technical assistance expert could help in planning the new effort, or that a definite program request should be submitted to UNDP.

Another source of direct suggestion to government is the technical assistance official already at work. Frequently these officials man key posts in planning or economics ministries or are general advisors to other ministries. In the countries observed, they were universally impressed with the shortage of officials with sophisticated skills suitable for general planning and supervisory functions, and they sometimes suggested obtaining additional help through the international agencies by which they were sent. Such suggestions, however, cannot be seen as the inevitable outcome of furnishing technical aid through international agencies; they depend far more on the situation and the views of the experts on the spot than on the indirect involvement of an international body.

This discussion of abstract and concrete approaches to influence by international organizations far from exhausts the possibilities. Some concrete approaches lead to emphasis on more abstract ones, as in the case of a technical assistance advisor who helps conceive and execute a national planning exercise which intentionally or incidentally conforms with generalized recommendations from the UN General Assembly. Some abstract approaches eventually lead to the creation of specific and concrete projects, as in the case of the UNESCO effort to combat illiteracy and its translation into literacy projects in many countries. Some approaches certainly result in trivial influence on the recipient governments or none at all. Others may have substantial effect in defining some economic and social goals and rejecting others. And some approaches open the way to administrative actions by international organization per-

169

sonnel that affect the national development programs. But data sufficient for reliable generalization has proved impossible to obtain so far. Indeed, it is a plausible hypothesis on the basis of observation that such a generalization cannot be made, except in the most general and nonpredictive terms, because of the rapid changes in personnel, external political situations, internal governmental shifts and the personalities of individuals involved.

III. SOME LONG-TERM EFFECTS ON THE INTERNATIONAL SYSTEM

If the United Nations and associated agencies could achieve their goals of economic development and social change, the international system would veer sharply towards multi-polarity.[19] The UN has set fairly modest goals for economic development, seeking a steady net growth of gross national product per person of at least 1 per cent per year in the poor countries of the world.[20] Even such a growth level, however, would create several and perhaps a large number of viable economies and social structures. And if the postulated growth rate by itself, is too low to develop a large number of newly-viable economies during, say, the next twenty years, the United Nations programs seeking to eliminate poverty have the same goal.

Additional viable economies, always framed by nation-states which are now conventionally conceived in international organization circles,[21] would imply new sources of in-

[19] Young refers to a fluid system, above, pp. 13-14.
[20] The Development Decade goal. See UN General Assembly Resolution 1710 (XVI), 19 December 1961. See also "United Nations Development Decade at Mid-Point," UN, Official Records, Economic and Social Council, Thirty-ninth Session, Annexes, document E/4071.
[21] Representatives of governments usually would rather turn to stone than admit that the nature of the nation-state with which they are associated might be changed, especially as the result of a consensual program. Therefore, the pages of international organization records contain little discussion of what might happen to the international system and to nation-states as a result of the programs undertaken under the rubric of the general welfare.

170

puts of the order of those emanating from any modern, highly-developed state. In the present international system a handful of states, mostly in the North Atlantic area, have a continuously wide influence, sometimes in spite of small size and relatively small populations. This ability to influence—to produce inputs of significance in the international system—results from a high level of economic development, a modern social structure, and the consequent articulated and efficient governmental structure. The new world produced by the success of United Nations programs might have dozens of such governmental entities, whose political stances and related economic actions could not be overlooked by other members of the system. Instead of only a few countries like France, Belgium, the Netherlands, or Sweden, there would be many.

The interdependence of the present international system permits the less highly-developed states to exert system-wide influence.[22] The future international system, based on a wider distribution of high economic development, would also be characterized by a high degree of interdependence[23]—which would not only extend farther but would also be tighter. One implication of interdependence is the reduction of the range of permissible individual action by members of the system. To disregard systemic effects of policies would cost any government dear; the calculation of policy would require sensitivity to reactions from other states if system-disturbing effects were to be avoided. This suggests that a change of style from the high-pressure tactics now sometimes evident in the United Nations would become necessary. So would institutional development: this future international system would require mechanisms for adjustment. Present international organizations provide means for consultation, reconciliation, and conflict-resolu-

[22] In this connection, see Miller's concluding question on the possible role of lesser powers, above, p. 149.

[23] In fact, the international organization programs referred to here begin with a perception of interdependence and look forward to increasing its intensity. See also Young, above, pp. 56-58.

tion. If these same institutions induce economic development and social change, it could be expected that the intergovernmental mechanisms for dealing with differences would also offer a greater range of options and pressures, and therefore would evolve to new effectiveness and wider scope.[24]

The international organizations would thus become more deeply involved than ever with national governmental policies, to which they would have access at many points.[25] Their authority as organizations could be expected to increase greatly as a result of their increasingly necessary role in the international system. This sort of development would promote what Young calls a system of qualitatively mixed actors.[26] The nature of the nation-state itself, or at least the nature of its role as actor in an international system, would change; so would that of the international organizations, which would find it easier to produce broader and more significant systemic influences than they do at present.

To pretend, however, that the United Nations will certainly or even probably succeed in its aims of economic change and social modernization, expressed specifically in its proclamation of the first Decade of Development and the planning for the second, would be misleading and falsely optimistic. Whatever progress occurs, the point must be made that international organizations now constitute but one, and in some cases the least important, source of outside economic aid and influence. If bilateral and regional sources of aid, which constitute alternatives and competitors to the universal international organization programs, were spread evenly over all countries, it would be much

[24] See Falk, below, pp. 218-222.

[25] The existing patterns of relationships already provide a great number of points of access of international organization officials to national officials and *vice versa*. See Gordenker, "Multilateral Aid and Influence on Governmental Policies," in R. W. Cox, ed., *International Organization: World Politics* (London: Macmillan, 1969), pp. 128-152.

[26] See Young, above, pp. 54-56.

172

simpler to project future tendencies. But if the pattern of the recent past holds, as seems likely, even in part, bilateral programs will remain highly selective and differential. Sometimes their own great size and great number of personnel will swamp international organization efforts, which begin with smaller potentials and tend to have to spread resources with less selectivity than bilateral donors. In other instances, bilateral donors prove rather indifferent to local needs. The international organizations then have the entire field. The following speculation, therefore, applies largely to instances where bilateral and regional programs are of much less importance than those of international agencies. This excludes some of the most interesting cases, such as India. Yet if bilateral programs continue to shrink, or to stay constant as populations burgeon, such instances may not prove entirely theoretical for some areas. Furthermore, despite the apparent lack of interest on the part of most donor governments in building up international organization programs, a reversal of these policies cannot be forever excluded. Therefore, some speculation may prove worthwhile.

Whatever else can be said about the ambitious aims of the Decade of Development, it is clear that actual results have fallen far short of hopes and plans. National policies have not been designed in accordance with the Decade of Development guidelines, especially in the highly-developed states. Measured in financial terms alone, support for United Nations programs does not increase along a steeply rising curve; it does not even keep pace with the population increase in the less-developed world.[27] And it is common

[27] As compared with 1962, the United Nations administrative budget increased for the next five years at an average of 10 per cent annually, while the average increase of population in the world, excluding North America, Europe, and the USSR, was just under 3 per cent. But the UN budget reflected mainly salary paid at the high rates (relative to local employment in the less developed areas) of the international civil service. This figure therefore has little importance.

What is more relevant is the recent trend in net movements of

173

knowledge that the voters, legislatures, and leaders in most of the highly-developed countries have little taste for expanding their total aid contributions. If present trends are projected ahead, there can be little confidence in United Nations programs of economic development and social change as a means for reconstructing the international system.

Yet even if these programs fall short of the postulated goals, they may have effects on the international system. Changes, certainly trivial and perhaps transforming, would appear first in the nation-state, where international organization programs exert new pressures and stimuli on at least some of the governmental decison-makers. By requiring recipient governments to meet some kind of international standard and by bringing government personnel concerned with policy into contact with international civil servants, some tendency toward change probably results, although it cannot be precisely measured. In any case, the scope of international organization activities widens.

A significant case in relation to the nature of the international system would be that of a state whose national development began closely to approach the goals set by international organizations without quite reaching the level where it could do without outside help. Because of its successful economic development, the government of such a state would probably have quite adequate administrative and policy-making equipment with which to exert some persuasive influence within the international system. In-

---

long-term capital and donation from developed market economy countries (which excludes the Soviet group) to less developed countries and multilateral agencies. By including the remarkable increase of 1964-1965, the average increase, based on 1962 totals, came out to 4 per cent. But in 1965-1966, the decrease compared with 1962 was nearly 10 per cent. There are indications of a possibility of an upturn as a result of new policies proposed by President Nixon, but the opposition in the U.S. Congress to large expenditures on foreign aid may not yet have changed. (This leaves aside the additional effect of a policy of tied aid.) Data from United Nations *Statistical Yearbook 1967*, Sales No. E/F 68. XVII.1., esp. pp. 688-689.

deed, on the basis of its development progress and its debts, it could bargain with its creditor organizations for a greater share of whatever aid was available.[28] Its improved structure, including better staffing and a well-articulated and skilled foreign office and development-planning mechanism, would give the state more influence on the policy processes of international organizations. It could have some confidence in its ability to direct and control its population and territory, and to execute its development plans. Such a situation would be seen from the outside as stability, a major advantage in attempting to deal with other actors in the international system. Furthermore, the state might be able to translate a considerable share of its economic resources into a military establishment—a matter of some weight, unless a utopian calm prevails in international relations.

Yet the government which developed such capabilities would be bound in numerous ways to the international organizations which helped it. These bodies would have prescribed to some extent the goals of development, and certainly the terms of assistance. It is conceivable that international civil servants would be in position to veto the planning of the next crucial stage. In any case, it is likely that international organization influence would have entered deeply into regions once considered as sheltered from outside factors. This penetration might result in changed views on the part of politicians and civil servants and could induce a strong "habit" of cooperation, perhaps strengthening the conflict-settling functions of the United Nations.

If the government concerned could not achieve its development goals without further aid, it would be in a particularly vulnerable position, for it would have inspired domestic hopes for further actions which were not in its power to take independently. If the aid were not forthcoming, severe internal repercussions could result. But the

[28] Susan Strange, "The Meaning of Multilateral Surveillance," in Cox, *op.cit.*, pp. 231-247.

government could not simply elbow its way to the cashier: it would not have yet reached a stage where it alone, in deliberative bodies, could reshape or redirect or veto international organization policies. Thus, its independence in making foreign policy determinations might be sharply reduced, or else its desires to make such policies would conflict directly with its new position in the international system. The appearance of states with the capacity for wide influence, but constrained by the need for cooperation with international organizations operating in the economic and social field, would represent a change in the international system.

Paradoxically, the government that avoids far-reaching economic development and social change and therefore receives relatively little aid and advice from international organizations would probably be able to retain its independence of policy but would not gain in ability to affect the international system. It would simply be able to ward off any growth of influence by international organizations and their representatives. As long as it produced no disturbances to which other actors reacted, it would be allowed to stagnate undisturbed.

This analysis supports a conclusion that fulfillment of the goals of international organizations with regard to economic development and social change implies far-reaching alteration in the international system. The degree of interdependence among actors would increase greatly; the nation-state would have less ability independently to determine its policies; it would then lose some of its independence to the international organizations, with the result that the actors in international systems would take on a much more mixed character.

The path toward such a change would no doubt be long, and marked by the inevitable tension between the traditional goals of the nation-state—expressed as independence of policy—and the need to conform to international goals and methods in order to procure the aid required for further development. Thus, digesting the influences of the international organization could be a turbulent process.

Whether or not the goals of the international organizations can be met, some states will approach them more closely than others. The most successful will find themselves tied most closely to the international organizations, and as the most modernized of the present crop of less-developed countries, they will be best equipped to influence those organizations. In the end, such influence will create a hierarchy of beneficiaries based on the degree of change supported by international agencies. Meantime, the nonconforming states will proceed at a much slower pace toward modernization and will have less and less influence on international bodies. Thus both centrifugal and centripetal tendencies will be encouraged by partially successful international organization efforts in sponsoring economic development and social change. Furthermore, some governments will embark on development policies, encouraged by international organizations, that will end in frustration unless new sources of aid and new policies appear among the highly-developed countries. Other governments may succeed in getting necessary aid from international sources, while still others will resist international organization efforts to produce harmonious development policies. Most of them can be expected to compete, some with great vigor, for international organization policies that they consider favorable to their own points of view.

Such competition could conceivably lead to new and disturbing inputs in the international system. Some governments will probably use new economic power to expand military capacity. The use or threat of use of these arms could even be connected with efforts to increase the economic benefits offered by some governments, either by blackmail of other members of the system or by forcing wider economic opportunities such as trade or mineral exploitation. Furthermore, international development programs cannot produce equal rates of economic development

177

in the member countries; rather, differential rates seem to be encouraged by the very structure of assistance. It is therefore conceivable that the international system would end more fragmented, even less integrated, and more sensitive to state behavior than it is today.[29]

IV. Gaps in Knowledge

Any conclusions drawn from the observations, interview results, and other data used in this chapter can only be regarded as tentative and lacking comprehensiveness. Even so, and despite the limited geographical and temporal scope of the observations, an effort to formulate some general conclusions may be useful in indicating how little is known and how much more should be known about the mutually influential relationship between the international organizations and member governments cooperating to carry out programs of economic development and social change.[30] Generally, this relationship may be expected to continue into the future, and it will produce changes in the nature of the state system and of the nation-state. It will be a fact in international relationships and must be understood eventually through descriptive and analytical theories.

International agencies themselves, because their programs project into the sensitive terrain of major national decisions on economic development and social change, join the often revolutionary forces producing new or different societies. Yet, beyond this general statement, it is extremely difficult to define precisely what kind of change, how much, and at what rate it takes place: to determine the specific causative role of international organization activity is even more difficult. In seeking greater exactitude and profundity, it may be possible to measure transaction flows, especially among members of elites and their groups. The

[29] Furthermore, the very process of economic development and social change can produce internal conflicts which have international ramifications of a disturbing sort. See Miller, Chapter 4 above.

[30] Sharp, *op.cit.*, makes some useful suggestions.

quality of inter- and intragroup relationships, and the lines and patterns of authority of the decision-makers involved with international organizations, might also be traced. But the basic statistics now available in many of the places where international organizations are at work—even the basic personnel data for international civil servants—can only be described as faulty. Data resulting from direct observation is scant, scattered, and often not comparable. Furthermore, much interesting observation of interpersonal relations among peoples of different cultures remains to be accomplished. While a relationship between international bodies and change may be expected intuitively, and perhaps on the basis of expenditure per capita in recipient countries—one figure that can be determined with mild accuracy—a great deal more study is clearly required if the process is to be understood.

At the same time, it seems likely that at least some significant changes will take place, or have already, in the attitudes of member governments and of international organization personnel as to the permissible level of intrusion in local affairs. (It is never explicitly called that.) Some of the discussion in this chapter strongly indicates that such changes, over the last two decades, have already reached important proportions. Yet no adequate conceptualization has been produced either by statesmen or by scholars.[31] More sophisticated concepts would make it possible to differentiate among various examples of the penetration of member countries by international agencies and their personnel. All that can now be said with some confidence is that such penetration has indeed taken place, but at differential rates depending on a wide range of factors—from welcoming or hostile attitudes on the part of national re-

[31] Harold Karan Jacobson, "ONUC's Civilian Operations: State-Preserving and State Building," *World Politics*, 17, 1 (October 1964), 75-107, provides some interesting insights into a situation in which international influence went very far into the domestic domain. See also Gordenker, *The UN Secretary-General and the Maintenance of Peace* (New York: Columbia University Press, 1967), Chapter xii.

179

gimes toward modernizing influences to the results of sharp political crises in the international system in general.

Manifold changes in relationships at many levels between international organizations and member governments cannot help but affect the nature and functioning of the international system. Yet a full understanding of the character, depth, and rate of this process and its outcome must await more information. Just how the international system is affected depends on how the relationships between international organizations and member governments change. If, for example, member governments in increasing numbers surrender a significant degree of their independence, in the course of decision-making processes dominated by international agencies and their personnel, one aspect of the international system will certainly have been altered: a more mixed system will have been created. But it is far from certain how this sort of change relates, if it does so at all, to other functions of the international system, such as the response to political disturbances that culminate in war.

The cooperative facade of the decision-making procedures of international organizations with regard to operational programs tends to produce a superficial appearance of interdependence. This is supported by a strong tendency toward "fair shares" as a principle of allocating resources,[32] for all the sharers tend to look to international organizations as a steady source of help. Yet even this rather obvious argument needs more attention. It is quite possible that despite the "fair-shares" tendency, governments proficient in securing aid will in time garner a major proportion of the available international resources. This aid would be used in part to improve their own governmental structures, enabling them to be even more influential in decision-making.[33] The outcome of this sort of process

[32] Andrew Shonfield, *The Attack on World Poverty* (New York: Vintage, 1962), pp. 18-20.
[33] Gordenker, "The New Nationalism and International Organization," *International Studies Quarterly*, 13, 1 (March 1969), 31-45.

might be a high degree of interdependence for some countries and what amounts to exclusion for the rest. Even if interdependence were to increase generally, it makes a significant difference with regard to the international system whether actors are mildly, strongly, or differentially interdependent, whether they are grouped around poles of interdependence or ranged across a wide continuum.

Both nation-states and international organizations seem likely to remain as actors, in their own fashions, in the international system. Yet international agencies cannot be viewed simplistically—as states writ large or as some variety of supergovernment which makes decisions followed slavishly by members. Instead, the member governments have the legal and political capacities to determine, when they wish, what intergovernmental agencies do and how they act. The way in which they in fact exercise these capacities varies sharply from government to government and situation to situation. Knowledge of the manner in which member governments deliberately attempt to shape the policies of international organizations in the economic and social field is hardly satisfactory.[34] Here clearer conceptualization would constitute a major advance.

Some speculation may, nevertheless, be worthwhile with regard to the way in which member governments deal with international organizations. Some few governments of less-developed countries have fostered or are likely to foster the expertness needed to make an impression in the complex decision-making processes of international organizations. But a highly-developed country can better afford such expertness, for it requires the backing of a society that puts a high value on technology, economic efficiency, rapid communication, and other characteristics common to the eco-

[34] For some useful light on this subject, see Harold K. Jacobson, "New States and Functional International Organizations: A Preliminary Report," in Cox, *op.cit.*, pp. 74-97. Also see Jacobson, *The USSR and the UN's Economic and Social Activities* (South Bend, Ind.: University of Notre Dame Press, 1963) and Alvin Z. Rubinstein, *The Soviets in International Organizations* (Princeton: Princeton University Press, 1964).

181

nomically most advanced areas. Furthermore, some of the less-developed countries cannot or will not develop the requisite expertness to cope with hundreds of international meetings, thousands of pages of documents and an infinite number of consultations. Thus, a particular national government's legal capacity to influence does not necessarily mean that the government will actually be effective in the policy process of a particular international agency. The entire range of organizations would probably present a diverse set of opportunities for influence.

In addition, the personnel of international organizations are in principle directed by deliberative organs in which governments are represented. But the international civil servants also exert powerful influences of their own on deliberative bodies,[35] as well as on policy processes within member states. The question may then be raised as to whether an international bureaucracy, operating within vague guidelines laid down by deliberative organs of undependable quality, will have an increasingly important role in shaping policy in a large number of countries without ever becoming fully subject to the clear direction of outputs from the international or national systems. At least one writer suggests that this may constitute a new form of colonialism.[36] Whatever evolves along these lines clearly needs more investigation by social scientists.

Finally, intriguing questions arise from the realization that international organizations routinely attempt some social engineering in their efforts to support national programs for economic development and social change. International organization programs, which include implicit theoretical goals, have been elaborated with relatively little

[35] See Stanley J. Michalak, "Peace-Keeping and the United Nations," *International Studies Quarterly*, 11, 4 (December 1967), 301-319, and Gordenker, *The UN Secretary-General* . . . , passim, for examples of the pervasive influence of secretariats in various international organization settings.

[36] Ronald C. Nairn, *International Aid to Thailand* (New Haven: Yale University Press, 1966), esp. Chapter 11.

critical attention from scholars. It may be asked what goals are set, how quickly they are supposed to be reached, what means may be used, what kind of world would be produced and by whom? What would happen if a somewhat higher, but not a satisfactory level of economic development and change emerged from international organization efforts? Who will deal with the resulting problems?

CHAPTER 6

The United Nations: Various Systems of Operation

RICHARD A. FALK

I. An Evaluative Outlook

Popular perceptions of the United Nations have tended to reach increasingly negative conclusions about its role in international society. These perceptions are heavily influenced by the gap that separates the goals proclaimed for the United Nations in its own Charter (and generally associated with its existence) from the behavioral actualities of international life. It is also influenced by a gap between the needs of world order and the capabilities of the Organization. These two gaps appear to be widening over time, and confirm the view that the sovereign state continues to be the only significant political actor in international society.[1]

Even the Secretary-General was led to say, in the Introduction to his Annual Report for 1968, that "this document must make gloomy reading."[2] U Thant evidently shares, to some extent, the widespread pessimism that has arisen in reaction to the inability of the Organization to close the gap between international behavior and the Charter. U Thant's most recent views seem somewhat negative about

[1] See, e.g., Stanley Hoffmann, *Gulliver's Troubles or the Setting of American Foreign Policy* (New York: McGraw-Hill, 1968), pp. 39-43. The multinational corporation has become an increasingly significant international actor in recent years. For one evaluation see Osvaldo Sunkel, "Some Notes on Development, Underdevelopment and the International Capitalist Economy" (April 1970, mimeographed).

[2] U Thant, "Introduction to the Annual Report of the Secretary General on the Work of the Organization." *UN Monthly Chronicle*, v, 10 (October 1968), 99.

UN accomplishments and prospects. He said in 1970 that "the United Nations born of the Charter has done well, but it has not done well enough." And in the Introduction to the 1970 *Annual Report of the Secretary-General* U Thant writes, "In the last two or three years, I have been constrained to report only a general deterioration of the international situation. This year, on the eve of the twenty-fifth anniversary session of the General Assembly, I am happy to be able to express some cautious optimism in this regard."[3]

The Secretary-General has made it plain that the prime deficiencies of the United Nations are not of a sort that call, at least initially, for organizational reform: "Nor is the structure of our world Organization, although admittedly imperfect, incapable of performing the tasks assigned to it. Indeed the machinery for international cooperation is as yet largely untested and untried." In his message on United Nations Day 1970, U Thant urged that "It is time for Governments to make a fresh start and to lift themselves again to the same high level, if not a higher level, of vision and determination as that of the authors of the Charter. We must give the Charter a real chance at last. We must pass from words to deeds."[4] U Thant apparently believes that the de-

[3] U Thant, "Message for United Nations Day, 1970," *UN Monthly Chronicle*, 7, 9 (October 1970), ii; and "Introduction to the Annual Report of the Secretary-General on the Work of the Organization," *ibid.*, p. 40.
The Charter is regarded, in this view, as embodying the new basis for international relations which had been evolved by statesmen to prevent the repetition of large-scale violence in the form of general warfare among principal states. In this view, the language of the instrument is taken literally, and disappointment is expressed with the failure of behavioral patterns of national governments to conform with the formal language. As a matter of idealistic polemics such an emphasis on constitutional imperatives may create some pressure for moderateness in international society. As analysis, however, it fails to acknowledge that the Charter made no effort to transform either the attitudes associated with sovereign prerogatives, or governmental access to the instruments of military violence that had produced wars in the past. A genuine peace system needs to implement aspirations with a feasible strategy for transforming behavior, or, in my terminology, for "bridging the gap."
[4] *UN Monthly Chronicle*, 7, 9 (October 1970), iii.

teriorating United Nations situation results from the non-supportive attitudes and patterns of behavior on the part of many national governments. In a similar vein, Emilio Arenales, President of the 23rd session of the General Assembly, said that a pessimistic view of the United Nations "is unfair and ought to be rectified."[5] Arenales' assertion embodies the view that the United Nations should be primarily understood as an instrumentality of governmental action rather than an autonomous actor with tasks that it either performs or does not perform.

More specialized commentary also takes account of 1) the gaps between Charter aspiration and United Nations actuality, and 2) of the extent to which the sovereign state persists as the dominant actor in international society. Ernst Haas has written that "the United Nations system is hyperdependent on its environment."[6] Stanley Hoffmann has expressed the same kind of judgment, observing that "the efficiency and authority of the organization depend ultimately, not on its Charter, but on the state of the world outside."[7] Such an acceptance of environmental determinism avoids the question of whether the United Nations has failed in conception or execution.[8] This analysis encourages

[5] See his UN Day Message, note 2, above, p. i; and on p. ii Mr. Arenales says: "A further reflection which we feel compelled to direct against the growing scepticism regarding the United Nations is that its weaknesses or limitations are not those of an organism with an independent life of its own or those of a super-State, but are rather the direct and unavoidable responsibility of the Member States, both those that founded the Organization and those that now belong to it."

[6] Ernst B. Haas, "Dynamic Environment and Static System: Revolutionary Regimes in the United Nations." In Robert W. Gregg and Michael Barkun, eds., *The United Nations System and Its Functions* (Princeton: Van Nostrand, 1968), pp. 162-197, at p. 172 (hereinafter cited as Gregg and Barkun).

[7] Stanley Hoffmann, "An Evaluation of the United Nations." In Falk and Saul H. Mendlovitz, eds., *The Strategy of World Order: the United Nations* (New York: World Law Fund, 1966), Vol. 3, 793-815, at 794.

[8] It seems misleading to regard an international organization as "a failure" because it acted in accordance with the limits set by the international environment. Such a perspective bases assessment on

a specification of those aspects of environment that determine the kinds of tasks that the United Nations can perform under various sets of international circumstances.[9] The Charter framework becomes virtually irrelevant to most close students of United Nations behavior; recently academic effort has concentrated upon trying to evolve functional categories of explanation that identify the tasks that the United Nations has actually performed.[10] A newer generation of specialists affirms the concrete, if modest, accomplishments of the Organization, and regards more grandiose conceptions of Charter goals or world community needs as incapable of much further realization in the present international system.[11] In this sense, United Nations

---

unrealistic expectations; the United Nations, or the League before it, "failed" only in relation to expectations that were utopian in the circumstances. To write of "failure," as does even such an acute commentator as F. H. Hinsley, is to fall into the trap of taking sides in the debate between utopians and cynics, thereby undermining any appreciation for actual role and accomplishment. In a discussion making many otherwise valuable observations about the League period Hinsley uses as his chapter title, "The Failure of the League of Nations," and includes in the opening paragraph this sentence: "Everything we know about the history and nature of international relations goes to show that the League, as it was constructed, was bound to fail; and that it was bound to be constructed as it was constructed." F. H. Hinsley, *Power and the Pursuit of Peace* (Cambridge: Cambridge University Press, 1963), pp. 309-322, at p. 309. In fairness, Hinsley is writing about the search for international peace—the end of war—and in this sense the League was indeed, as it was indeed bound to be, a failure.

[9] For a good example of this style of systemic analysis see Young, Chapter 1 above; a parallel, although quite distinct, approach is taken by Professors Gregg and Barkun in their volume of readings cited in note 6, although it is better exemplified in their editorial comment, especially the Introduction, pp. 3-9, than in the readings themselves, which seem rather ill-adapted to the theoretical compartments developed by the editors to cover "the field."

[10] Compare older approaches based upon an explication of Charter provisions and of the institutional forms laid down in the Charter. See, for example, the selections by Clyde Eagleton and Leland Goodrich reprinted in Falk and Mendlovitz, Vol. 3, cited note 7, pp. 10-16, 17-35.

[11] The point is to shift attention to the actual tasks performed rather than to emphasize or gloss over the gap between Charter

civil servants, peace groups, and public officials tend to keep alive the sense of "the two gaps," whereas more specialized scholars tend to redefine inquiry so as to maintain a descriptive and analytic focus on the Organization as an evolving actuality.[12]

My aim here is to lay a foundation for disciplined inquiry into the normative issues of world order.[13] Social science can contribute to problem-solving by careful analysis of issues and solutions.[14] The false utopianism of the past characteristically proposed a new system of world order, and then assumed that the progressive role of reason in human affairs would assure its adoption.[15] Few people now believe that the future will be an automatic improvement upon the present—quite the contrary. In fact, the loss of hope is so widespread and immobilizing that we must now demon-

---

language and organizational achievement. The Charter does not, in the literal terms used in Articles 1 and 2, provide adequate tests by which to assess United Nations performance.

[12] The professional outlook of academic specialists is well illustrated by the two sources cited in note 9. This outlook generally reflects the effort of political science to develop more "scientific" (in the sense of disciplined) procedures of inquiry.

[13] This chapter is a very preliminary effort to evolve a disciplined procedure for assessing the degree to which the United Nations has met, is meeting, and will meet the needs of international society. The character of these needs is the subject of my book, *This Endangered Planet* (New York: Random House, 1971). The argument of the book is that there are a series of challenges, the cumulative impact of which is likely to be catastrophic, unless drastic changes in the structure of international society are brought about by the end of the century. My depiction of United Nations behavior is in light of this overriding concern.

[14] For the basis of such a configurative approach see Myres S. McDougal, Harold D. Lasswell, and W. Michael Reisman, "Theories about International Law: Prologue to a Configurative Jurisprudence." *Virginia Journal of International Law*, 8 (April 1968) 188-299; and their contribution to Falk and C. E. Black, eds., *The Future of the International Legal Order*, I (Princeton: Princeton University Press, 1969).

[15] For a review of this kind of false utopianism see Hinsley, note 8; Walter Schiffer, *The Legal Community of Mankind* (New York: Columbia University Press, 1954); Stefan T. Possony, "Peace Enforcement," *Yale Law Journal*, 55 (1946), 910-949.

strate that the future can be beneficially shaped at all.[16] This essay takes the position that an evaluation of the United Nations properly combines descriptive analysis with normative appraisal. It is part of the scholarly function to clarify what has taken place; it is also part of this function to appraise performance in light of explicit goals and to recommend courses of action that might bring future behavior into closer conformity with preferences. In this sense my undertaking is one scholar's attempt to respond to U Thant's plea for moral strength.

II. Elements of Analysis

A series of well-analyzed and convincingly evidenced ideas provide an intellectual base for evaluating the United Nations. Several of these ideas are set forth in the following paragraphs to clarify my orientation:

The Two Gaps

The Charter conception of the United Nations is distinct in several important respects from the United Nations as an operative political entity.[17] The interaction between Charter goals and UN action is a relevant perception and it is one that can be used as the basis for mobilizing political support.[18] Furthermore, the United Nations has had a dif-

[16] In this regard see Erich Fromm, *The Revolution of Hope: Toward a Humanized Technology* (New York: Harper, 1968); Gerald Feinberg, *The Prometheus Project—Mankind's Search for Long-Range Goals* (Garden City, New York: Doubleday, 1969).

[17] Throughout this chapter for purposes of convenient reference I refer to the "United Nations" as if there were some concrete entity to which the label corresponds. Except as a convenience, such a form of reference is a misleading kind of reification. The United Nations consists of many distinct organs and organizational settings; also the specific organ does not "act" in any way analogous to the way a person acts. Instead, actions are taken in accordance with procedures by individuals who are assigned different roles that they play in quite different ways. This concreteness and specificity of event should be kept in mind throughout this discussion conducted at higher levels of abstraction.

[18] It is in this respect that an official of the United Nations, such

ferent center of organizational activity at each of the various stages of its existence. Therefore, there is an analytic need to differentiate these stages, especially by reference to shifts in coalition patterns and the bearing of these patterns upon the prospects for implementing various categories of claims and counterclaims that are asserted within the United Nations.[19]

The second gap, as we have said, is created by the distance between the United Nations as an operative system and the problems of world order that exist as these were set forth in Articles 1 and 2 of the Charter. This second gap does not imply organizational deficiencies, but rather takes account of those features of the international environment that identify the limits of United Nations capacity. It calls attention to the capacities that would be needed to attain certain world-order goals involving the minimization of violence, the maximization of human dignity, and the promotion of social and economic progress.

An awareness of these two gaps helps to orient inquiry into the significance of the UN in the present world: What would be likely to change if the United Nations were to be removed from the world scene? What would be the impact upon world affairs of a greatly strengthened United Nations?[20] Note that such questions are unrealistic to the extent that unidentified environmental changes would have to occur to create the occasion of the removal or strengthening of the United Nations.[21]

---

as U Thant, invokes the gap between Charter language and statecraft to mobilize public and elite opinion in favor of more moderate international behavior.

[19] Haas develops an interesting conception of "stages" in the article cited in note 6, pp. 171-172. For his more recent thinking in the context of collective security see "Collective Security and the Future International System." In Falk and Black, eds., *The Future of the International Legal Order*, I.

[20] See discussion of the United Nations' significance by Hoffmann in terms of "abyss" and "ambiguity," note 7, esp. pp. 793-795.

[21] That is, there is no current demand for the elimination of the United Nations from the international scene. It is possible to inquire

The United Nations Is an Actor in the International System

Despite the dependence of the United Nations on environmental factors, the Organization has a distinct identity and certain autonomous and semi-autonomous roles. These roles were probably not very fully envisioned by the drafters of the Charter, and their character has changed from one stage to another in the history of the Organization. Furthermore, the United Nations as actor builds up a certain momentum of its own that produces an organizational identity that influences to varying degrees, on varying issues, the attitudes and behavior of its members.[22]

The United Nations is an integral part of the complex pattern of international politics.[23] In observing that the United Nations is highly dependent on the character of the international environment there is implicit the expectation that the main currents of political conflict will influence the action of its main organs, particularly the more political ones. However, there is a refraction effect discernible, such that the United Nations setting may be said to influence the ways in which conflicts are conducted and justified. The prospect and actuality of UN discussion seems to have had a marginal moderating and conditioning impact on the behavior of governments, although such an assertion is difficult to establish and must be regarded as vague and speculative.[24] This refraction effect will have a differential

---

as to what changes in the international environment would have to occur before such a demand might be made in a serious fashion. The question is unrealistic because it does not posit these conditions.

[22] E. B. Haas has described the character of this momentum in great detail and to very instructive effect in his study of the ILO. See *Beyond the Nation-State* (Stanford: Stanford University Press, 1964).

[23] This point about the character of political determination is made very persuasively by the works cited in notes 9 and 15.

[24] Convincing evidence in support of this assertion will be difficult to obtain until foreign office archives are available. The assertion in the text is based upon impressionistic indications of influence, although it is supported by the recollections of participants in such

impact depending on the government concerned, the issue-area presented, and the concrete setting of a particular concern. Also patterns of refraction effect will vary with the specific tradition of the institutional arena within the overall United Nations setting.[25]

Susceptibility to environmental influences will also vary in extent and quality from organ to organ within the United Nations system. Of the principal organs, the International Court of Justice is probably the least responsive to the international environment, and the General Assembly the most responsive. The voting procedures in the General Assembly, based on the principle of sovereign equality, do not accurately reflect the grossly unequal distribution of power within the overall international system. Therefore, the General Assembly often tends to refract environmental shifts in an unreliable or partial fashion. For instance, the collapse of colonialism has apparently not increased the pressure on South Africa to abandon apartheid within the international system as a whole nearly so much as it has increased the scope and magnitude of the General Assembly's concern and pressure. This situation illustrates the refraction effect created by the ability of the Afro-Asian states to dominate, increasingly since 1955, the agenda and claiming process of the General Assembly while remaining unable to command the capabilities which would assure implementation of the claims endorsed by the Assembly.[26] To vote in favor of a

---

international crisis situations as the Cuban Missile Crisis of 1962 and the Suez Campaign of 1956.

[25] There is obviously a need for a framework of inquiry and a collection of data that examines the refraction effect over time, for distinct issue-areas, and within the various United Nations organizational arenas.

[26] The Afro-Asian group has been unable to induce the United Nations to make available the resources needed to mount a serious military effort or to persuade any of the more powerful states to move along these lines outside the framework of the Organization. There is a virtually universal endorsement of Afro-Asian aims, but the more established sovereign states are not prepared to generate the means needed to achieve or even to threaten a humanitarian

course of action is quite different from taking steps to obtain the results, such as making available resources needed to make a claim effective, or even credible.[27] The General Assembly exhibits so great a refraction effect in relation to the international environment that it engenders cynicism among its own membership. Failure of implementation, especially if the claim is put forward on a series of occasions and receives the support of an overwhelming consensus, calls dramatic attention to the modest extent of UN enforcement capability.[28] The disjunction between words and deeds encourages the view that the United Nations is "at most, a debating society," and, what is more destructive, lends some credence to the position that justice claims (claims advanced by groups to change their relative status, wealth, or power within the political system and supported by appeals to the justice of the demands) will only be satisfied to the extent that they can be enforced by violent means. Failures of implementation by the United Nations encourage strategies of violent implementation.[29] The Goa

intervention. Compare the willingness of powerful states to police deviance within their spheres of influence (e.g., Czechoslovakia) or to commit huge amounts of resources to the struggle for geopolitical ascendancy (e.g., Vietnam).

[27] A gap between endorsing a claim and acting to assure its fulfillment is in some sense analogous to the gap between Charter ideals and United Nations behavior.

[28] At the same time, as has been suggested already, there are other functions that may be served by the mere assertion of a claim, including a gradual mobilization of support for violence within the international community and an eventual recourse to some kind of sanctioning process. The United Nations is neither primarily an enforcement agency nor the basis of a restraint system; its principal roles are more typically to clarify a consensus, formulate demands, and set some standards for distinguishing permissible from impermissible uses of force. In the case of apartheid, United Nations pressure has occasioned a greater degree of world awareness and has even had a role in inducing blacks in the United States to identify with the anti-apartheid movement.

[29] This encouragement comes about in three ways: 1) frustration with persuasive approaches that rely on legality and nonviolence; 2) a gradual legitimation, or at least toleration, of violent approaches as a consequence of refusal to make voluntary concessions; 3) a belief that

193

model of social change is instructive in this respect: India's years of futile effort to eliminate the Portuguese colonial presence through UN intervention offer a sharp contrast to the efficacy of violent takeover in December of 1962.[30]

The major point here is that, given the absence of autonomous capabilities on the part of the United Nations,[31] it is important to correlate the Organizational claims against behavior with prospects for reasonably prompt and effective implementation, as well as with the capacity to muster a constitutional majority in support of a UN resolution. The quality of this double-dimensioned correlation is difficult to assess in particular instances, because there may be a variety of objectives underlying the assertion of a claim, including the creation of some kind of legitimizing basis for recourse to violence outside the United Nations framework.[32] Careful research is needed, and analysis of the effects of different degrees of correlation for different issues at different stages of United Nations history.[33]

violence alone works, a belief that is reinforced on every occasion that ineffectual strategies of persuasion have been replaced by effectual violent strategies.

[30] The Goa incident is illustrative of a double failure of implementation that leads both sides in the dispute to be critical of the United Nations; 1) the Afro-Asian side is critical because of the prolonged inability of the Organization to secure compliance with the anti-colonial demand put forward by India; 2) the conservative states of international society are critical because of the inability and unwillingness of the Organization to take steps on behalf of a Member state, Portugal, that has been a victim of "aggression" directed at its territorial boundaries.

[31] But as the Korean action has illustrated, the absence of such capabilities can be occasionally overcome by the *ad hoc* assignment of capabilities by Member states.

[32] Recourse to the United Nations in search of a persuasive solution is part of the contemporary process of exhausting all pacific remedies before recourse to violent remedies. Nondefensive recourse to force for legislative purposes that have been approved by the world community is not explicitly allowed by the Charter or positive international law, but such recourse does seem to enjoy some status to the extent that formal and authoritative expressions of the will of the international community can now be regarded as the fundamental law-creating process.

[33] There is a need for in depth case studies examining the conditions under which different kinds of capabilities are and are not

To regard the UN as an actor within the international organization can transform international politics without endowing the organization with military and police capabilities and missions.[34] At the same time, UN arenas are to a variable and uncertain extent separated from national arenas and capable of inducing a sum greater than its parts. There is a common normative basis of communication, even within highly political organs, that certainly influences rhetorical style and, perhaps, gradually socializes participants toward more cosmopolitan values.[35] Furthermore, there is an international civil service built up over time in the secretariat of each international institution that interacts with the nationally oriented missions of the membership.[36] Such data may not yet appear significant, but it would seem to reinforce the efforts of cosmopolitan constituencies within nation-states to diminish reliance upon sovereign prerogatives and to build up confidence in the prospects for a world community. These constituencies appear especially active within the liberal democracies in the

---

available to implement different kinds of claims on behalf of the United Nations (Chapter 3, above, represents research in this direction). "The financing dispute" has illustrated a serious effort by important states to withhold financial resources on a *post hoc* basis to discourage certain kinds of peacekeeping operations by the Organization. Part of the issue, of course, is the extent to which the political execution of the United Nations position was correlated with the specific preferences of the states being assessed for the cost of an operation. And part of the issue, especially as reflected in Soviet behavior, is an effort to prevent the easy operation of UN System I (see pp. 215-216 below for a discussion of the operation of a United States-dominated United Nations).

[34] Transformation is circular. The moment that the Organization is entrusted with adequate capabilities its need for them is likely to diminish. Part of the present problem arises from the consequences of governments wanting to have the discretion that would be lost, or diminished, if a more effective United Nations existed.

[35] Such an observation is not meant to contradict the continuing dominance of national governments within the United Nations setting, and the continuing reliance of the main decisional procedures upon nationalistic modes of participation. The increasing use of world community rhetoric is a social fact with certain attitudinal and behavioral consequences even if these consequences remain very subordinate for most purposes.

[36] See Gordenker, Chapter 5 above.

developed countries of the world at this time,[37] but social-ist and centralized societies might experience a sharp shift of outlook in reaction to the growing evidence that man-kind cannot long expect to endure the hazards and costs at-tendant upon "a world of sovereign states."[38]

The United Nations Plays Multiple Roles and Has Multiple Functions[39]

More often than not the performance of the United Nations is related to its success or failure in the area of war and peace. The UN emerged as a direct consequence of World War II, just as the League of Nations was estab-lished as a reaction to the breakdown of international order in 1914.[40] The Preamble of the Charter talks of "saving suc-ceeding generations from the scourge of war," and both utopian and cynical perceptions of the United Nations con-verge on its role as an agency of war prevention. The more configurative views emphasize that the Organization is poorly endowed to maintain peace, and that the interna-tional environment does not reinforce these Charter goals except in those very special and limited circumstances where principal states perceive their interests as converg-ing upon an endorsement (or indulgence) of a peacekeep-ing or peace-enforcing role for the United Nations.

But the United Nations has acquired functions other than the maintenance of peace and security during its history that have, in fact, grown to be its main preoccupations:

[37] There are numerous proposals along these lines now being made in the United States: 1) Senator Hartke has led the effort to estab-lish a Department of Peace within the Executive Branch; 2) the suggestion has been made that President Nixon establish a National Commission on World Order; 3) there are various schemes for secur-ing a United Nations source of direct revenue, such as a share in the revenues from ocean mining.

[38] An argument to this general effect is the principal subject of *This Endangered Planet* note 13, above.

[39] See sources cited in note 9, especially Young, Chapter 1 above.

[40] The League Covenant, for a variety of complicated reasons, including the quest for ratification by the United States Senate, was formerly included as a section of the Versailles Peace Treaty.

a) the promotion of social change (e.g., decolonialization, economic development); b) the aggregation of claims by "the new states" for the reform of the structure of international trade and investment; c) the facilitation of technical forms of cooperation, including standard-setting and the exchange of information; d) the publication and censure of certain classes of violations of human rights (e.g., apartheid); and e) the formulation of a world public interest with respect to subject-matter of global dimension (e.g., status of nuclear weapons, pollution).

Each of these complex areas of endeavor is more successfully pursued in certain UN organs than others, and is more prominent at certain stages of UN history than others. Here also careful research and analysis is needed to present a sophisticated profile of the multi-dimensional role of the United Nations.[41]

Depending on the politics of the Organization there is constantly present within it a bargaining process and potential to encourage trade-offs and compromises between opposed groups of states. For instance, the United States may exchange its support for anti-apartheid resolutions to obtain African support or abstention on the issue of Chinese representation. Such bargains may be tacit, implicit, or explicit. It is difficult, of course, to gain insight into the dynamics of this bargaining process and virtually impossible to acquire data on specific bargaining patterns. Nevertheless, the bargaining process that takes place in various United Nations arenas determines to a great extent the shape of action that is undertaken.[42] Often the bargaining concerns only an exchange of verbal commitments, thereby accentuating the problems associated with failures of implementation, and calling dramatic attention to the disjunction

[41] For useful inquiry along these lines see Gordenker, Chapter 5 above.

[42] The analysis of the bargaining nexus of United Nations operations has been well analyzed in a number of distinct settings by Ernst B. Haas. For a succinct statement of his approach to bargaining relations within the United Nations see the article cited in note 6.

between implementing capabilities within and outside the Organization.

Shifts in the International Environment Produce Changes in Characteristic Patterns of United Nations Operation

The United Nations is a quasi-dependent international actor, to a far greater extent reflecting changes elsewhere in the international system than initiating changes by its existence and undertakings. It is a quasi-dependent international actor that serves member states as an instrument of confrontation and cooperation. It also has certain active potentialities which allow it to coalesce a viewpoint or create a moral presence in an area where otherwise an action vacuum might exist.

Indicators need to be developed to draw attention to changes in the international environment that are likely to have significant impacts upon United Nations operations.[43] Such a task lies outside the main concern of this chapter, but it seems appropriate to offer a few tentative suggestions.

The Type of Correlation between Patterns of United Nations Authority and Structures of Power and Influence within the International Political System

The effectiveness of the United Nations is likely to vary directly with the correlation between authority patterns and the distribution of power in international society.[44]

[43] Such a correlation has not yet been made in any systematic fashion. Useful light is shed on some of these problems by Oran R. Young, "Trends in International Peacekeeping." Research Monograph No. 22, Princeton Center of International Studies; see also Ernst B. Haas, "Collective Security and the Future International System." In Falk and Black, cited note 19.

[44] The Security Council is more likely to advance effective claims than is the General Assembly because the voting rules in the Council emphasize the participation and assent of principal states to a far greater extent than do Assembly voting rules. The International Court of Justice, should it become seized of a case bearing on ques-

Such a correlation is more significant for peace and security issues than other issues, and in the political arenas than other arenas. Achievement of a positive correlation between power and authority within the United Nations is impeded by: 1) the postulate of sovereign equality, especially in the General Assembly, giving states of greatly unequal power an equal influence in the formulation of authoritative policy;[45] 2) the fact that the permanent membership of the Security Council has been defined to refer to the principal members of the alliance that achieved victory in World War II, thereby giving status to states of diminished importance in the present world (Great Britain and France) and excluding from participation on a permanent basis more important states (e.g., India, Brazil, UAR)—an authority pattern fostering the anachronistic idea that the major European states are among the most important actors on the international scene;[46] 3) the continuing ex-

---

tions of importance, is even less likely to posit an effective claim than the General Assembly, because its behavior is least likely to be responsive to political constraints. The highly unpopular decision in the South West Africa Cases is illustrative of a determination that is so unresponsive to these constraints as to undermine the authority of the institution as well as the assertion of the particular decision. Specialized agencies with clear lines of authority to facilitate technical cooperation among national governments may be more or less able to neglect the actualities of power and conflict in international society.

[45] A study sponsored by the United States Government in 1963 indicated that United States positions appeared to be better protected by the one vote/one state formula than by any of the main proposals for weighted voting. For the text of the conclusions see Falk and Mendlovitz, Vol. 3, cited note 7, pp. 297-299. There is no evidence at this time that a greater correlation between relative size and relative authority would carry with it any assurance that the preferences of a particular state might carry increased "weight" within the Organization.

[46] With the special exception of China representation in the Security Council may not appear so anachronistic if the possession of nuclear weapons or the level of gross national product are selected as the decisive criteria of relative power. The assertion in the text is based on the importance of diverse participation in the decisional process and, therefore, the growing insistence that roles in authority structures be parceled out to allow principal cultural, ethnic, and ideological

199

clusion of mainland China from participation in the affairs of the United Nations and the insistence on the cold war fiction that the Taiwan regime represents China for UN purposes; and 4) the failure to confer direct UN status of some sort upon regional and, possibly, transnational functional, cultural, and even ideological actors, which may express the main political perspectives on many international issues in a more meaningful way than do separate states.

These four expressions of a negative correlation between the United Nations and the international political system suggest some of the reasons why the Organization has not assumed greater importance. There is also a basic circularity present—part of the reason why the United Nations has the structure that it does is to assure that its role will be marginal.[47]

United Nations Capabilities and World Order Tasks

The scale and character of United Nations operations is very much confined by the budgetary and other resources at its disposal. Limits upon assured resources generally exclude the United Nations from an autonomous and central role in major international conflict situations. In special circumstances an *ad hoc* political consensus may form to assign a mission to the UN and even to provide some confidence that the mission can be financed. The Congo Operation gave rise to the so-called financing dispute. The related controversy over the reorganization of the Secretariat illustrated the outer limit of such an *ad hoc* operation within a

---

constituencies to participate on the basis of equality. In such a calculus of relative power the Security Council appears very Eurocentric, top-heavy with Caucasian representation, and weighted toward Christian perspectives.

[47] This argument is a persistent theme of scholars who criticize the naïve expectations of idealistic strains of thought among proponents of world government. See references cited, notes 8 and 15. The failure to make use of the potentialities of the United Nations is a consequence of deliberate policy on the part of all major governments. The level of nationalism seems to correlate with capability much more than with ideology or culture.

setting where the political consensus authorizing the mission disguised sharp disagreements among principal states as to the character and outcome of the UN role. The learning experience provided by the Congo Operation has induced a sense of modesty about what might be expected from the United Nations in a situation where the scale and stakes of the conflict are sufficiently great to undermine the stability of the initiating consensus.[48]

The lack of autonomous United Nations capabilities is itself a way of maintaining the preeminence of principal sovereign states and of sustaining traditional modes of diplomatic interaction. World-order tasks, whether involving peace and security, economic development, or human rights, are of a magnitude so clearly exceeding normal UN capabilities that its role is certain to be both subordinate and marginal. The United Nations tends to stress roles and discharge functions that are not concerned with the direct resolution of conflicts and controversies that imperil peace. These roles and functions make use of the Organization as a facility for the articulation and exchange of claims and for the conduct of conference diplomacy at various levels of overtness.[49] Therefore, the importance of the United Nations at any given time, as one of a variety of diplomatic forums available in international society, depends directly

[48] A United Nations peacekeeping role involves a process normally initiated by a collective decision. As such a decision must be acted upon in an extremely unstable environment of conflict, choices are likely to be made that are antithetical to the policies of major members. The politics involved in building the initial consensus may have deliberately introduced certain ambiguities into the definition of goals attached to the United Nations assignment so as to mobilize wide support. Later on, in more concrete settings, these contradictory expectations about goals are likely to induce a severe sense of disappointment about what the United Nations is doing. Distinct policy inputs may also be introduced by members of the UN staff. The Congo Operation exemplified the differences between obtaining a consensus to assign the United Nations a role and sustaining that consensus throughout the various phases of executing that role.

[49] A role is conceived of as a form of characteristic behavior by an actor, whereas a function is conceived of as a valued task that an actor performs within a social or political system.

on the degree to which diplomacy within the UN appears propitious to either parties or observers. A judgment of censure is one way to use the political arenas of the United Nations in a setting in which other modes of adverse response might seem both too dangerous and too costly.[50]

Capabilities for coercive action remain heavily concentrated within the principal states of the world. The refusal of these states to endow the United Nations with some greater measure of complementary capabilities is a clear expression of an unwillingness to depart from a system of largely decentralized management for the vital affairs of international society. This unwillingness is deep-seated, being embodied in the original Charter drawn up by the victorious powers in World War II during a period in which these governments seemed to share a commitment to world peace; therefore the meager powers assigned to the United Nations cannot be adequately explained by reference to patterns of intense conflict that subsequently emerged in its early years.

The Character of Secondary International Conflicts: Moderateness of Means and Ends

The United Nations was not intended to resolve intense conflicts between its principal members. However, the hope existed that it might keep secondary international conflicts within tolerable limits or bring them to an end. The Organization has played such a role with varying degrees of success.[51]

A critical indicator of the extent of the United Nations role is whether parties to a dispute are prepared to accept a solution that involves a political compromise. The UN

[50] The political organs of the United Nations can be used to register displeasure by the world community about some specific policies of a major state. The West has used the Organization frequently to censure Soviet behavior in Eastern Europe as a way of adopting a position without risking any action. Such verbal denunciations may even serve to dilute domestic demands for a more militant response. Also see Miller, above, p. 145.

[51] See Lande, Chapter 3 above.

lacks autonomous capabilities and, since the Congo Operation, has not enjoyed enough confidence among enough of its membership to take a major part in matters of peaceful settlement. The most characteristic role in the years ahead is likely to involve assisting parties to maintain a stalemate or establish a negotiated compromise.[52] The political organs will also serve to register reactions of world opinion to particular complaints about violations of sovereign rights, and perhaps in certain cases to mobilize different publics, for or against one side in an international controversy. Since June 1967 the United Nations (especially the Security Council) has served in this capacity in relation to the conflict in the Middle East, arousing sentiments in favor of the Arab countries and increasingly putting Israel in a position of diplomatic isolation.[53]

Moderateness of scope, means, and ends facilitates all modes of nonviolent conflict resolution, including those modes involving varying degrees of UN participation. The existence of irreconcilable conflicts, those where the minimum terms of the revisionist actor are clearly unacceptable to the status quo actor, appear to be least susceptible to settlement by UN intervention unless possibly the Organization can be mobilized to take the side of one part in the conflict.[54] Such mobilization is likely to occur effectively

[52] There is a well-established distinction between "peaceful settlement" and "peacekeeping." The latter kind of operation involves an active military presence, although its nature can vary from symbolic buffering to participation in large-scale belligerency. It seems likely that the United Nations may play major peacekeeping roles in future in the Middle East, either to supervise a cease-fire or to implement and sustain part of a political settlement.

[53] With respect to peaceful settlement the United Nations has been playing a significant role: 1) Security Council Resolution 242, Nov. 22, 1967, has established agreed guidelines for a settlement (although there are many "open" issues and Israel appears unlikely to accept any solution that involves restoring the territorial status quo as of June 5, 1967); 2) Gunnar V. Jarring, as Special Representative of the Secretary-General, has been seeking to find bases for a negotiated settlement and has had significant contact with all governments concerned with the issues.

[54] The United Nations might also act to avert disaster by interposing a corps of observers in a situation of tension and hostility.

when the principal states of the Organization agree about the direction, rate, and outcome of influence to be exerted. The attack upon apartheid is an instance of irreconcilable conflict, where the United Nations has taken sides and where the principal states share an original consensus as to the character of change that is desirable.[55] However, this consensus hides contradictory attitudes toward the rate and outcome of change and toward the appropriate limits of external influence. The conflicts between the Arab countries and Israel and between India and Pakistan over Kashmir also seem to be of an irreconcilable character. The United Nations might nevertheless help, in these settings, to prevent a deterioration of the status quo or to restore a condition of nonviolent confrontation by facilitating and sustaining a cease-fire.

Another kind of immoderateness results from hegemonic claims exerted by principal states over dependent or lesser states situated within a clearly delimited zone of influence.[56] The United Nations is denied an active role in such settings as Eastern Europe and the Caribbean by the pre-emptive presence of a state with the capabilities to enforce its will by coercive means, subject only to challenge by another principal state willing to risk a major conflagration.

If any major state pursues an expansionist policy by overt military means, then there is likely to be little role for the United Nations in the area of peace and security.[57] Serious

[55] There is evidence that the consensus that can be obtained to support verbal denunciations could not be sustained in the event that sanctions were voted to bring increasing diplomatic, economic, and military pressure upon South Africa.

[56] See discussion of "spheres of influence" in Young, pp. 15-16 above, and Falk, "Zone II as a Structure of Political Domination."

[57] The Organization is not equipped to contain a determined aggressor state and shows no real disposition to turn itself into an instrument of genuine collective security. National security in the nuclear age, more than at any previous point in world history, depends upon the operation of a deterrent strategy at the national level. Critical risk-taking and reactions to risks continue to be national decisions made in periods of international crisis and confronta-

challenges to the present distribution of power in international society continue to be dealt with through increases of defense spending at the national level and intensification of cooperative efforts at the alliance level. It is hardly surprising that the Soviet occupation of Czechoslovakia in August 1968 had a far greater impact on United States-Soviet relations and on NATO-Warsaw Pact relations than it did upon the operations of the United Nations.

Exclusions, Withdrawals, and Nonmembers

The authority of the United Nations depends considerably upon its claim to be a universal organization speaking on behalf of the whole of international society. Significant nonparticipation by states, regardless of reason, weakens this claim. Also, nonparticipating states are likely to be strongly opposed to accepting a UN role for disputes to which they are a party. The opposition of China and North Vietnam to *any role* for the United Nations in settling the Vietnam War is one salient demonstration of the effects of nonparticipation upon the willingness of states to make use of the United Nations as an agency for problem-solving.

THE PRECEDING pages have discussed some aspects of the international environment that influence the role of the United Nations at a particular period of time. Environmental changes will have to be much more precisely linked to specific operations of United Nations organs before hypotheses can be formed and tested and causal propositions of explanation and prediction formulated.

III. SOME PRINCIPAL SYSTEMS OF CHARTER
CONCEPTION AND UNITED NATIONS OPERATION

Existing approaches to the United Nations are sensitive to several sets of distinctions: 1) among the Charter as a formal conception and the United Nations as a network of

tion. See O. R. Young, *The Politics of Force* (Princeton: Princeton University Press, 1969).

political actors; 2) among successive phases of United Nations operation; and 3) among distinct issue-areas of UN concern. A stress upon each of these distinctions is an important part of any adequate conception of the United Nations role at any particular time.

However, there is little sense of how to specify the dominant aggregate trends of United Nations activity. In this section a preliminary attempt will be made to specify the principal modes of operation, both as contemplated in the instrument of incorporation, the Charter, and as exemplified in the experience of the Organization in relation to distinct issue-areas and during distinct phases of its history. Each main pattern will be characterized as a "system."[58] The objective is to facilitate comparison among distinct subject-matters and time periods, and the various systems are delineated to highlight distinctive patterns of expectation and operation. They can be conceived either in analytical terms as hypothetical alternatives or in sociohistorical terms as condensations of United Nations history.[59]

[58] See discussion of a comparable use of the word "system" for United Nations activities in Gregg and Barkun, cited note 6, pp. 3-5. Gregg and Barkun offer two reasons for their use of system: "In the first place, we simply wish to avoid the use of expressions such as 'world community,' which suggest a non-existent consensus. . . . In the second place, the concept of system is useful because it suggests actors interacting within environmental constraints, and this is precisely the picture which we wish to conjure up" (p. 3).

[59] It is also possible to go backwards in the history of international society and formulate distinct organizing *de jure* and *de facto* images for each period. For instance, it would certainly be useful to compare the Covenant Conception with the various League "Systems" that emerged in relation to different issue-areas and during the main phases of its existence. Sir Alfred Zimmern in a book first published in 1936 writes that the Covenant "embodies five different systems, each with its appropriate method" (p. 270). Zimmern's conception of "a system" is very close to my own, although he does not stress the distinction between the Covenant as a formal document and the League as a political actor. For an outline of the five systems see Zimmern, *The League of Nations and the Rule of Law 1918-1935.* (London: Macmillan, 2nd ed. 1939; repr. Russell, 1969), pp. 270-280. The most complete effort to deal with international history as a whole in this systemic way is to be found in Richard N. Rosecrance, *Action*

The clarity of the boundaries of each system are somewhat overrated, and therefore it may be desirable to make intra-systemic as well as intersystemic comparisons.[60] My purpose is to outline an approach to UN studies through the conceptualization of these main systems, which should be associated with other efforts to produce greater analytic clarity and substantive understanding about the United Nations.

A basic distinction is made between the formal system embodied in the instrument of incorporation and the life history of the resultant organization.[61] The instrument of incorporation, the United Nations Charter, is susceptible to multiple perceptions and interpretations because of its complexity, its inclusion of contradictory and complementary norms and procedures, and its vagueness about the relative priority of concerns. In part, a formal instrument of incorporation is intended only to sustain a minimum original consensus among the founding members of an organization to create a frame for action within which different lines of development, depending on the political climate, can unfold. The formal level of system planning is important in any project to strengthen the United Nations.

---

and Reaction in World Politics (Boston: Little, Brown, 1963); see also Stanley Hoffmann, "International Systems and International Law." In Falk and Mendlovitz, cited note 7, Vol. II, 134-166.

[60] It is possible to compare the treatment of issue-areas and phases within a single system as well as to compare one system with another. The boundaries of a system are to some extent artificial, imposed on subject-matter that cannot be confined altogether to abstractly formulated categories.

[61] The formal system embodied in an instrument, say, the United Nations Charter, can be perceived in distinct ways. These perceptual images may be quite different on many key issues involving role and expectation. Stanley Hoffmann, writing about the League of Nations, points out "that the main authors of the Covenant did not agree on what they expected from the organization, and that the post-war world fitted the expectations of none of them." Hoffmann, cited note 7, p. 795. The various images of the formal system might also be specified and compared, but for the purposes of this paper there is "one" Charter, although its meaning yields different perceptions on any controversial occasion.

The Charter system establishes certain constraints and opportunities for behavior, although under some circumstances the constraints will be eroded and under others the opportunities will go unused. Several points follow from the distinction between Charter systems and United Nations systems: 1) the clarity of the separation between the idea of the United Nations and its actual realization; 2) the complex interactive relationship between the idea and its realization through time; 3) the limited capacity to predetermine the behavioral patterns of a political actor by agreeing upon an instrument of incorporation; 4) the shaping role of the overall environment within which an actor operates.[62]

The following presentation differentiates a series of systems, outlined with a clarity not reproduced in actual experience. These systems induce blurred images in experience because observers approach them with distinct preconceptions, assess them on the basis of different readings of facts and preferences, and bring to bear quite different ideas about evaluating the behavior of the Organization.

Charter System I

The United Nations Charter is premised on a series of norms, procedures, and institutions that incorporate a set of political assumptions and expectations about the resulting organization. The document is coherent and can be explicated as such without any consideration of United Nations history.[63] The basic goal of the Charter is to contribute

[62] Such an observation is especially applicable to international society where law habits are weak and the ethos of self-help continues to prevail on matters of critical concern to sovereign governments.

[63] It could also be compared with other formal conceptions for global organization that might be notated as Charter IIa, IIb, etc. Even as to a single document there exists the problem of divergent perception discussed in note 61. There is also the altering content of the formal instrument, as it acquires (and loses) meanings through adaptation to a series of concrete situations. The United Nations Charter is in 1971 a different instrument in some respects from what it was in 1945.

to the maintenance of peace and security in international society. The basic political assumption is that an international institution can be set up for this purpose only if the powerful states of the world are assured that the Organization will not act against their wishes, and that harmony can be attained within a framework of orderly cooperation among sovereign states. The states of primary rank were defined as the principal powers victorious in World War II.[64] The main device used to assure deference to these states was to confer upon them alone permanent membership in the Security Council. Permanent members were given a power of veto by the voting rules of the Council, and it was entrusted with exclusive decision-making authority and with primary competence on matters of peace and security. The Organization was endowed with almost unlimited potential authority to implement any consensus of the victorious states of World War II, including the competence to undertake further action against the defeated countries, promote a buildup of United Nations enforcement machinery, or intervene in the affairs of smaller countries.

The Charter also embodied several central ideas of normative constraint: 1) a prohibition on the discretionary right to use force; 2) an insistence that claims to act on self-defense be subject to community review by the Security Council; 3) an obligation to use procedures of pacific settlement in the event of a dispute. There were certain inadequacies in this pattern of normative constraint, aside from the political problems of implementation: 1) no clear delimitation of the idea of self-defense; 2) no assured procedure for passing on alleged recourse to self-defense; 3) no prospect of an impartial determination of claims about

[64] It is true that the five permanent members of the Security Council are the five states that possess nuclear weapons at the present time (overlooking the Chinese representation issue). But aside from nuclear weapons, India, Japan, Brazil, and West Germany might have better status claims than either France or the United Kingdom.

aggression and self-defense; 4) no assured policing procedures to impose the will of the Security Council.[65]

Geopolitical calculations and ideological solidarity proved far stronger influences than did a commitment to adhere to the UN framework of action. States voted in the United Nations in light of these traditional affinities and often did not allow their positions to be shaped by the merits of a controversy. This strongly political content of the deliberations led states in minority positions in the United Nations into an adversary relationship with the Organization; real credibility was never established for the Charter claim that the Organization would act on behalf of some neutral and transcendent world interest, as specified by the Charter in normative terms. The rivalry and tension of the world political setting was not excluded from the UN arena; indeed it is possible to maintain that this atmosphere of intense rivalry defeated Charter expectations and made it impossible for the UN to carry out its intended role. But it should be understood that the Charter was never intended to transform the structure of international society and that there was no reason to suppose that international conflicts of a severe sort would not emerge after 1945. The Charter embodied only a commitment to create a flexible instrument of collective action that would be continuously readapted to the dominant trends of international life.

Several developments shaped the role of the United Nations in directions not fully anticipated in the explicit terms of the Charter. First, the postwar political alignments meant that the main structures of conflict split the perma-

[65] There were also failures to posit norms and procedures that were adapted to the main technologies of violence: 1) nuclear weaponry; 2) low-visibility commando operations. The Charter ideas of "aggression" and "self-defense" were evolved to deal with conventional warfare between regular military forces. International lawyers have been slow to evolve new and more relevant functional categories, better adapted to actual patterns of behavior.

nent membership of the United Nations.[66] Second, the development of a nuclear missile technology established a rather clearly delimited structure of hierarchical power in international society, and introduced an element of moderation into adversary relations among principal states. Third, liberation movements and civil strife came to have a central and controversial role in international society. Fourth, the unexpectedly rapid decolonialization of Asia and Africa and the entry into international society of a large number of new states altered the balance of political influence within the United Nations. Fifth, the outcome of the Chinese civil war and the continuing representation of China in the Organization by the Western-oriented Chiang regime distorted the authority structure of the Organization.

These developments are part of the explanation as to why the enforcement provisions of the Charter were never carried out. No political consensus of a continuing kind made possible sustained cooperation among the Permanent Members of the Security Council. The United Nations was denied autonomous capabilities and the main issues of peace and security were handled by traditional Westphalia methods (national defense, alliances, spheres of influence) and newer regional arrangements of a quasi-institutional variety.[67] At the same time in the early United Nations period the United States' political dominance of the Organization led to its partial conversion into an instrument of foreign policy on issues of peace and security.[68] Therefore,

[66] The Charter was negotiated in an atmosphere still influenced by the wartime alliance, and by an image of the main line of international conflict as between the Allied and Axis powers. It was set up to enable clear, concerted action against the states defeated in World War II, and its procedures were not encumbered at all in relation to such an undertaking, provided only that the principal victorious states agreed on a course of action.

[67] Some regional organizations are, of course, disguised hegemonies, or at least disguised hegemonic alliances. The Warsaw Pact and the Organization of American States are two prominent examples.

[68] For a positive account along these lines see Lincoln P. Bloomfield, *The United Nations and U.S. Foreign Policy* (Boston: Little,

211

some *ex parte* missions were entrusted to it, most notably the conduct of the defense of South Korea. A rather indefinite United States-Soviet convergence on certain aspects of an anti-colonialist position has also been evident in certain United Nations action.

The Charter distribution of functions between the General Assembly and the Security Council was altered by a series of developments: 1) the desire of the United States to circumvent the Soviet veto and obtain a United Nations mandate for its international policies; 2) the growing insistence by Afro-Asian states that issues of human rights and residual colonialism be given prime attention.[69]

Several conclusions can be stated about this Charter system: 1) there existed a set of normative imperatives that were at sharp variance with Westphalia modes of international behavior; 2) there was no serious effort to evolve procedures within UN settings for implementing these normative imperatives; 3) several sharp discrepancies between the Charter conception of international society and its empirical character became apparent during the first decades of the United Nations' existence; 4) the net effect of these two kinds of discrepancy has resulted in a rather marginal role for the UN in the area of peace and security, a role restricted to the moderation of conflict and the facilitation of social change.[70] As a result, the Organization has

---

Brown, 2nd rev. edn., 1967). The idea of formulating national strategies of participation within the United Nations seems to be a desirable one, but if the state has the power to shift the Organization into a partisan role in the central international conflict then the role of the Organization as a meeting ground for principal adversaries is jeopardized.

[69] The most dramatic instance of this shift was accomplished by means of the Uniting for Peace Resolution during the early period of the Korean War when government officials in the United States were eager to use the Organization to support national policies, especially those involving action against the Soviet Union. For text and consideration of the Uniting for Peace Resolution, GA Res. 377A (V), see Falk and Mendlovitz, cited note 7, Vol. 3, 250-269.

[70] On the relation of social change and maintenance in the Charter system, see Gordenker, above, pp. 171-178.

displayed its inability to secure compliance with the Charter's own prescriptions about international behavior.[71]

The question remains as to whether a more useful or effective United Nations could be derived from a new and different Charter. The answer depends on whether it is practical to suppose that it would be possible to negotiate a new Charter—given the present composition of the Organization and given the current international environment. The world political climate today is such that it would be impossible to agree on a Charter at all, much less a greatly different one. There are no indications whatsoever that governments of principal states would endow the community of states or a political majority of states with the competence and implementing resources to override sovereign discretion on central matters of security and development, or even encourage the autonomy needed if the Organization is to evolve over time a world position of its own on vital questions of war and peace. It was only the war-sustaining consensus that provided the degree of solidarity needed to bring the United Nations into being. If the project had been put off until the 1950s, it would be hard to conceive of the Soviet Union and the United States agreeing on joint sponsorship of a world peace organization of even such modest proportions as the United Nations.

The Charter system is not seriously inadequate, given the character of international society. There is no consistent evidence of governmental disposition either to create stronger implementing machinery or to abandon altogether the normative ideals of a world without war. The Charter has been flexible enough to accommodate itself to an international system differing in several key respects from what had been anticipated. Without a strong disposition to dis-

[71] These generalizations are provisional and subject to quite sharp reversal. The principal states acknowledge their converging interests in peacekeeping from time to time, and may at any point act jointly to create a world police unit of real military capability, say 40,000, to be used to prevent or moderate conflict or to restore or maintain order.

solve or reconstitute the framework established by the Charter, its system seems to be a durable, if ambiguous and uncertain, element of the current international system.[72] Part of this durability, of course, arises from the capacity of the United Nations to alter its main forms of behavior within the Charter framework. The cost of such flexibility is a weak tradition of constitutional adherence, itself a factor inhibiting the growth of real authority over behavior —this, however, may not interfere with the role of the Organization as a forum for communication, political mobilization, and interest articulation.

United Nations System I

The United Nations during the early years of its existence was dominated by a Western alliance led by the United States. The Organization operated principally as an instrument of United States foreign policy in war/peace issues arising out of a competitive bipolar relationship with the Soviet Union. The Soviet role in the United Nations was to obstruct the Organization from operating at more than a verbal level, and to sustain the existence of an open forum for the assertion of its position. The United Nations also provided a channel for continuing communication and diplomacy among rival governments at whatever degree of overtness or covertness was desired, whether as a forum for propaganda or for secret talks. The UN role in the Korean War was the most pronounced case in which the Organization was used as a partisan instrumentality for the execution of the foreign policy directives of the leading state. Such a use of the United Nations was not solely a consequence of the ability of the United States to command a sufficient number of votes to assure that its political preferences would prevail. The nature of the United States' position in

[72] "Ambiguous" is used in the sense of being susceptible to divergent lines of authoritative interpretation depending on the wishes of the governing consensus at certain points. There are few non-ambiguous directives embodied in the Charter.

the Korean controversy also seemed consistent with the basic normative imperative in the Charter about force—the prohibition of aggressive force and the toleration of defensive force—as well as with the commitment of the Organization to fight on the side of a victim of aggression. Thus the foreign policy of the United States in the Korean War might be understood as fulfilling the Charter conception, rather than distorting it.

More controversial instances of the partisan manipulation of UN machinery have included the successful efforts of the United States to deny mainland China access to United Nations affairs, including its success in supporting the Chiang regime as China's representative in the Security Council for all these years.

The point is that one main United Nations system of operation—not in accord with Charter procedures—has been to execute in selected instances the foreign policy of the politically preeminent member over the opposition of other members accorded a veto power. The outcome of the financing dispute, by interposing a French and Soviet "financial" veto, suggests one of the limits of United Nations System I. Nevertheless, the continuing ability of the United States to avoid censure for such uses of force as the Dominican intervention of 1965 or for its involvement in Vietnamese affairs after 1954 suggests an immunity from United Nations criticism in bipolar settings that is not enjoyed by the Soviet Union.[73] In Afro-Asian settings, such as the debate on the propriety of the Stanleyville Operation or that on sanctions against the Smith regime in Rhodesia, there is some evidence that the United States political capability has been declining in recent UN history.

The Afro-Asian control of the General Assembly since the late 1950s has made this arena less available for partisan United States manipulation than is the Security Council.

[73] For instance, the Soviet occupation of Czechoslovakia in August, 1968, was immediately subject to adverse debate in the Security Council.

The availability of the Soviet veto in the Council prevents formal decisions of matters of substance from being reached in that body, although this forum can always be used prominently to express an international mood of censure, even in circumstances where no formal decision can be reached by the Council.

United Nations System II

Convergence of United States-Soviet policy perspectives and interests leads to support for occasional, or sporadic, cooperation in the United Nations on the part of these two dominant rivals. The role of the Organization in responding to the Suez Campaign in 1956 and in the early stages of the Congo Operation in 1960 serve to illustrate bipolar cooperation and its limits. In such circumstances there is a greater tendency to evolve an autonomous and central United Nations role—which in the complexity of its execution is likely to disappoint one or the other superpower, or even both, as became the case during the long period of UN involvement in the affairs of the Congo. This kind of cooperative role is most likely to endow the United Nations with the sort of functions suggested by an optimistic view of the potentialities of Charter System I. Successful implementations, if sustained and not interspersed with serious reversions to UN System I, might create more confidence in the positive potentialities of the Organization, producing an expanded budget, more assigned tasks, greater deference to claims, and a generally enhanced stature.

The United Nations as an arena for bipolar cooperation varies with the subject-matter and time period. United Nations System II, in the presence of serious forms of US-Soviet cooperation, could allow the UN to become an instrumentality to facilitate and disguise bipolar hegemony. The quality of UN System II depends in part on the extent to which bipolar cooperative steps accord with or appear to violate the normative framework embodied in Charter

System I, as well as its interactions with the sentiments, interests, and capabilities of other groupings of states.

One conclusion is clear—given the bipolar political structure on matters of strategic security, UN System II seems to bring about a closer correlation between the structure of power in international society and the assertion of United Nations authority than results from UN System I. Of course, to the extent that the United States became the preeminent world power and bipolarity became supplanted by unipolarity the correlation between power and United Nations authority would be established for UN System I, but at the expense of any normative pretense of a cooperative framework of universal and pluralistic character. The tendency of UN System I is to convert the Organization in the direction of serving as a dominant political alliance of a hegemonic character. Such a conversion results in the loss of authoritativeness for United Nations decisions and recommendations.[74] One positive consequence of Afro-Asian participation in the United Nations has been to diminish the relevance of UN System I to operations. The attitude of nonalignment is sufficiently dominant to discourage United States policy-makers from making partisan use of the General Assembly.[75]

United Nations System II has most chance of controlling the situation in those settings where the United States and the USSR have distinct, but convergent interests that each feels can be safely or usefully advanced under United Nations auspices.[76] The setting of standards with respect to arms developments (demilitarization of outer space) and the management of intraregional conflicts (Middle East,

---

[74] Exclusion or withdrawal of significant states has the same diluting impact upon United Nations recommendations and decisions.

[75] The potency of UN System III has induced some pressure to activate UN System II in certain contexts, for instance, with regard to the Middle East.

[76] The convergence may be either primarily positive (to attain some common goal) or primarily negative (to avoid a disaster).

217

Indo-Pakistan) are areas in which UN System II might achieve prominence in the near future. The scope and significance of UN System II reflects the orientations of the domestic regimes and foreign policies that prevail in the United States and the Soviet Union at a particular period of time, including the relevant images of an appropriate role for the United Nations held by the two governments, and the extent to which foreign policy objectives are perceived in convergent terms on key issues.

United Nations System III

United Nations System III has emerged as a consequence of the Afro-Asian control of the General Assembly and the voting majority at the disposal of a caucus of the poorer countries. It represents the claims made on behalf of the Organization and expressed by a consensus (at least $\frac{2}{3}$ of the General Assembly. UN System III posits demands, asserts interests, seeks to mobilize public opinion, and seeks especially to induce the more powerful and rich states to make more of their resources available for economic development in the poorer ones.

The most characteristic illustration of UN System III is the crusade against apartheid that has been carried on in various ways throughout almost the entire history of the United Nations.[77] The Afro-Asian priority schedule involves putting pressure upon the white regimes of southern Africa on the ground that these regimes are racist and colonialist. The Soviet voting bloc endorses these Afro-Asian demands, but there has been as yet little Soviet willingness to endow the United Nations with the capabilities needed to implement them. The United States position is similar, although its government shows a greater deference to Charter System I and may be more concerned with sustaining the credibility of actions of censure under UN System I; it is also true that the United States has a greater conflict of

[77] For some materials on the United Nations role in opposing apartheid see Falk and Mendlovitz, cited note 7, pp. 364-407.

interest about the resolution of this set of issues as a consequence of its heavy investments in that part of Africa and because these regimes are anti-Communist in their outlook. At the same time, the dynamics of the rivalry with the Soviet Union for third-world allegiance as well as the problems of domestic race relations mount pressure upon the United States Government to lend increasing support to Afro-Asian objectives.

The Afro-Asian outlook, often reinforced by the Latin American countries in the area of aid and trade, is also very much concerned with finding ways to overcome national and regional poverty, mass misery, and economic backwardness. UNCTAD is a product of UN System III, as is the whole emphasis on the so-called North/South split within the United Nations context. In fact, the agenda and acts of the General Assembly have been since 1957 increasingly governed by UN System III.

In UN System III there is a maximum disjunction in the Organization between power capabilities and authority claims. Such a disjunction engenders disrespect for the United Nations on the part of those who assess its success or failure by reference to successful enforcement of its authority claims.[78] This disrespect is deepened concomitantly with the failure of UN System I and II to operate in relation to peace and security issues. In UN System III the Organization does not usually attempt to deal with the grave war/peace issues of the day, except to propose some general goals and standards with respect to the status of nuclear weapons or the desirability of drastic disarmament. One problem with UN System III is that the only apparent outcome of the political process is to intensify verbal demands. There is neither a gradual buildup of commensurate capabilities, nor any genuine prospect of such a buildup. There is also some indication of a tacit willingness by the principal states to concentrate action functions in the Security Coun-

[78] Cf. Charter II variants for ideas of international organizations possessing greater capacity to implement their decisions.

cil, an organ wherein the voting rules work against the operation of UN System I or III.

Considerable intersystemic bargaining, as we have noted, takes place from time to time within the United Nations. The United States has supported some of the projects of UN System III in exchange for some Afro-Asian support of its own projects (e.g. Chinese representation), which it insists on treating as a UN System I issue.

The future of UN System III depends very much on the extent to which the Afro-Asian majority begins to command some capabilities, whether within or without the Organization, that might make some of their major claims credible or successful. The Afro-Asian attitude toward the United Nations as a whole will be largely determined by whether UN System III begins to operate beyond the threshold of interest articulation. If implementation by UN System II of UN System III projects takes place, then the relevance of the Organization to Afro-Asian affairs is probably assured. If not, Afro-Asian disenchantment with the United Nations may lead to an increasing emphasis on regional and special diplomatic forums. The continuing possibility also remains that the more militant or dissatisfied Afro-Asian states might form a counterorganization comparable to that proposed by Sukarno after Indonesia's brief period of withdrawal from the United Nations in 1965.[79]

United Nations System III represents the most serious explicit assault upon Charter System I. Some of the claims put forward involve direct violations of basic Charter norms, such as those involving deference to sovereignty, respect for domestic jurisdiction, and renunciation of non-

[79] Sukarno proposed creating a world organization of Newly Emerging Forces, including in its membership Indonesia and possibly mainland China. The project never proceeded very far, being completely abandoned when later in the same year the anti-Sukarno countercoup took over the government of Indonesia. But the challenge was instructive in suggesting the fragile base on which the United Nations' claims of world authority rest. This fragility underscores the importance of realizing the ideal of universal membership.

defensive uses of force. The Afro-Asian majority demands, above all, the use of coercive means to achieve social change and the toppling of constituted regimes in southern Africa in the process. Such objectives can be somewhat reconciled with the human rights provisions of the Charter, but the proposed means of attainment cannot. In this sense, then, UN System III, to the extent it is implemented, involves the most severe strain upon Charter System I. The diplomatic representatives of South Africa have pointed to this strain as part of their overall contention that UN System III is in its totality "unconstitutional" and *ultra vires.*

A serious implementation of UN System III with respect to several projects might be argued to create a *de facto* revision of the Charter.[80] The abridgement of domestic jurisdiction as a result of the use of force by the United Nations to implement legislative claims would amount to a major modification of Charter expectations.[81] In contrast, UN System II is quite clearly within the scope of Charter System I, whereas UN System I has been substantively, but not procedurally, quite compatible with Charter System I. The whole effort of the United States to engineer a shift of emphasis from the Security Council to the General Assembly was designed to circumvent the Soviet veto and enable United Nations action despite the opposition of a permanent member of the Security Council.[82] This intended redistribution of functions is essential for the operation of UN System I, but it has been difficult to implement since the Afro-Asian control of the General Assembly, and it is difficult to reconcile with the expectations of Charter System I. It should be understood that the constitutional criterion is

[80] If such a revision proceeded far enough a new normative framework could be indicated by the notation Charter System I (*de jure*)/ II (*de facto*).

[81] Such a development would be the inverse of the underfulfillment of the provisions in Chapter VII for evolving a United Nations military capability.

[82] There may be some effort to invoke the Uniting for Peace Resolution in a UN System III setting even though it was initially designed as an instrument for UN System I.

221

certainly not the decisive one in assessing United Nations developments.[83]

United Nations System IV

There is a less evident area wherein the decisions of the United Nations are reached after an assessment of the merits of contending claims. These decisions seek to assess claims by primary reference to the relations between Charter norms and behavior. In UN System IV, the search for an impartial determination of the facts in dispute is dominant. In UN Systems I, II, and III the violation of Charter norms by the target country may well intensify the claim and is a factor taken into account during debate, but the nature of the decision and voting behavior is largely shaped by patterns of political affiliation that persist outside the halls of the United Nations; by hearing which state is making what sort of claim it is possible to predict who will vote how.

As to peace and security issues, especially prior to the heavy Soviet involvement since 1965, the Middle East has provided a context in which the political organs of the United Nations have often and largely behaved in accordance with the postulates of UN System IV. The most dramatic example of this kind of behavior was the joint United States and Soviet insistence that Great Britain, France, and Israel restore the *status quo ante* after the Sinai Campaign of 1956. The United States' failure to uphold its prime allies and its possible sacrifice of geopolitical advantage on that occasion was widely scored as involving a gesture of "legalistic" deference to the Charter.[84] Supporters of the United Nations in the area of peace and security have always hailed UN System IV as the optimal mode of be-

[83] Cf. Myres S. McDougal and Richard N. Gardner, "The Veto and the Charter: an Interpretation for Survival." In McDougal and Associates, *Studies in World Public Order* (New Haven: Yale University Press, 1960), pp. 718-760.

[84] See, e.g., Ernest W. Lefever, *Ethics and United States Foreign Policy* (New York: Meridian Books, 1957).

havior for members of the Organization. UN System IV entails a measure of depoliticization of state behavior within the political organs of the United Nations. Depoliticization has not generally occurred except in instances when the comparative geopolitical merits of a dispute were either clouded or marginal for principal states. The expansion of UN System IV would mean that international politics have been increasingly subordinated in favor of a more law-oriented approach to the settlement of disputes. Such a transformation of behavioral patterns would seem first to require a shift in priorities and traditions at the national governmental level of principal states. There is no real trend-line visible at present. Up to this time, UN System IV has come into play only in very exceptional circumstances.

Nevertheless, states attempt to solicit support for their various contentions by talking as if the Organization normally functions according to the terms of UN System IV. Political decisions by national governments are reached by reference to UN Systems I-III, whereas the debate is carried on in the form of UN System IV. This incongruence facilitates the rejection of a United Nations claim by a target state. South Africa, Israel, the Soviet Union have all been repeatedly subject to adverse votes that reflect their minority position, given the operation of UN Systems I-III at certain times for certain issues. These votes are political expressions of preference couched in legal and moralistic rhetoric taken from the Charter and cannot be regarded as a fair application of Charter norms after impartial and full-scale inquiry.

The International Court of Justice is an arena wherein UN System IV prevails to a far greater extent than elsewhere in the Organization. It is not possible to predict how most of the judges will vote merely by looking at the geopolitical status of the adversary positions, and there is no strong correlation between the judicial behavior of a judge and the foreign policy of his country.[85] The fact that most

[85] At the same time, if a judge is a national of a state that is a

international disputes are not deemed suitable for judicial settlement is one expression of the minor role accorded UN System IV in the present international political system.[86] The exceedingly unpopular outcome in the South West Africa Cases aroused Afro-Asian resentment about the way in which the International Court of Justice was using UN System IV. The Afro-Asian countries expected that the International Court would reach a result in accordance with the political logic of UN System III, regardless of the perception of the relative merits of the factual and legal arguments.[87] It seems clear that a United Nations institution cannot achieve importance unless it is somewhat responsive to the political dimension of international society, and that the International Court of Justice is unlikely, even if it allows political factors to exert more influence on the recruitment of judges in the future, to be entrusted with a major role in settling politically significant disputes. Governments are reluctant to entrust vital issues to tribunals not so much because they are concerned about biased decision being rendered against them but because they are unwilling to risk an adverse outcome of an unbiased decisional process. The real point is that national adversaries are still unwilling to allow their vital concerns to be compromised by third-party

party to a dispute brought before the International Court of Justice, then he is likely to adopt a judicial position that conforms to the national policy. In fact, such conformity is actually encouraged by the Statute of the International Court of Justice which makes provision for the appointment of a national judge in the event that a party appearing before the Court is unrepresented by a national on the bench.

[86] For excessive optimism about judicial potentialities see Arthur Larson, *When Nations Disagree* (Baton Rouge, La.: Louisiana State University Press, 1961).

[87] It is possible to contend that the role of the International Court of Justice would be greater if there was more evidence of responsiveness to the political will of the international community. There are limits to judicial autonomy which, if exceeded, lead to a disregard of a court because it is unable to fulfill a prevailing sense of justice. The United States Supreme Court has oscillated between the poles of excessive autonomy and excessive responsiveness in the course of its experience.

procedures, no matter how reliable these procedures may appear to be. Naturally, if the outcome of a UN System IV inquiry is likely to vindicate a national position, then it is good politics to advocate and accept such an approach; or if, as in the case of South Africa, the outcome of the political processes is so much worse than the worst plausible result of a UN System IV approach, then it may make sense to accept the International Court of Justice as a forum for decision even if an adverse result is expected.[88]

It may be useful to summarize the presentation of UN System IV: 1) given current behavior patterns states will seldom approach important controversies in the spirit of UN System IV (although part of the myth of Charter System I is the general prevalence of UN System IV in United Nations operations); 2) UN Systems I-III are mainly ways of formulating claims to control behavior, expressive of the political sentiment of a voting majority; these claims may or may not be consistent with the results that would be reached by a UN System IV approach; 3) the implementation of a UN System IV outcome is by no means assured if the result is an unpopular one.

The continuing primacy of politics in world affairs results in a minor role for UN System IV. It is not possible to expand the scope of UN System IV operations until other changes in attitude and behavior lead principal governments to depoliticize international society.[89]

United Nations System V

A very brief mention should be made of certain recent indications that the Organization may be increasingly useful to mobilize world political opinion on general issues of

[88] The International Court of Justice as a forum for dispute-settlement also presents a wide range of opportunities for delay and evasion on the part of the losing side, both in the course of litigation and in response to an adverse decision.

[89] Of course, there is a circle implicit here: UN System IV will only expand in the event of depoliticization, but depoliticization will be signalled by an expanded UN System IV.

global concern such as pollution, population, policy, and resource conservation. In this setting there is less effort to resolve conflicts than to clarify an international concern about an existing situation. The claims posited by the Organization are likely to be made under the leadership of middle-rank moderate states (Sweden, Canada, Japan) that have accepted as their function the responsible articulation of urgent matters of world community interest. Such a development of this range of concerns was not really anticipated by the Charter to be a major activity of the United Nations.

These issues are likely to attract growing attention as their seriousness to national and world welfare becomes more apparent. UN System V will probably work initially to clarify the objective situation and then proceed toward the recommendation of cooperative action on behalf of a global interest. Within a decade one can imagine the declaration of "a world ecological emergency."[90] By the end of the century UN System V is quite likely to become the most important activity of the Organization.

These concerns with the fundamental conditions of human existence should be sharply distinguished from issues of technical cooperation that have been handled by functional international agencies since the formation of the International Telecommunications Union of the Universal Postal Union in the nineteenth century.[91] UN System V should also be distinguished from the broad efforts at standard-setting and knowledge-dissemination that have been made by the International Labor Office and UNESCO. UN System V will undoubtedly generate various kinds of political pressures, especially because the issues will tend to point up the need for greater political integra-

[90] As a consequence of various forms of pollution, ranging from noise to radioactivity, and of resource depletion, environmental hazards may grow enough to necessitate a single, coherent, global response organized within a central political framework.

[91] One would expect that the expanding network of international relationships and the increasing technological capacity for centralized forms of cooperation would lead to the further rapid growth of these kinds of "functional" institutions.

tion at the world level.[92] Therefore, formal acts of UN System V are likely to impinge upon sovereign prerogatives to an increasing extent. However, the issues likely to concern UN System V are of such a character as to make normal political alignments unlikely to exert predominant influence; it is also hard to tell whether the main governments will find that the United Nations provides a useful set of arenas within which to cope with these problems, and whether United Nations action will proceed beyond the stage of fact-gathering and interest articulation.[93]

Charter Systems II a . . . n

It is possible to contemplate the adoption of a new Charter designed to shift capabilities to international institutions. The Clark-Sohn plan and the Chicago proposals are two prominent examples; both propose to convert the United Nations into a form of limited world government, but the latter emphasizes the regionalization of political influence to a far greater extent than the former.[94] Constitution-building as an intellectual exercise (as distinct from a political proposal) may clarify alternatives to the present structure of international society, as well as give some sense of content and direction to a strategy of change. Normally such constitutional models are put forward as

[92] Cf. Kenneth E. Boulding's ideas about "the great transition" set forth in his provocative book entitled *The Meaning of the 20th Century* (New York: Harper, 1965); also see books cited in note 16.

[93] Most accounts of the future of international society, especially those that are most apocalyptic about the urgency of drastic change in political structure, do not give the United Nations a very prominent role in this process. The Organization is neglected rather than denigrated, rather as if its existence hardly penetrates the present imagination. See, e.g., works cited in previous note and H. Brown, *The Challenge of Man's Future* (New York: Viking, 1954); H. Brown, James Bonner, and John Weir, *The Next Hundred Years* (New York: Viking, 1957); Barry Commoner, *Science and Survival* (New York: Viking, 1965); Herman Kahn and Anthony J. Wiener, *The Year 2000* (New York: Macmillan, 1967).

[94] See Grenville Clark and Louis B. Sohn, *World Peace through World Law* (Cambridge: Harvard University Press, 3rd rev. ed., 1966); "A Constitution for the World," Papers on Peace (Santa Barbara, Cal.: Center for the Study of Democratic Institutions, 1965).

mere exercises in advocacy with no appreciation of political obstacles or consideration of implementing transition processes. As a consequence, there is a considerable tendency to dismiss Charter II systems as wishful thinking.

It also appears true that existing limits on the usefulness of the United Nations result more from the character of the international environment than from the deficiencies of Charter System I. In fact, Charter System I seems to have established an adequate framework to facilitate growth or contraction of United Nations activity depending on the relative weight of political pressure on a given issue or at a particular time. No political disposition presently exists to adopt a Charter System II that would do away with the present behavioral patterns. The main issue posed for world-order reformers is how to generate a political disposition favoring change in national orientation and international structure. The projection of Charter System II may help clarify the reorientation that would be required, but it does not constitute any evidence that such a reorientation is at all likely to occur. As in Frederick the Great's time, the successful creation of world government still awaits a crop of political leaders who have experienced a complete conversion to cosmopolitanism "and a few other trifles." However, the emerging imperatives of UN System V, combined with the persisting (if not increasing) danger of nuclear warfare and other varieties of catastrophe, emphasize the unprecedented vulnerability of the present basis of human organization. Nothing less than the survival of the human species may be finally at issue. Charter II projections, then, are part of a new political terrain on which world order reform movements might be expected to play an increasingly significant role.

United Nations Systems a ... n

It would also be necessary, but beyond the scope of this chapter, to project the main implementing systems that would be likely to result from the adoption of the main al-

ternative conceptions of Charter System II. Obviously one
system of importance would be some kind of autonomous
structure of United Nations administration in the area of
peace and security. As we know from current UN operations a realistic assessment of the role of the Organization
should be closely associated with the prevailing patterns of
political influence and their correlation with implementing
capabilities. The same effort at projection might improve
our understanding of how alternate systems of world political organization might be expected to operate.[95]

IV. Concluding Comments

The idea of explicating variations in system is to help identify principal modes of United Nations operation and facilitate comparison with past and future practices of international organizations. The focus upon distinct systems of
operations suggests the importance of consensus patterns,
implementing prospects, and national strategies of participation to the understanding of how the United Nations
works in relation to a given issue-area during a particular
phase of its existence. These initial mapping exercises need
to be continued and refined, thereby making possible a
gradually sharper discernment of principal patterns.

The entire orientation stems from an acceptance of the
primacy of political factors in explaining United Nations
activity. As such, we are working within an intellectual
tradition which holds that the explanation of these political
factors is not antithetical to the United Nations idea, but on
the contrary, that politics is at the basis of any effective role
for international institutions. At the same time, a formal in-

[95] The World Order Models Project of the World Law Fund is a
major undertaking that is moving in this direction. The Project is
organized on a global basis with "teams" of scholars in the United
States, Europe, Latin America, Africa, India, Japan, and the Soviet
Union each formulating a model of a preferred (and attainable)
system of world order by the last decade of the century, the 1990's.
The focus of the project is upon the functional efficacy of various
systems of political organization at the global level.

strument of incorporation and a special sense of normative mission conditions both the rhetoric and behavior of states in any governmental or parliamentary setting. The United Nations provides a distinctive set of arenas for the conduct of international politics, and it is up to students of this subject-matter to find appropriate methods of interpretation.

A social scientist has special skills, complementary to those of the political analyst, diplomatic historian, legal analyst, and commentator that should be brought to bear. These skills involve building up a conceptual environment for the classification and presentation of the mass of information generated by the existence of a complex network of entities such as is embraced by the United Nations label. This conceptual environment aspires to be at once parsimonious and comprehensive. As greater conceptual sophistication is achieved it becomes desirable to obtain statistical and other forms of empirical verification by formulating and testing propositions about principal processes. A series of case studies would provide evidence about the usefulness of the hypothetical systems outlined in the text to describe the main forms of United Nations activity.

At present, one high priority for social science is to promote disciplined inquiry without indulging in formalistic or sentimental modes of analysis. Discussions about whether the United Nations has been or is likely to be a success or a failure are not likely to be very illuminating unless the criteria of judgment are put forward in a challenging fashion. Similarly, narrations of the formal procedures by which United Nations organs have dealt with a controversy or an issue-area are not likely to promote understanding unless tied to a theory of United Nations politics, which in turn needs to be interpreted as one subsystem of the overall international political system.

INDEX

Aaland Islands controversy, 80
Aden problem, 21
Africa, international stability and 38; military coups and fall of leaders in, 143
African states, UN as political instrument for, 20, 30, 215, 218; UN scope and, 140; settlements "imposed" by, 144
Afro-Asian bloc, aims of, 192n; attitude toward UN, 219-20; control of General Assembly by, 20, 30, 215, 218; demands of, 218-21; U.S. support of, 219
aggression, definitions of, 136; first-shot conception of, 37
Alker, H. R., Jr., 94n
Anglo-German Naval Agreement, 83
Annual Report of the Security Council, 184-85
apartheid, crusade against, 193n, 218; decolonization and, 191
Arenales, Emilio, 186
Aron, Raymond, 66n
Asher, Robert E., 153n
Asia, great-power diplomacy and, 42; international stability and, 38-39; UN failures in, 19-20. *See also* Afro-Asian bloc
authority, decision-making and, 67; power structures and, 198-200

bailing-out exercises, UN and, 21-22
balance-of-power politics, 25n, 50
Barkun, Michael, 186n, 187n, 206n
Berlin issue, 1948 referral of, 22
Bienen, Henry, 130n

bipolarity, cooperation through, 216-17; decline of, 35, 41; international organization and, 101; League of Nations and, 97; vs. multipolarity, 47-48; UN and, 97-98, 216-17
Bizerte dispute, 64
Black, Cyril E., 46n, 150n, 188n, 198n
bloc issues, League of Nations and, 97-98; UN and, 87, 98
bloc system, and international organization, 101. *See also* Afro-Asian bloc
Bloomfield, Lincoln P., 211n
Bonner, James, 227n
Boulding, Kenneth E., 227n
Bozeman, Adda B., 25n
Brown, H., 227n
Burton, M. E., 97n

Calvocoressi, P., 70n
Carelia conflict, 85
Carr, E. H., 69n
Carter, G. M., 69n
Castro, Fidel, 73n, 75, 87
Cefkin, J. Leo, 144n
Center of International Studies, Princeton University, 6
change, international 34, 45-47, 198
Charlesworth, James C., 104n
Charter conception, principal systems of, 205-29. *See also* United Nations Charter
Charter System I, 228
Charter Systems II *a . . . n*, 227-29
China, League of Nations and, 85. *See also* Peoples Republic of China (Communist)
civil strife, intervention in, 134-36; national discretion and, 134. *See also* internal conflict

231

BOOKS WRITTEN
UNDER THE AUSPICES OF THE
CENTER OF INTERNATIONAL STUDIES
PRINCETON UNIVERSITY

Gabriel A. Almond, *The Appeals of Communism* (Princeton University Press 1954)

William W. Kaufmann, ed., *Military Policy and National Security* (Princeton University Press 1956)

Klaus Knorr, *The War Potential of Nations* (Princeton University Press 1956)

Lucian W. Pye, *Guerrilla Communism in Malaya* (Princeton University Press 1956)

Charles De Visscher, *Theory and Reality in Public International Law*, trans. by P. E. Corbett (Princeton University Press 1957; rev. ed. 1968)

Bernard C. Cohen, *The Political Process and Foreign Policy: The Making of the Japanese Peace Settlement* (Princeton University Press 1959)

Myron Weiner, *Party Politics in India: The Development of a Multi-Party System* (Princeton University Press 1957)

Percy E. Corbett, *Law in Diplomacy* (Princeton University Press 1959)

Rolf Sannwald and Jacques Stohler, *Economic Integration: Theoretical Assumptions and Consequences of European Unification*, trans. by Herman Karreman (Princeton University Press 1959)

Klaus Knorr, ed., *NATO and American Security* (Princeton University Press 1959)

Gabriel A. Almond and James S. Coleman, eds., *The Politics of the Developing Areas* (Princeton University Press 1960)

Herman Kahn, *On Thermonuclear War* (Princeton University Press 1960)

Sidney Verba, *Small Groups and Political Behavior: A Study of Leadership* (Princeton University Press 1961)

Robert J. C. Butow, *Tojo and the Coming of the War* (Princeton University Press 1961)

Glenn H. Snyder, *Deterrence and Defense: Toward a Theory of National Security* (Princeton University Press 1961)

Klaus Knorr and Sidney Verba, eds., *The International System: Theoretical Essays* (Princeton University Press 1961)

Peter Paret and John W. Shy, *Guerrillas in the 1960's* (Praeger 1962)

George Modelski, *A Theory of Foreign Policy* (Praeger 1962)

Klaus Knorr and Thornton Read, eds., *Limited Strategic War* (Praeger 1963)

Frederick S. Dunn, *Peace-Making and the Settlement with Japan* (Princeton University Press 1963)

Arthur L. Burns and Nina Heathcote, *Peace-Keeping by United Nations Forces* (Praeger 1963)

Richard A. Falk, *Law, Morality, and War in the Contemporary World* (Praeger 1963)

James N. Rosenau, *National Leadership and Foreign Policy: A Case Study in the Mobilization of Public Support* (Princeton University Press 1963)

Gabriel A. Almond and Sidney Verba, *The Civic Culture: Political Attitudes and Democracy in Five Nations* (Princeton University Press 1963)

Bernard C. Cohen, *The Press and Foreign Policy* (Princeton University Press 1963)

Richard L. Sklar, *Nigerian Political Parties: Power in an Emergent African Nation* (Princeton University Press 1963)

Peter Paret, *French Revolutionary Warfare from Indochina to Algeria: The Analysis of a Political and Military Doctrine* (Praeger 1964)

Harry Eckstein, ed., *Internal War: Problems and Approaches* (Free Press 1964)

Cyril E. Black and Thomas P. Thornton, eds., *Communism and Revolution: The Strategic Uses of Political Violence* (Princeton University Press 1964)

Miriam Camps, *Britain and the European Community 1955-1963* (Princeton University Press 1964)

Thomas P. Thornton, ed., *The Third World in Soviet Perspective: Studies by Soviet Writers on the Developing Areas* (Princeton University Press 1964)

James N. Rosenau, ed., *International Aspects of Civil Strife* (Princeton University Press 1964)

Sidney I. Ploss, *Conflict and Decision-Making in Soviet Russia: A Case Study of Agricultural Policy, 1953-1963* (Princeton University Press 1965)

Richard A. Falk and Richard J. Barnet, eds., *Security in Disarmament* (Princeton University Press 1965)

Karl von Vorys, *Political Development in Pakistan* (Princeton University Press 1965)

Harold and Margaret Sprout, *The Ecological Perspective on Human Affairs, With Special Reference to International Politics* (Princeton University Press 1965)

Klaus Knorr, *On the Uses of Military Power in the Nuclear Age* (Princeton University Press 1966)

Harry Eckstein, *Division and Cohesion in Democracy: A Study of Norway* (Princeton University Press 1966)

Cyril E. Black, *The Dynamics of Modernization: A Study in Comparative History* (Harper and Row 1966)

Peter Kunstadter, ed., *Southeast Asian Tribes, Minorities, and Nations* (Princeton University Press 1967)

E. Victor Wolfenstein, *The Revolutionary Personality: Lenin, Trotsky, Gandhi* (Princeton University Press 1967)

Leon Gordenker, *The UN Secretary-General and the Maintenance of Peace* (Columbia University Press 1967)

Oran R. Young, *The Intermediaries: Third Parties in International Crises* (Princeton University Press 1967)

James N. Rosenau, ed., *Domestic Sources of Foreign Policy* (Free Press 1967)

Richard F. Hamilton, *Affluence and the French Worker in the Fourth Republic* (Princeton University Press 1967)

Linda B. Miller, *World Order and Local Disorder: The United Nations and Internal Conflicts* (Princeton University Press 1967)

Wolfram F. Hanrieder, *West German Foreign Policy, 1949-1963: International Pressures and Domestic Response* (Stanford University Press 1967)

Richard H. Ullman, *Britain and the Russian Civil War: November 1918-February 1920* (Princeton University Press 1968)

Robert Gilpin, *France in the Age of the Scientific State* (Princeton University Press 1968)

William B. Bader, *The United States and the Spread of Nuclear Weapons* (Pegasus 1968)

Richard A. Falk, *Legal Order in a Violent World* (Princeton University Press 1968)

Cyril E. Black, Richard A. Falk, Klaus Knorr, and Oran R. Young, *Neutralization and World Politics* (Princeton University Press 1968)

Oran R. Young, *The Politics of Force: Bargaining During International Crises* (Princeton University Press 1969)

Klaus Knorr and James N. Rosenau, eds., *Contending Approaches to International Politics* (Princeton University Press 1969)

James N. Rosenau, ed., *Linkage Politics: Essays on the Convergence of National and International Systems* (Free Press 1969)

John T. McAlister, Jr., *Viet Nam: The Origins of Revolution* (Knopf 1969)

Jean Edward Smith, *Germany Beyond the Wall: People, Politics and Prosperity* (Little, Brown 1969)

James Barros, *Betrayal from Within: Joseph Avenol, Secretary-General of the League of Nations, 1933-1940* (Yale University Press 1969)

Charles Hermann, *Crises in Foreign Policy: A Simulation Analysis* (Bobbs-Merrill 1969)

Robert C. Tucker, *The Marxian Revolutionary Idea: Essays on Marxist Thought and Its Impact on Radical Movements* (W. W. Norton 1969)

Harvey Waterman, *Political Change in Contemporary France: The Politics of an Industrial Democracy* (Charles E. Merrill 1969)

Richard A. Falk and Cyril E. Black, eds., *The Future of the International Legal Order*, Vol. I, *Trends and Patterns* (Princeton University Press 1969)

Ted Robert Gurr, *Why Men Rebel* (Princeton University Press 1969)

C. S. Whitaker, Jr., *The Politics of Tradition: Continuity and Change in Northern Nigeria, 1946-1966* (Princeton University Press 1970)

Richard A. Falk, *The Status of Law in International Society* (Princeton University Press 1970)

Henry Bienen, *Tanzania: Party Transformation and Economic Development* (Princeton University Press 1967, rev. edn. 1970)

Klaus Knorr, *Military Power and Potential* (D. C. Heath 1970)

Richard A. Falk and Cyril E. Black, eds., *The Future of the International Legal Order*, Vol. II, *Wealth and Resources* (Princeton University Press 1970)

Leon Gordenker, ed., *The United Nations and International Politics* (Princeton University Press 1971)

Cyril E. Black and Richard A. Falk, eds., *The Future of the International Legal Order*, Vol. III, *Conflict Management* (Princeton University Press 1971)

Harold and Margaret Sprout, *Toward a Politics of the Planet Earth* (Van Nostrand Reinhold Co. 1971)